# WORLDLY ETHICS

# WORLDLY ETHICS

⸗

*Democratic Politics and*

*Care for the World*

ELLA MYERS

DUKE UNIVERSITY PRESS

DURHAM AND LONDON    2013

© 2013 Duke University Press

All rights reserved

Printed in the United States of America on acid-free paper ⊛

Designed by Heather Hensley

Typeset in Whitman by Tseng Information Systems, Inc.

Library of Congress Cataloging-in-Publication Data appear
on the last printed page of this book.

FOR MARK

=

CONTENTS

ACKNOWLEDGMENTS  ix

INTRODUCTION
Tracing the Ethical Turn  1

CHAPTER ONE
Crafting a Democratic Subject?
The Foucauldian Ethics of Self-Care  21

CHAPTER TWO
Levinasian Ethics, Charity, and Democracy  53

CHAPTER THREE
The Democratic Ethics of Care for Worldly Things  85

CHAPTER FOUR
Partisanship for the World: Tending to the World
as Home and In-Between  111

EPILOGUE
Self/Other/World: Forging Connections and
Fostering Democratic Care  139

NOTES  153

BIBLIOGRAPHY  195

INDEX  207

ACKNOWLEDGMENTS

Though writing can often feel like a solitary pursuit, I am quite aware that I did not create this book on my own. I am deeply grateful for the institutional support, intellectual stimulation, and plain old encouragement I have received along the way.

I most likely would never have found my way to political theory or discovered its many pleasures and challenges were it not for the tremendous good fortune of crossing paths with Peter Euben and Wendy Brown early in my undergraduate studies at the University of California, Santa Cruz. I can still recall the excitement I felt every time I attended Euben's legendary, manic "Political Freedom" class and the inquisitiveness and ambition that Brown's demanding seminars awakened in me. I am grateful to both of them for showing me what engaged scholarship and teaching look like and for encouraging me to see graduate school and an academic career as real possibilities in my life.

I began this project at Northwestern University, as a member of a lively and growing political theory community there. Linda Zerilli was an invaluable interlocutor and critic, tirelessly reading and discussing many drafts of this project in its early stages. Her rigorous intellectual engagement with my ideas was invigorating, flattering, and exhausting. My work today is better for it. Bonnie Honig also provided sharp commentary and expert guidance. Her original, incisive readings of texts and events always push me to consider things anew. I am especially appreciative of Bonnie's ongoing interest in my work and her willingness to offer practical advice in addition to sharp conceptual insights.

I am lucky to be a faculty member of the Political Science

Department and Gender Studies program at the University of Utah, where I am surrounded by talented and interesting colleagues and students. I am especially indebted to Mark Button, who read the complete manuscript and offered characteristically probing and careful comments. I am grateful for our many conversations over the past several years and for the reassuring words he has offered at crucial moments. Steve Johnston, a more recent arrival to our department, has brought great energy with him, and I look forward to our exchanges in the future. Many other colleagues from across campus have also become good friends. Matt Basso, Beth Clement, Ben Cohen, Kellie Custen, Gretchen Dietrich, Nadja Durbach, Edmund Fong, Lela Graybill, Monty Paret, Richard Preiss, Paisley Rekdal, Angela Smith, Kathryn Stockton, and Jessica Straley have all helped make Salt Lake feel like home, providing not only intellectual companionship but warm meals, laughter, and commiseration. Finally, my students have helped me think differently and better about the questions pursued in this book, and they have reliably kept me on my toes.

Many other people have played an important role in helping this book see the light of day. In addition to those I've already mentioned, I want to acknowledge Paul Apostolidis, Crina Archer, Jason Frank, Michael Hanchard, and Patchen Markell—all of whom have read and commented on parts of the project at various points, posing tough questions and offering fruitful suggestions. Thanks also to two anonymous readers who provided astute, provocative, and very helpful comments on the manuscript. My work has been shaped in ways big and small by discussions over the years with Cristina Beltrán, Michaele Ferguson, Kristy King, Jill Locke, Lida Maxwell, Sara Monoson, Jeanne Morefield, Chris Skeaff, Matt Voorhees, and Lena Zuckerwise. Demetra Kasimis deserves special mention for the many hours she has spent discussing this project and for providing good cheer when most needed.

Earlier versions of some of this book's arguments were presented at the American Political Science Association meetings in 2007 and 2009 and at the Western Political Science Association meetings in 2009 and 2011. Part of chapter 1 was published as "Resisting Foucauldian Ethics: Associative Politics and the Limits of the Care of the Self" in *Contemporary Political Theory* 7, no. 2 (2008), and I am grateful for permission to use this material here. I am thankful for critical financial support I received from the University of Utah. A semester's leave allowed me to complete the first full draft of the manuscript, and a Faculty Fellow Award from the University

Research Committee at precisely the right moment allowed me to revise and polish the final version. Thanks also to Duke University Press, especially to my editor, Courtney Berger, who has been supportive, responsive, and wise.

As I have worked on this project I have been sustained by extraordinary friends whose intelligence, humor, and care have seen me through. I especially thank Paul Adelstein, Tony Bianchi, Mike Bosia, Phil Dracht and Heather Huffman-Dracht, Jason Given, Roshen Hendrickson, Martine Hyland, Demetra Kasimis, Nick Markos, Jon McCoy, Paul North, Christine Pirrone, Laura Scott, Mike and Heather Simons, David Singer, Friese Undine, Liza Weil, and Eva Yusa. Thanks also to my sister, Brooke Myers-Awalt, for listening, understanding, and being hilarious. I want to thank my parents, Robyn Wagner and Tom Myers, for their love and support and for fostering in me a sense of curiosity, a love of books, and a desire to keep learning. And to Solomon, who arrived as this project was coming to completion: my gratitude for your smile, your sweet curiosity, and all the surprises to come.

Finally, I owe the most to Mark Schwarz. I dedicate this book to him in appreciation of the wit, patience, and warmth he brings to our life together. He has always believed unwaveringly in this project and, even more important, in me, with or without a book. His distinctive voice and vision make the world more intriguing and my place in it more sure.

# TRACING THE ETHICAL TURN

The category of ethics is ascendant in recent democratic thought—that much is clear. Even a brief review of contemporary political theory reveals a development notable enough to have garnered a name: the "turn to ethics."[1] This phrase, though helpful, is also misleading since it suggests a unified phenomenon, an implication belied by the multiple, competing understandings of ethics and ethos that shape the current conversation. The prevalence of an ethical vocabulary is undeniable, but this signals less the pursuit of a common purpose than a struggle over signification.

Still, one feature of contemporary democratic theory's multivalent obsession with ethics is striking. Again and again, across work taking inspiration from highly disparate sources, ethics emerges as an indispensable treatment for a crippled democratic politics.[2] That is, despite divergent conceptions, ethics is cast as a response to (sometimes ill-specified) problems plaguing democracy today. Ethics is figured repeatedly as an animating supplement to politics, supplying democracy with something it cannot give itself but urgently requires. Indeed, perhaps the only belief uniting the diverse work identified with the turn to ethics is the conviction that ethics constitutes that missing something that can help cure what ails democratic life. This conviction increasingly circulates in non-academic circles as well—ethos figures prominently in mainstream diagnoses of the ills afflicting liberal democracies.[3]

This book provides a sympathetic critique of the quest for a democratic ethos, cautioning against the directions this search often takes, while seeking to forge a different path. I affirm the significance of the democratic ethos question, yet I argue that prominent efforts to specify an ethics suited to democracy are, in the end, not especially democratic. Formulations of ethics inspired by the work of Michel Foucault and Emmanuel Levinas, I show, are inclined to undermine, rather than enhance, citizens' democratic activity. These therapeutic and charitable modes of ethics, which center on care for the self and care for the Other, respectively, may be admirable in their own right, but, despite claims to the contrary, they are ill-equipped to nourish associative democratic politics. The dyadic relations that are labeled ethical in both of these cases narrow attention to the figures of self and Other and obscure the worldly contexts that are the actual sites and objects of democratic action.

I elaborate and defend here an alternative ethos, one which focuses not on an individual's practice of care for the self or care for the Other, but on contentious and collaborative care for the world, an idea I develop with and against Hannah Arendt's political theory. The worldly ethics advocated here rests, first, on an account of democratic relations that highlights the sense in which citizens' joint action concerns some*thing* in the world, a simultaneously common and contested object that is the focus of mutual attention, advocacy, and debate. A viable democratic ethics honors this dynamic, recognizing that democratic relations are never simply intersubjective but involve relations between multiple actors and specific features of the world they struggle to shape. A world-centered democratic ethos aims to incite and sustain collective care for conditions, care that is expressed in associative efforts to affect particular "worldly things." Moreover, this ethos is tied to an explicitly normative conception of world as both a shared human home and mediating political space. Thus care for the world, which lies at the heart of democratic ethos, is expressed not only by associative action that tends to conditions but also by action that pursues particular substantive ends.

We must first ask, however, what gives rise to the turn to ethics in recent democratic thought? If, as I argue, this move often falters, it is nonetheless prompted by genuine concerns of the present. Two broad conditions are especially significant, in my view, providing the context in which the question of democratic ethos has been posed: widespread citizen disengagement within the U.S. polity and the so-called fact of pluralism. The first, well-documented situation is characterized by Americans' low levels of participation across multiple sites and forms of citizen activity. The growing disaffection of many and the seeming withdrawal of large segments of the population from public life throw into question the basic premise of self-government. It also creates a vacuum that tends to be filled by the most extreme and dogmatic voices, which threaten to monopolize or at least greatly distort public discourse. In light of these circumstances, the concept of democratic ethos emerges as a way of thinking about what can inspire or motivate ordinary citizens' participation in democratic politics. Efforts to define an ethics for democracy are usually concerned with elaborating sensibilities or orientations that, if fostered, might draw more people into democratic activity. The challenge is, furthermore, to develop orientations that can encourage impassioned participation in the difficult, frustrating labor of democratic politics while avoiding the vitriol and demonization that characterize so much political debate today.

The belief that ethics of one kind or another can inspire and nourish democratic politics relies upon an implicit understanding of politics as irreducible to the formal features of government—a regime's institutions, laws, and procedures. Indeed, the inquiry into ethos asks one to think about the spirit of democracy, that is, the constellation of dispositions, habits of feeling, and qualities of character that serve to animate and sustain practices of self-government. If this spirit is in some sense weakened or even missing today, how might it be cultivated?[4] What affects or sensibilities does it call for? And can such qualities be fostered among a varied citizenry in ways that respect diversity and liberty? The search for ethics is at least partly a response to a nominally democratic order characterized by only minimal democratic activity.

The second important context for understanding the proliferation of ethics talk is what Max Weber referred to at the beginning of the twentieth century as our "inescapable condition," or what today often goes by the name "the fact of pluralism." Growing recognition of the competing and irreconcilable goods, faiths, and ways of life that characterize human existence has thrown into question the idea of a single morality that would ground political life. In light of this development, the topic of ethics has assumed new importance. If politics can no longer be imagined as the instantiation of a universal Good in a world marked by multiple, incompatible comprehensive views, the ideas of ethics and ethos seem to open up ways of thinking about the normative dimensions of politics in non-absolutist ways. The foray into ethics signals an attempt to wrestle with questions of value, character, and commitment in a pluralist age.

But if the inquiry into ethics is partly in response to the fact of pluralism, now widely accepted as the starting point for political theorizing, this investigation should be distinguished from the influential work of Jürgen Habermas and John Rawls and their intellectual heirs, which also presents pluralism as the starting point. Although both Habermas and Rawls treat the existence of multiple, irreconcilable comprehensive doctrines or conceptions of the good life as a given, each responds to this condition in ways that the turn to ethics challenges.

On the one hand, Habermas acknowledges that no single answer to the question of the good life is possible; answers to that question are rooted in particular traditions and cultures that diverge and conflict without the promise of reconciliation. Yet he also claims that a moral point of view can be attained through fidelity to a special procedure of justification. This moral point of view is rational and universal, irreducible to concrete forms of *Sittlichkeit*, or ethical life.[5] Habermas acknowledges a multiplicity of ethical values and corresponding ways of life as the lot of modernity, yet this ethical plurality is qualified and limited by a proceduralist morality that retains for liberal-democratic politics a form of universal normativity. Rawls, on the other hand, famously endeavors in his later work to provide a political, rather than moral, justification for his conception of justice, one which remains neutral between competing moral outlooks. The fact of pluralism itself leads Rawls to alter his theory of justice in such a way that its justification is held to be independent of any comprehensive moral ideal. Justice as fairness does not aspire to universality but is instead, according to Rawls, self-consciously rooted in a particular historical context, that of modern constitutional democracy. But while Rawls seeks to avoid the moral universalism that Habermas retains, his nonmetaphysical account of justice includes a defense of "public reason" that strictly limits the expression of pluralism in political life. Although the nuances of Rawlsian public reason continue to be heavily debated, its function is clear: it specifies the kind of reason giving and argumentation that Rawls holds should and should not characterize public debate in a diverse, liberal society.[6] Under conditions of pluralism, Rawls writes, "there are many nonpublic reasons but only one public reason."[7]

The turn to ethics in postfoundational democratic theory takes pluralism as a point of departure, then, but its orientation toward this fact is distinctive from both Habermasian and Rawlsian approaches in two primary ways.[8] First, when ethics of one kind or another is offered up as nourishment for democratic life, the gesture usually disavows more conventional forms of morality. Work that draws on Foucault and Levinas, for example, presents ethics as an explicit challenge to morality, however formal or procedural. Indeed, ethics in this vein is sometimes called post-moral in recognition of its departure from familiar moral traditions that are thought to deny or do violence to the plurality of values, goods, and faiths. Speaking very schematically, ethics is understood to be more particular and affective than universal, reason-governed models of morality. While conventional moralities tend to aspire to the status of law, ethics privileges the cultivation of dispositions over rule-following, suggesting a way of being in the world that cannot be formulated in codified, universal terms.[9] Second, the pursuit of post-moral ethics is usually understood as an effort to expand, rather than contain, the expression of pluralism in public life. For thinkers like William Connolly, Judith Butler, and Simon Critchley, for example, who draw on Foucauldian and Levinasian ethics in support of radicalized democracy (and whose work I address in the following chapters), the task is not primarily understood to be one of limiting the presence of pluralism in political debate and decision making.[10] Instead, the aim is to conceptualize and develop the qualities of character and habits of feeling that might enable lively and respectful exchange across deep difference, fostering even further pluralization of collective life. What virtues, they ask, might guide and animate citizen action in a liberal-democratic polity marked by competing and irreconcilable comprehensive views, which are not and cannot be left at the door?[11]

If the search for a democratic ethos is motivated largely by these distinctive problems of the present, we can see that it also revives some very old concerns within political theory. Although the history of political thought does not offer any simple consensus on the matter, it reveals a persistent preoccupation with the question of how ethics might be connected to politics, a preoccupation that spans time and competing intellectual traditions. Several important strands of that lineage, including ancient, civic republican, and liberal, constitute the backdrop against which the latest inquiry into ethos is taking place.

Most notably, the recent reappearance of the term *ethos* in political theory points to its original ancient Greek context, in which *ethos*, "the characteristic spirit, prevalent tone of sentiment, of a people or a community," was understood to be a crucial complement to *nomos*.[12] Together, they were thought to constitute a "universalizing pair" in which the principles of order, written and unwritten, were joined with a particular, shared sensibility.[13] The Greeks' defining belief in a mutually influential relationship between city and soul, elegantly captured in Plato's references to "the *politeia* of the soul," was informed by the conviction that the soul, though belonging to an individual, was shaped and directed by the surrounding political order, consisting of both official institutions and a communal spirit or character, nomos and ethos, which together served as a source of moral education for its members. "Soulcraft" was closely bound up with the organization of collective life, in both its legal and extralegal dimensions. Ethos in this context referred neither to a code of rules nor to an attribute of the individual, but to a distinctive, shared way of being that complemented but was irreducible to the government's formal structure. In the work of Plato, Aristotle, and other thinkers of the period, *ethos* connotes disposition, character, and bearing, understood in collective rather than strictly personal terms and held to be susceptible to purposeful shaping and cultivation.[14] The ethos of a city or constitution was its "moral ambience," coloring a whole way of life and exerting an important influence on the children reared there.[15]

The belief that political life is inevitably inhabited by an ethos also characterizes the civic republican tradition, which approaches the topic largely through the conceptual vocabulary of civic virtue. Republican thinkers regard such virtue as fundamental to sound citizenship, insisting that a healthy republic depends not only on well-designed institutions capable of upholding the rule of law, but also on citizens' qualities of character, which orient them toward pursuit of the public good. While the tradition ranging from Cicero to Machiavelli to Tocqueville is far from unified, the attention devoted to the question of citizens' "habits of the heart" is one of its defining features.[16] Inspired by classical thought and practice, republicans understand the formation of subjects to be a central problem for politics. According to Tocqueville, for example, American institutions of self-government both cultivated and required citizens who shared certain dispositions and orientations, such as a felt sense of collective responsibility and a spirit of continual improvement. From the civic republican vantage point politics and ethics are distinguishable, with politics referring to a community's institutional arrangements and ethics to its citizens' character and sensibilities, but they are necessarily bound up with one another in a relation of reciprocal influence and together constitute a society's political culture.

Finally, although not always as readily recognized, liberal thought through the ages has focused attention on those qualities of character or ethical preconditions thought to make a successful liberal order possible and investigated how these might be encouraged. An anemic account of liberalism, according to which liberals are entirely unconcerned with the good life and seek only an impartial umpire in government, still circulates, despite the difficulty of finding any liberal thinker, past or present, who actually articulates such a position. Yet many contemporary liberals affirm the significance of citizen virtue to present-day liberal orders and have brought to light the extent to which canonical liberal political theory has been concerned with its own version of civic virtue from the start.[17] Peter Berkowitz, for example, has shown that the achievement of a liberal way of life for Hobbes, Locke, Kant, and Mill, among others, depends upon certain virtues which are not automatically generated by liberalism's central institutions and which are sometimes even discouraged by them.[18] Similarly, Mark Button has convincingly argued that the social contract, so central to liberal thought from its inception to today, is more than a device for conceptualizing legitimacy (as is usually assumed). It also serves to theorize a "transformative ethos" that can foster in citizens the "civic character" and "ethical sensibility" that a liberal order requires.[19] What Berkowitz, Button, and others help identify is less a unified account of liberal virtues across thinkers than a shared conviction that there *are* such virtues, quite variously defined, and that their cultivation is a difficult but pressing question for liberals. The abiding interest in an ethics that animates liberal politics is complicated, however, by liberalism's core commitment to individual liberty and skepticism toward government intrusion. Liberal thought is characterized by simultaneous enthusiasm for and aversion to virtue.[20] Without discounting this ambivalence, it is important to acknowledge that enthusiasm for virtue, sometimes overlooked, is a prominent feature of liberal political theory. The inquiry into ethos and its role in political life is integral, then, not only to classical and civic republican thought but also to liberal philosophy.

When thinkers today turn to ethics or ethos (usually used interchangeably) to address contemporary democracy, they tap into these traditions.

They draw on ancient Greek insights, for example, even as they put them in the service of visions of political life that bear little resemblance to the classical *polis*. Most significant, they take their bearings from the ancient conviction that character and disposition matter politically, that is, by the belief that a polity is irreducible to its formal features. From this perspective, every political community is shaped, for good or ill, by its collective spirit no less than by its laws. Many contemporary democratic theorists, explicitly or not, are returning to an ancient concern and affirming the Greek notion that "just as the *ethe* and the *nomoi* of a city are closely connected, so too the study of 'ethics' is itself a part of 'politics.'"[21]

Likewise, the quest for a democratic ethos revives a central feature of republican thought by asking after the habits of the heart that could enable more robust, respectful forms of participation by a broader range of citizens in a diversifying American polity. Contemporary thinkers seeking an ethics for democracy are reimagining civic virtue for the present, exploring which sensibilities and orientations can prepare citizens for co-action with one another and how these virtues, which seem to be in rather short supply, might be promoted under current conditions. At the same time, proponents of the turn to ethics, though focused on the question of cultivation, evince some of liberalism's ambivalence, remaining alert to the danger of paternalism that attends any effort to shape citizens' character. Theorists of democratic ethos strive to conceptualize a kind of moral education that avoids normalization and, further, actually aids pluralization.

Given the extent to which contemporary democratic theory builds on these prior strands of political thought, it is tempting to label the turn to ethics a *return* to ethics. Yet while ancient and modern influences are undeniable, recent inquiries into ethics are not simply continuous with earlier modes of thought. Most important, ancient and civic republican sources connected ethos and civic virtue, respectively, to fairly homogeneous and self-contained political communities, characterized largely by face-to-face relations within relatively small territories.[22] The question of ethos today takes its bearings from a very different set of conditions, as the previous discussion of pluralism noted, and asks whether the idea of citizen virtue can be adapted and reimagined for a diverse, mobile, and expansive society. Are there certain habits of the heart uniquely suited to the practice of democratic politics among a vast, heterogeneous, increasingly globalized citizenry?[23] And can desirable dispositions be nurtured in ways that protect and extend plurality rather than seek monistic unity?

While proponents of the ethical turn answer these questions affirmatively, today's search for a democratic ethos is not without its critics. I want to clarify the nature of these objections and explain why my project critically participates in, rather than rejects outright, the ethical turn.

A major charge leveled by skeptics at those seeking an ethics for democracy is that such efforts are poorly disguised exercises in moral absolutism. That is, while ethics is usually presented as a less rigid alternative to conventional forms of morality, some critics of the ethical turn allege that the attempt to locate an ethics for democracy expresses the desire to ground democracy in an extrapolitical foundation.[24] For example, Ernesto Laclau argues that "ethicization" reverts to a discourse of "first philosophy." To seek an ethics for democracy is to seek an ultimate authority beyond political practice; it is an attempt to evade politics' "radical contingency."[25] Chantal Mouffe voices a similar concern when she claims that the tendency among contemporary democratic theorists to adopt an ethical vocabulary is driven by the fantasy of a "final guarantee" that authorizes political arrangements. The hunt for ethics, she avers, is the hunt for a "more profound or more solid" ground than "the practices, the language games that are constitutive of [a] particular form of life."[26]

The worry is not just that proponents of the ethical turn posit a ground where there is none, but that the preoccupation with the category of ethics, however soothing, signals a very real "contraction of political ambitions."[27] Wendy Brown, for example, warns against the temptation to embrace a moralizing imperative that substitutes for engagement in the messy, frustrating work of struggling for power, with and against others, in the field of politics.[28] Like Mouffe, who labels the turn to ethics "a retreat from the political," George Shulman argues that part of the allure of ethics is its apparent promise of a truth that precedes or is external to political contestation—a truth that would seem to relieve citizens of the difficult work of organizing together to make public demands and mobilizing others on behalf of the demands they advocate.[29] He notes further that the obsession with ethics is a symptom of despair over the prospects for such collective action today. Perhaps there is comfort in the thought that one's task consists in affirming the right ethical outlook, from which desirable political consequences will hopefully follow. When "action in concert" appears to be rare or unlikely,[30] we may be attracted to the notion that democracy can be rescued by something other than itself, namely, the discovery of the proper ethics.[31]

Although these claims are compelling, it is a mistake to dismiss the turn to ethics as a dead end. Rather than eschew the category of ethics in the name of the autonomy of the political or insist upon the primacy of politics, this project interrogates, but also contributes to, democratic theory's investigation of ethos. The critics cited earlier are partly correct: the turn to ethics can assume absolutist forms and at times does signal an attempt to evade the realities of democratic struggle, points I have insisted upon elsewhere.[32] But this is not necessarily so; ethics is not a monolith. There are many competing conceptions of ethics, just as there are of politics. Some versions of ethics are likely to discourage rather than inspire collective action by democratic citizens. Two of my chapters, in fact, focus on the problems posed by ethical models that center on dyadic relations of care—a serious limitation largely overlooked, even by those who are otherwise skeptical of the ethical turn in democratic thought. Yet it is also possible to conceptualize and defend an ethos that is uniquely suited to the challenges of associative democracy, as this book's account of worldly ethics will show.

Ethics, I believe, remains a valuable idiom for thinking and talking about the normative and affective orientations and sensibilities that are inevitably part of political life. It is not a matter of whether we want to bring ethics into politics; the phenomena that tend to travel under these names are already combined, for better or worse. Indeed, the language of ethics and politics renders as separate dimensions of cultural existence that are actually quite difficult to pull apart. Nonetheless, ethics continues to provide a useful, albeit imperfect, conceptual vocabulary for investigating those elements of democratic life that are left out of strictly institutional and rationalist accounts. More specifically, my book deploys an ethical vocabulary in order to consider the spirit that already inhabits associative democratic action—which I name care for the world—and to argue for its importance and purposeful cultivation. In doing so, I resist the tendency to cast ethics per se as unworldly in opposition to the worldly character of politics. Bonnie Honig, for example, rightly insists, following Arendt, that politics is both in and about the world and that the romance with ethics may serve as an escape from the "exposure" worldly engagement entails.[33] But if politics is not confined to formal procedures and institutions, what dispositions and sensibilities are at work when citizens undertake the demanding, uncertain, but also often pleasurable work of world-centered democratic action? Certainly, as I will show, some forms of ethics—which I conceptualize as therapeutic and charitable in character—can aptly be characterized as unworldly and therefore as generally unsupportive of democratic activity. But it is a mistake to declare that ethics as such is always and only alienated from the world, understood as the messy, power-laden, varied space of democratic association. This book argues, on the contrary, for a distinctively worldly ethics, not only as a possibility but as a reality, one that is already expressed and enacted today by admirable forms of joint action.

This is a critical and constructive project. The argument offered here aims to reveal unacknowledged costs of the turn to ethics. I demonstrate that Foucauldian and Levinasian approaches, each focused on a different dyadic relation of care, are inclined to enervate rather than enrich associative action by democratic citizens. My critique does not conclude with a call to abandon the quest for a democratic ethos, however. Instead, I conceptualize and defend an alternative ethical orientation, one focused on inciting citizens' collective care for worldly things. And I argue that worldly ethics, implicit in certain collective citizen efforts, is a promising resource for democratic action today.

The book's case for worldly ethics centers on an associative conception of democratic politics that emphasizes joint action by citizens aimed at shaping shared conditions.[34] This view of democracy grants primacy to public practices in which differentiated collectivities struggle, both with and against one another, to affect features of the world in which they live. The term *associative* refers to three interlocking features of such a politics: (1) it involves collaborative and contentious action, born out of association among multiple citizens; (2) such action is not confined to the official channels of government but frequently appears at the level of civil society, within so-called secondary associations; and finally, most significant: (3) democratic actors are both brought together and separated from one another by common objects. In other words, they always associate around something.

First, *associative* signals a nonholistic understanding of democratic collectivity. Relations of association are ones in which distinct individuals coordinate their actions with others in order to pursue goals not achievable by a single actor.[35] Democratic politics thus understood does not depend on the existence of a unified demos or a single people. Rather, associative democratic politics involves collectivities that are constituted by multiple "co-actors."[36] In addition, these relations of solidaristic association are situated within broader, more contentious forms of association in which competing collectives vie publicly with one another over specific practices, laws, policies, and norms.

Second, although certain political institutions and spaces serve as enabling conditions for the enactment of associative democratic politics, this politics is not confined to the official channels of government. As many of the most powerful examples of associative democratic politics in recent American history indicate, these projects frequently involve creative forms of advocacy that take place on the margins of or in opposition to the state apparatus. Whether in pursuit of African American civil rights, environmental protections, a humane AIDS policy, or economic policies that benefit the so-called 99 percent, direct collective action has typically involved the creation of new institutions and the reconfiguration of public space, not simply the occupation of preexisting political venues. We cannot fully anticipate where or how associative democratic politics will appear.[37]

Finally, *associative* indicates that democratic relations are not simply intersubjective, if by that we mean they involve two or more subjects. Rather, democratic politics involves relations among plural individuals which are mediated by shared, yet also disputed, objects of attention. These third terms around which democratic actors associate serve as sites of mutual energy and advocacy. Citizens are simultaneously brought together and separated from one another by specific, worldly matters of concern, which "*inter-est*" or lie between them.[38] Relations of both cooperation and antagonism among democratic constituencies are mediated by something in the world that is the focal point of their activity.

This portrait does not claim to depict democracy as such; certain features of democratic politics are emphasized at the expense of others. Nonetheless, it is important to recognize that associative activity by ordinary citizens is central to almost every conception of democratic politics, including philosophical formulations and practical understandings alike. Citizen association is certainly not always interpreted in the way sketched above—indeed, as I will show, the central role played by mediating worldly things is especially neglected—yet there is a pervasive, shared understanding that the "art of association" is absolutely central to any satisfactory account of democratic politics.[39] David Held's influential *Models of Democracy*, for example, reveals the extent to which associative activity by citizens is regarded as a distinctive, indispensable characteristic of democracy, even according to competing philosophies which otherwise diverge considerably.[40] It is not only direct democrats, but also Dahlian pluralist democrats and more conventional liberal democrats, among others, who assign an important role to citizen association when defining democracy.[41]

Moreover, everyday language suggests that people regularly identify associational practices by which plural citizens aim to affect their environment as specifically democratic, even in the context of regimes that would not themselves be so categorized. For example, media coverage in the United States in early 2011 often described the collective protests in Egypt leading up to the revolution as part of a "democratic uprising" or as the expression of "democratic freedom."[42] These characterizations, also prevalent in informal conversations among nonexperts, indicate that people tend to understand public action in concert precisely as an enactment of democracy, wherever it occurs. The identification of the protests in Tahrir Square in the spring of 2011 as democratic had less to do with the fact that some participants were calling for democratizing reforms than with the shared insight that the protesters were already practicing democracy by joining together to generate power and produce effects collectively that they could not alone.

If associative action is integral to nearly every philosophical and practical definition of democracy, then this book's investigation of ethos is perhaps of some general interest. The book's central questions — Does the practice of associative democracy have an ethos? How should it be characterized? Can it be purposely fostered? How? — will, I hope, resonate with democrats of varying stripes who share the conviction that ordinary citizens' joint action, and not merely individuals' right to vote, is essential to democratic life.

The book's initial, ground-clearing project centers on work that takes inspiration from Foucault and Levinas. Theorists who turn to these thinkers in order to develop an account of democratic ethos are typically interested in nourishing activist forms of democracy that involve significant associational activity among citizens. Yet, as I show, the ethical orientations they conceptualize are ill-suited to enriching the associative dynamics outlined above, in which collaborative and contentious forms of action take place in plural sites and are mediated by disputed common objects. In particular, care for the self and care for the Other describe ethical orientations that celebrate dyadic relations in which the primary actor, a single self, tends to herself or to another. These models of care cannot simply be extended to associative democratic politics. Neither the face-to-face immediacy of the Levinasian encounter nor the reflexive intimacy of Foucauldian arts of the self leaves room for the crucial third term, a common and disputed object, that inspires democratic projects and draws citizens into relations of support and contestation with one another. In response to this neglect, the book elaborates an alternative ethics, also centered on practices of care. Yet the care that is central to associative democracy, I show, is enacted by many persons, not one. And the recipient of that care is neither a self nor even selves but a particular feature of shared conditions—a worldly thing—that is both a common and contentious object of concern.

One final note, before offering a map of the book's contents: the three central thinkers in this project, Foucault, Levinas, and Arendt, whose work and its appropriation by others I examine in relation to the question of democratic ethics, are heirs to a specific, shared intellectual heritage.[43] This lineage, existential phenomenology in general and Martin Heidegger's thought in particular, is not the focus of my inquiry, yet the fact that all three theorists' writings are shaped by and responsive to this singular theoretical tradition is important.[44] Most notably, it may help to explain why their work is especially fertile ground for today's investigations into ethos, investigations which, as discussed earlier, are undertaken from a nonessentialist, postmoral vantage point.[45] Despite the distinctiveness of their respective approaches and the unique relations of care each conceptualizes, Foucault, Levinas, and Arendt can be regarded as participants in a common theoretical endeavor, one which is marked, first of all, by a "critical orientation to rationalism, abstract system-building, and other objectifying modes of thought such as positivism."[46] In addition, the focus of existential phenomenology on "worldly relations" and "concrete lived experience" rather than on "mental contents" is evident in all three thinkers' work and connects with their readers' interest in ethos as an embodied, enacted way of being.[47] Finally, because the existential-phenomenological perspective is especially alert to "non-rational dimensions of human existence: habits, non-conscious practices, moods, and passions," it is unsurprising that writings emerging from this tradition have captivated contemporary audiences interested in ethics, where ethics is understood as dispositional and affective, an important extra-rational aspect of political life.[48] The following analysis focuses primarily on exploring the differences between therapeutic, charitable, and worldly ethics, which take their bearings from Foucault, Levinas, and Arendt, respectively. These competing approaches to ethics are not simply or only at odds with one another, however; a shared existential-phenomenological orientation informs the work of all three and seems to resonate with those seeking a democratic ethos today.

The book's argument proceeds as follows. Chapter 1 focuses on how Foucault's late work has been taken up by theorists seeking a contemporary democratic ethos. Foucault's interest in ancient aesthetic/ascetic modes of self-elaboration, which he describes as an ethics of "care of the self," has intrigued those interested in cultivating new forms of democratic subjectivity that might spur deeper, more respectful forms of citizen engagement. Building on Foucault's recommendation that the ethics of self-care might be reinvented for the present and help to foster selves who "play games of power with as little domination as possible," William Connolly, for example, has advocated ethical tactics performed by the self on herself as indispensable for contemporary pluralist democracy.[49]

In this chapter I examine both Foucault's and Connolly's work, focusing on Connolly's contention that arts of the self, or "micropolitics," have a vital role to play in inspiring and shaping collective democratic action, that is, "macropolitics." I argue that although this idea is appealing, an ethics capable of animating associative democratic activity cannot take the self's relationship to itself as a starting point. Even though Foucault and Connolly conceptualize a self that is continually recrafted rather than discovered in its ultimate truth, their work nonetheless advances a therapeutic ethics, which treats the self's relationship with itself as primary and envisions democratic activity as a consequence or extension of that reflexive relation. The chapter illuminates this therapeutic ethical orientation and tries to dispel the belief that it is by caring for oneself that one comes to care for the world. I argue that unless the self's relationship to itself is driven from the start by shared concern for a worldly problem, there is no reason to believe that it will lead in an activist, democratic direction. Indeed, focused care for the self too readily substitutes for tending to the world that is shared with diverse others.

In light of the critical perspective cast on Foucauldian ethics, I turn in chapter 2 to Levinas's ethical theory, which condemns egoism in the name of the self's infinite responsibility to the Other. This understanding of ethics, centering on the Other and its summons to the self, privileges an intersubjective rather than an intrasubjective relation.

For theorists such as Simon Critchley and Judith Butler, this focus on the self's obligation to tend to a needy Other appears especially useful to a democratic ethos because it confronts self-interest, calling on us to concern ourselves with the fates of others. My readings of Levinas, Critchley, and Butler, however, show that it is a mistake to assume that a charitable ethics, centered on the self's provision of aid to a singular, suffering other, can support collective democratic endeavors. The tendency to present a Levinasian-inspired ethical truth as the key to political transformation is falsely reassuring; it evades the difficulties of democratic mobilization by implying that associative action simply awaits acceptance of an indisputable ethical reality: the self's total obligation to the Other. Yet an ethics focused on the self's care for the Other, even if understood in less foundational terms than this, is unable to nourish associative democratic action. Levinasian ethics may be compelling, but it revolves around a dyadic, hierarchical relation that is focused on addressing immediate needs. Such charitable relations have value, but, as I show, they are distinct from, even at odds with, democratic ones, which involve collaboration among co-actors who struggle to tend not to a singular Other, but to the worldly conditions under which selves and others live.

I argue that the therapeutic and charitable models of ethics promoted by Foucault, Levinas, and key interpreters such as Connolly, Critchley, and Butler are unlikely to inspire and sustain collective democratic activity, in which participants cooperate and contend with one another in an effort to affect worldly conditions. Care for oneself or care for the Other, though perhaps valuable, does little to encourage associative relations among citizens. Moreover, it is a mistake to assume that forms of democratic engagement somehow follow from proper care for the self or for an Other. Indeed, I show that the therapeutic and charitable orientations others have advocated in the name of a democratic ethos need to be resisted if we seek to foster activist forms of democratic citizenship.

Chapters 3 and 4 are dedicated to theorizing a world-centered ethos.[50] I argue that the spirit of care for the world, which already animates some associative democratic projects, deserves to be explicitly thematized and purposefully cultivated. The first step toward elaborating this ethical orientation, which I argue is especially important to democratic life, is to articulate the central concept of world. Chapter 3 develops this notion, first, by defining *world* as the array of material and immaterial conditions under which human beings live—both with one another and with a rich variety of nonhumans, organic and technological. This portrait draws on Arendt's understanding of world as an "in-between," that is, both the site and object of politics, yet, as the above statement indicates, I challenge her restriction of world to what is man-made. In addition, I claim that coaction among citizens is best understood not as being directed at the world per se, as Arendt would have it, but at particular worldly things, which are more plural, dynamic, and disputed than her theory recognizes. In reference to *thing*'s original meaning, worldly thing, a central concept in this book, indicates not a generic object but a "matter of fact" that has been reconstituted as a public "matter of concern."[51] This thing, I show, is crucial to every democratic undertaking; it is the contentious third term around which people gather, both in solidarity and division. A viable democratic ethos honors this dynamic, seeking to inspire mutual care for worldly conditions.

Chapter 3 engages with the work of Arendt, John Dewey, Bruno Latour, and others in order to reveal the structure of citizen association in which worldly things both connect and divide constituencies, a structure that is eclipsed by dyadic models of ethics. Chapter 4 builds on this account of the crucial role played by worldly things in democratic politics in order to specify the normative ends that care for the world pursues. This chapter clarifies that not all forms of collective organizing in relation to a worldly thing or matter of concern count as instances of care for the world. The democratic ethos I defend is refined to mean care for the world *as* world. Here I advance an explicitly normative conception of world—as both a shared human home and mediating political space—that allows for critical distinctions to be made between competing projects undertaken by democratic actors. The chapter elaborates these concepts by examining contemporary organizations and movements, including No More Deaths/ No Más Muertes, the Beacons programs in New York City Public Schools, and the Right to the City Movement, which embody the democratic ethos I advance.

A brief epilogue revisits the distinctions between care for the self, care for the Other, and care for the world that inform the book's argument in support of an ethos that can and does animate associative democratic politics. Here I consider whether and how the dyadic, intimate modalities of care emphasized by Foucauldian and Levinasian ethics can be transformed into collaborative practices of care focused on shaping collective conditions. What strategies of politicization, for example, can activate feelings of care and concern and direct them toward worldly things? I consider the techniques that can help foster care for the world even under circumstances seemingly inhospitable to it.

One image in particular, from the margins of Arendt's work, can help illuminate the distinctive orientation that defines worldly ethics. In the summer of 1963, Gershom Scholem, the renowned Jewish scholar, wrote a letter to Arendt concerning her recently published book *Eichmann in Jerusalem*, which reported on the trial of the former ss officer Adolf Eichmann.[52] At the time of its appearance *Eichmann in Jerusalem* was the subject of intense dispute, debates that continue to shape its reception today. One of the most controversial points in the book was Arendt's charge that the Judenräte, or local Jewish governing structures, had, in their maintenance of Jewish public order in the ghettoes, enabled the Nazis to slaughter greater numbers of Jews with greater efficiency than they might otherwise have done. Many people, Jews and non-Jews, were shocked by this seemingly harsh and unempathic claim. Scholem's letter to Arendt accuses her of adopting a "heartless" tone in her discussions of "Jews and their bearing in the days of catastrophe." By way of elaboration, Scholem explains to Arendt, "In the Jewish tradition, there is a concept, hard to define and yet concrete enough, which we know as *Ahabath Israel*: 'Love of the Jewish people.'" And he declares that he finds "little trace of this" in her book.[53]

In her response to Scholem, Arendt directly addresses this charge. She writes of the "love of the Jewish people," "You are quite right—I am not moved by any love of this sort." She states, "This 'love of the Jews' would appear to me, since I am myself Jewish, as something rather suspect. I cannot love myself or anything which I know is part and parcel of my own person." And she writes, as a point of contrast, that "the greatness of this people was once that it believed in God, and believed in Him in such a way that its trust and love towards him was greater than its fear. And now this people believes only in itself? What good can come of that?—Well, in this sense I do not 'love' the Jews, nor do I 'believe' in them."[54] Arendt's response to Scholem calls into question the self-oriented nature of *Ahabath*

*Israel*, the love of the Jewish people by the Jewish people. She reminds him of the real "greatness" of the Jews, which concerned their trust in and love for an entity outside themselves in relation to which they came to be: God, who acted as a common object of devotion and thus constituted a shared world for them, an in-between. It is not the Jews' love for themselves or even for one another that Arendt wants to recall and honor, but their regard for a third term, their God, around which they constituted a community.

This book invites readers to see in Arendt's exchange with Scholem a nascent democratic analogy. Scholem's invocation of a self-oriented relation of love and faith (of Jews to themselves) evokes a dyadic ethical relation of the sort I call into question. Arendt's radical shift in perspective, which brings into view a relation involving multiple individuals and a shared object of love and faith, offers a religious analog to the democratic relations with which this book is concerned. The third term, God, is akin to those secular, worldly objects that, as I argue, inspire the labors of democratic actors and mediate relations among them. The book tracks how these democratic modes of relation—in which individuals are connected to and separated from one another by a common object which they attempt to affect—are occluded by popular ethical approaches. And it urges us to see that a sensibility focused on collective and contentious care for worldly things is an ethos uniquely fit for democracy.

CHAPTER ONE

‗

# CRAFTING A DEMOCRATIC SUBJECT?

The Foucauldian Ethics of Self-Care

Care for others should not be put before the care of oneself. The care of the self is ethically prior in that the relationship with oneself is onto-logically prior.

— MICHEL FOUCAULT

Change the World. Start with Yourself.

— BUMPER STICKER

The oft-heard complaint about contemporary Americans' political apathy, their apparent disinterest in the basic activities of citizenship, is coupled with another, seemingly distinct objection: that those who do participate, particularly in public debates and protests, do so in ways that are aggressive, close-minded, and unlikely to contribute to meaningful discussion or reflection. The so-called decline in civility, though arguably a characteristic of political actors on the right and the left, was especially evident early in President Barack Obama's administration, as citizens opposing his health care proposals commandeered town hall meetings with Democratic officials, yelling angrily over one another while frequently likening Obama to Hitler.[1] Tea Party protesters challenging big government drew national attention in late 2009 with vitriolic and racist words and images of the president. In these instances, citizens are far from withdrawn and indifferent; yet the form and style of their engagement are disconcerting to many. Indeed, this version of active citizenship threatens to give apathy a good name.

While citizen inaction, on the one hand, and the confrontational, angry demeanor of some citizen groups, on the other, may seem to pose wholly separate problems, these phenomena actually raise some similar questions about democratic subjectivity. What kinds of selves are apt to venture into and are capable of enduring the demands and frustrations of contemporary political life? What proclivities or sensibilities inspire ordinary individuals not only to vote but also to attend meetings, organize protests, form associations, and speak publicly when many others turn away in exhaustion or disgust? Moreover, what habits, dispositions, and character traits encourage individuals to pursue forms of public involvement that are impassioned yet respectful, oppositional without being antagonizing? What allows people to enter into democratic contest in such a way that their convictions do not foreclose other voices and demonize those who disagree? These related questions focus on identifying the personal qualities that equip an individual to participate deeply in democratic politics and to do so in a certain spirit.

This is hardly a new inquiry. Political theorists through the ages have struggled with the question of how to create not only a polity suited to its potential members but also members who are themselves suited to the polity. From the *Republic*'s account of the wide-ranging, exacting techniques required to mold inhabitants so they can assume their proper roles in the ideal city to Rawls's interest in a public culture that inculcates in citizens the desire to be the kind of person that acts in accordance with the principles of justice, the making of citizens is a perennial as well as a fraught concern in political thought. Contemporary inquiries into civic virtue in liberal-democratic contexts address not only the means by which the cultivation of virtue might occur, but also the abiding tension between projects of citizen formation and ideals of liberty, individuality, and diversity.

As I suggested in the introduction, the quest for a democratic ethos is similarly motivated by the insight that political institutions and practices depend for their vitality and endurance on the attitudes, emotions, and habits of thought of citizens. The inquiry into ethos aims to address the affective and normative dimensions of democratic subjectivity while rejecting the idea of a single, universal morality that would ground collective life. Revived interest in ethics among postfoundational thinkers reflects a desire to consider the connections between character and democratic activity, while remaining cautious about the imposition of uniform ways of being.

It is perhaps not surprising, then, that a conception of ethics centered on care for the self holds such appeal. The idea, drawn from Foucault's intriguing unfinished work on ancient Greco-Roman culture, holds out the hope that people can transform who they are, that is, develop certain qualities of character that allow them to conduct themselves differently, through reflexive relations with themselves. An ethics defined in terms of arts of the self emphasizes the individual's capacity to consciously shape or reshape herself and acquire an admirable style of existence largely detached from the enforcement of a general moral code. As we will see, Foucault's work invites us to explore the possibilities of a reworked ethics of self-care in the present and gestures toward its potential political significance, yet it is ultimately ambiguous about the purpose and effects of such an ethics. Contemporary political theorists, however, captivated by the idea of self-care, have placed great, arguably disproportionate, weight on this facet of Foucault's work.[2] Drawing on his evocative discussions of self-care, Foucault's readers have insisted that techniques of the self have an important role to play today in preparing individuals for the challenges of democratic struggle.[3] The cultivation of citizenly desires and dispositions, it is suggested, can be a self-guided "practice of freedom" rather than the task of large-scale social and political institutions intent on making good subjects.

This chapter offers a critical analysis of care for the self (*le souci de soi*) as an ethics for democratic politics. Beginning with an examination of Foucault's writings, lectures, and interviews on the topic, I assess the appeal of and the difficulties posed by his account of care for the self. In particular, although Foucault implies that arts of the self can provide the basis for a contemporary ethics and even avers that such a reflexive ethics, focused on the self's relationship to itself, can alter the broader field of intersubjective power relations, the connection between self-care and sociopolitical dynamics is only weakly and inconsistently articulated. In light of this gap in Foucault's thinking, the work of William Connolly is intriguing. He argues that Foucauldian techniques of the self, or "micropolitics," are crucially important for enabling and guiding collective democratic action, or "macropolitics," and he seeks to articulate the relation between the two.

I argue here that the care for the self is a flawed basis for elaborating a democratic ethics. Although the notion that purposeful work on the self can contribute to collective citizen action is no doubt appealing, an ethics capable of animating associative democratic activity, I show, cannot take the self's relationship to itself as its starting point. The therapeutic ethics that emerges from Foucault's and Connolly's work tends to treat democratic activity as a consequence or extension of self-care, a view that overlooks the unique orientation toward shared conditions that associative democracy requires. Unless the self's reflexive relationship to itself is driven from the start by concern for a worldly problem, there is no reason to believe that self-intervention will lead in an activist, democratic direction. Any reflexive relationship that might enhance democratic subjectivity depends upon collective political mobilizations that both inspire and continually guide work on the self. A viable democratic ethos should focus less on inciting and enriching individual care for oneself than on activating collaborative concern for social conditions. Only in tandem with such world-centered practices of care can arts of the self acquire democratic significance.

### "Man Is One and the Other at the Same Time": Foucault's Ancient Ethics

Foucault locates in antiquity a very particular understanding of ethics, conceptualized as *rapport à soi*, or, more specifically, as "the kind of relationship you ought to have with yourself."[4] The self was regarded as both subject and object of ethical action in Greco-Roman culture, according to Foucault, and this is the central idea that captured his attention and subsequently his readers' as well. But what exactly is the reflexive relation at the heart of this ethics? And what possible connection could exist between that uniquely ancient perspective and the present time and place?

Foucault's work on ancient ethics is often quite dense, consisting of detailed analysis of sometimes obscure texts. It is nonetheless possible to identity four distinguishing features of Foucault's account of ancient ethics that merit scrutiny: the emphasis on the aesthetic dimension of the care of the self, the significance of *askesis* (exercise, training) in order to achieve self-control, the identification of care for oneself with the practice of freedom, and the distinction drawn between ethics and morality. Grappling with these elements is a necessary prelude to consideration of whether such an ethics, reimagined and reinvented, might serve to support associative democracy today. Because the larger question of democratic ethos guides this encounter, my analysis is less concerned with judging the historical veracity of Foucault's account than with exploring the connections between the (admittedly partial and creative) story he tells about ancient ethics and the conditions of the present. While valid objections have been made to inaccuracies in Foucault's treatment of Greco-Roman ethics,[5] his "unabashed contemporary orientation" gives one reason to approach this work as a narrative constructed at least partly in relation to present-day concerns.[6]

The first feature of ancient ethics that Foucault stresses is the aesthetic character of *epimeleia heautou*, the injunction to "take care of yourself." This principle, traceable from classical Greece through the imperial era, despite undergoing important changes during that period, called for treating "one's own life as a personal work of art."[7] The practice of self-care Foucault explores in texts ranging from the first Platonic dialogues to the major texts of late Stoicism is a project of self-creation. Care consists not in the nurturing of an already constituted self but in the efforts by which a self is brought into existence as a distinctive entity to be recognized by others.[8] This "aesthetics of existence," involving concerted attention and ongoing work directed at cultivating the self, stands as a striking alternative to the later Christian hermeneutic tradition of confession and self-renunciation.[9] Timothy O'Leary argues that, for Foucault, "The modern hermeneutics of the self is both historically preceded and normatively surpassed by the ancient aesthetics of the self."[10] But if this is so, what is normatively compelling about this aesthetic pursuit? What does it mean to regard the self as a creative production elaborated through form-giving activity?

Foucault elaborates: "What I mean by the phrase [arts of existence] are those intentional and voluntary actions by which men not only set themselves rules of conduct, but also seek to transform themselves, to change themselves in their singular being, and to make their life an *oeuvre* that carries certain aesthetic values and meets certain stylistic criteria."[11] This passage is striking in several ways. First, it depicts the arts of the self as intentional, voluntary, and guided by self-set rules of conduct. These arts, Foucault contends, are undertaken freely and in accordance with standards that are not simply imposed from without but taken up and endorsed by the individual who seeks to meet them. I want to focus here on the specifically aesthetic qualities ascribed to the care for the self. This passage is marked by an ambiguity that runs throughout Foucault's account, an ambiguity born of two competing understandings of *aesthetic*. On the one hand, the activities of self-care seem to be aesthetic because they aim to create a life that is beautiful, a work of art, or, as Foucault says above, an *oeuvre* that realizes certain stylistic criteria. On the other hand, he depicts caring for the self as aesthetic largely because the self is related to as a site of work and transformation; here the emphasis is on *travail* rather than *oeuvre*. So does the aesthetic quality of the practice of self-care primarily concern a process or an outcome? Is caring for the self aesthetic because the self is treated as material in an ongoing project, susceptible to lifelong form-giving and alteration, or because the self is likened to a finished art object, modeled in accordance with certain standards of beauty?

The latter possibility, most pronounced when Foucault explains, for example, that one's life, no less than a lamp or a house, might be seen as an art object, has elicited charges of dandyism.[12] Richard Bernstein and Pierre Hadot, for example, worry that the care for the self pursues stylization for its own sake and therefore cannot serve to inspire an ethics worthy of consideration today.[13] Art for art's sake as it applies to the formation of the self, the argument goes, is a superficial, even normatively bankrupt pursuit.

Yet as Thomas Flynn and O'Leary have pointed out, the implied opposition between beauty and substantive, moral ends is troubled by the identification of the beautiful with the morally good in ancient thought, as evidenced by the term *kalos*, which referred to both beauty and moral worth.[14] This indicates that even if beauty was sometimes the aim of the care of the self in antiquity, this need not be interpreted in superficial or amoral terms.[15] Moreover, Foucault repeatedly insisted—both in his readings of ancient techniques of the care of the self and in his references to a possible reworking of such techniques in the present—that such care is directed at an end distinct from beauty per se: limiting and controlling one's domination over others. Thus the ambivalence of the term *kalos*, along with Foucault's emphasis on the minimization of domination, directs one away from the assumption that the "aesthetics of existence" is about the pursuit of beauty, at least in any conventional modern sense of the term. Indeed, the stress in Foucault's work on ethics lies on the aesthetic mode of relation, which regards the self as something to be crafted and recrafted over time, rather than on the notion that caring for oneself is synonymous with making the self beautiful.

Second, the activity of self-constitution Foucault identifies with ancient Greek ethics involves not only *techne* but also askesis, continuous training and exercise. The ancient focus on self-formation was, Foucault writes, a matter of "constant practice" and "regulated occupation," not merely an idea or attitude.[16] This work, though it assumed various forms over time, entailed both mental and physical exercises involving self-examination, "control over representations," and practices of "abstinence, privation, and physical resistance" focused on three domains of the "arts of self-conduct": bodily regimen, household management, and erotics.[17] The array of techniques, though vast, is characterized by a common theme: the establishment of a relation with oneself characterized by "domination," "mastery," "*arkhe*," and "command."[18] As Foucault explains, "The effort that the individual was urged to bring to bear on himself, the necessary ascesis, had the form of a battle to be fought, a victory to be won in establishing a dominion of self over self, modeled after domestic or political authority."[19] The "domination of oneself by oneself," or *enkrateia*, requires the constitution of part of oneself as a "vigilant adversary," akin to a fighting soldier or wrestler, who confronts and attempts to subdue the "inferior appetites" that threaten to overtake the self.[20] On Foucault's telling, success within the terms of this ethical struggle was imagined not as the complete expulsion of desires but as the "setting up of a solid and stable state of rule of the self over the self."[21] The desires and pleasures did not need to disappear; what was required was that one "construct a relationship with the self that is of the 'domination-submission,' 'command-obedience,' 'mastery-docility' type."[22]

Third, the aesthetic and ascetic undertaking that Foucault labels care of the self is also framed as a "practice of freedom." This claim is complicated by the fact that the ancient culture Foucault examines was home to more than a single notion of freedom (as he sometimes acknowledges), making it difficult to pin down the exact meaning of this identification of reflexive ethics with freedom. On the one hand, disciplined self-elaboration among the classical Greeks was generally understood to be an activity reserved for a certain class: free citizens, those who were not ruled by others. The ethical practice of self-care was not a universal pursuit but was typically undertaken by those who enjoyed civic freedom, itself defined in opposition to slavery. On the other hand, as Foucault is well aware, this understanding of outer freedom coexisted, somewhat tensely, with a conception of inner freedom, developed most influentially in Plato's philosophy, in which the master–slave relation is installed within the self, in the soul.

According to this understanding of freedom, as it was most forcefully articulated by the later Stoic thought of Epictetus, a slave who is master of himself, such that his reason reigns over the passions, may be freer than Alcibiades, who enjoyed a powerful social and political status but was beholden to the tyrannous elements within himself.[23] Foucault does not specify how he is using the term *freedom* when he declares the care of the self to be an instance of its practice. But his comments indicate that he means to link self-care to some measure of outer freedom, understood as a necessary condition for the exacting project of aesthetic and ascetic self-formation. Such reflexive activity, Foucault seems to believe, requires a degree of outer freedom, such that one is not enslaved or dominated by others. Care of the self amounts to an advanced, rigorous, and by no means automatic enactment of that basic freedom. He writes, "Freedom is the ontological condition of ethics. But ethics is the considered form that freedom takes when it is informed by reflection."[24] In other words, a measure of civic freedom, or what Foucault elsewhere calls liberation, is required for the ethics of self-care to be a meaningful possibility.[25] But the exercise of self-care, the attempt to form oneself through a demanding reflexive relation, is, to Foucault, an example of what it means to practice freedom actively, that is, to put one's freedom to use and thereby experience it as something other than a static condition: "What is ethics if not the practice of freedom, the conscious practice of freedom?"[26]

The conscious practice of freedom consists in "extensive work by the self on the self," but this work is not private; it is manifest in one's interactions with others. Foucault says of the Greeks, "*Ethos* was a way of being and of behavior. It was a mode of being for the subject, along with a certain way of acting, a way visible to others." While this mode of being involved a rich, reflexive relation of disciplined craftsmanship, a person's ethos was externalized and evident in everything he did: what he wore, the way he walked, how he responded to events. Ethos, as the "concrete form of freedom," was on display for others: "A man possessed of a splendid *ethos*, who could be admired and put forward as an example, was someone who practiced freedom in a certain way."[27] For the ancients, Foucault explains, freedom was exercised in the development of a style of existence visible to others.

The prominence of freedom in Foucault's account of self-care is especially notable because it seems to mark a shift in his work away from a portrait of the subject as an effect or conduit of power (which dominated his middle-period writing) and toward a conception of the subject as a purposeful actor, capable of giving shape to himself. What does one make of the appearance of this figure, who engages in "practices of liberty"? Is Foucault invoking a premodern self untouched by the operations of disciplinary and bio power? Or is he seeking to replace or amend the theory of the subject as constructed by regimes of power? Although some commentators have suggested that the inquiry into the care of the self marks a decisive break in Foucault's thinking, even an embrace of autonomous individuality, the shift in emphasis in his later work is nonetheless consistent with earlier analyses.[28]

Addressing his interest in the care of the self, Foucault explained, "Perhaps I've insisted too much on the technology of domination and power. I am more and more interested in the interaction between oneself and others, and in the technologies of individual domination, in the mode of action that an individual exercises upon himself by means of the technologies of the self."[29] While previous scholarship centered on the subject's relation to "coercive practices," the turn to the ancient ethics of self-creation is partly an inquiry into the "practices of liberty" that, together with "practices of subjection," constitute the subject.[30] And in 1984, on the occasion of the publication of volumes 2 and 3 of *The History of Sexuality*, Foucault explained that what bothered him about his previous books was that he considered only two of three major problems or "domains of experience"—the problem of truth and the problem of power—while neglecting the third, the problem of individual conduct, which he now sought to take into account.[31]

While these comments lead some readers of Foucault to interpret his ethical work as the much-longed-for answer to the problems posed by his earlier analysis of the production of compliant subjects, the concept of subjectivation (*assujettissement*) actually connects the middle and later work, revealing continuity rather than rupture between the two.[32] Subjectivation, as Foucault explained in the first volume of *The History of Sexuality*, refers to human beings' constitution as subjects "in both senses of the word."[33] Foucault's turn to ethics corresponds to one side of this ambivalent structure of subjectivation. If subjectivation refers to the fact that power both initiates the subject and constitutes the subject's agency such that the subject is "*neither* fully determined by power *nor* fully determining of power (but significantly and partially both)," then Foucault's earlier work can be considered primarily an analysis of the way in which subjects are constituted, while his late work on ethics aims to consider the constituting capacities of subjects.[34] This mapping of Foucault's work helps guard against the facile taking of sides in which one affirms either Foucault's account of the subject-as-effect-of-power or, alternatively, his account of subject-as-artistic-practitioner-of-freedom and encourages instead an attentiveness to the ways in which these two portions of Foucault's scholarship speak to what Judith Butler calls "the double aspect of subjection," that "the subject, taken to be the condition for and instrument of agency, is at the same time the effect of subordination."[35]

The dynamic of subjectivation helps to clarify that the freedom exercised in self-care occurs within social constraints; it is not outside or beyond power relations. Indeed, the practices of liberty that allow the subject of antiquity to form himself, Foucault argues, are based on "the rules, styles, inventions . . . found in the cultural environment."[36] Even the self-fashioning subject is simultaneously limited and enabled by the repertoire of norms and techniques available in his social setting. The practices of the self, as a manifestation of freedom, are possible only on the basis of models that are "proposed, suggested, imposed" by one's culture, society, or social group.[37] Self-formation can be understood as a "struggle for freedom within the confines of a historical situation."[38]

Finally, aligning ancient ethics with the practice of freedom enables Foucault to establish a distinction between morality and ethics. Whereas morality centers on rule-following, ethics, he claims, is not primarily about obedience to a code but about the manner in which one forms oneself as an ethical subject, how one conducts oneself.[39] Foucault recognizes that these typologies coexist in practice: "Every morality, in the broad sense comprises . . . codes of behavior and forms of subjectivation."[40] Nonetheless, Foucault asserts that in certain moralities "the main emphasis is placed on the code, on its systematicity, its richness, its capacity to adjust to every possible case and to embrace every area of behavior," while in others, "the strong and dynamic element is to be found in the forms of subjectivation and practices of the self." Foucault associates the former type of morality with Christianity and the latter with antiquity: "Moral conceptions in Greek and Greco-Roman antiquity were much more oriented toward practices of the self and the questions of askesis than toward codifications of conducts and the strict definition of what is permitted and what is forbidden."[41]

The contrast between ancient ethics and Christian morality is deepened by Foucault's depiction of ancient ethics as being concerned with the cultivation of "singular being" rather than focused on processes of "normalization" involving a "pattern of behavior for everyone."[42] Foucault depicts the aesthetic ethics of self-creation as a matter of "personal choice," and creative elaboration that lacks any relation to "the juridical per se," "an authoritarian system," or a "disciplinary structure."[43] At the heart of these comparisons is the idea that later, Christian-based moralities impose a general code of conduct, universal in scope, which centers on compulsory precepts supported by the penalty both of the norm and of the law.[44] Ancient ethics, on the contrary, Foucault holds, operated relatively independently of "any social—or at least legal—institutional system." The questionable veracity of this claim notwithstanding, Foucault was drawn to what he regarded as rigorous, austere work on the self that was not simply imposed via law or religion but was "a choice about existence made by the individual."[45] The aesthetics of existence was voluntarily pursued as a "supplement" or "luxury" involving the individual stylization of activity.[46] The reference to luxury signals that the ancient ethics Foucault depicts was primarily the practice of an elite, "the smallest minority of the population."[47] Yet his critical remarks on the exclusions and oppressions characterizing ancient Greece suggest that what Foucault is drawn to is not the idea of an ethics that is the purview of an elite class, but the possibility of an ethics centered on the self's reflexive relation, an ethics that is willingly pursued apart from an "authoritarian moral system" consisting in "deep and essential prohibitions."[48]

These four features of ancient ethics—aestheticism, asceticism, freedom, and stylization over codification—are not merely matters of antiquarian curiosity for Foucault. His inquiry is consistently guided by the insight that "our problem nowadays" might be similar to that of the Greeks, because he asserts (rather hopefully?) that "most of us no longer believe that ethics is founded in religion, nor do we want a legal system to intervene in our moral, personal, private life."[49] Foucault believes that modern circumstances may be particularly well suited to and in need of an ethics centered on care for the self, characterized by the four features addressed above. He rejects the notion that ancient ethical practices could simply be imported into the present, arguing that contact with the past may "produce something, but it must be emphasized that it would be something new."[50] Nonetheless, he continually links the inquiry into ancient ethics to the conditions of the present.[51]

Crafting a Democratic Subject?

*Crafting a Democratic Subject?*

—

It is the Greek and Greco-Roman emphasis on practices of self-formation rather than on a prescriptive and proscriptive moral code that leads Foucault to wager that there may be something to learn from ancient ethics.[52] He situates his inquiry in relation to contemporary conditions: "From Antiquity to Christianity, we pass from an ethics that was essentially the search for a personal ethics to a morality as obedience to a system of rules. And if I was interested in Antiquity it was because for a whole series of reasons, the idea of morality as obedience to a code of rules is now disappearing, has already disappeared. And to this absence of morality corresponds, must correspond, the search for an aesthetics of existence."[53] Here Foucault claims that we live in something like a post-moral era, having left behind the aspiration for a universalizable code of rules, a situation that opens up the possibility of an ethics of self-care.[54] Although Foucault wavers as to whether we are truly beyond the morality of rule-following or still somewhat beholden to it, he consistently maintains that the ethics of self-cultivation he traces through antiquity is worthy of attention here and now.[55] He seems to think there is something to be learned from an ethics defined in terms of reflexive self-creation and transformation. As Paul Veyne notes, Foucault believed that "in the modern world, it was impossible to ground an ethics" and that under these conditions, one element of Greek ethics, "namely, the idea of a work of the self on the self" might be "capable of reacquiring a contemporary meaning."[56]

But if Foucault maintains that we need an ethics today, why is this so?[57] To what problem might the ethics of self-care serve as a response? What is its purpose? Its potential?

## The Aims of Self-Care

One way of understanding the purpose or *telos* of arts of the self in contemporary contexts is in terms of what James Bernauer and Michael Mahon have described as the two sides of resistance articulated by Foucault.[58] Perhaps the value of self-care lies in the role it can play in the project Foucault describes in "The Subject and Power": the task of simultaneously refusing the kind of individuality that has been "imposed on us for several centuries" and "promot[ing] new forms of subjectivity."[59] This approach to conceptualizing the meaning of self-care is appealing for its elegance. It suggests that an ethics centered on reflexive self-(trans)formation is intended, in a rather direct way, to challenge existing forms of subjectivity and create alternative forms. While this casting leaves open the normative question of which subjectivities ought to be resisted, which pursued, and on what grounds, the seemingly linear route from purposeful efforts at self-crafting to the creation of new and different kinds of subjectivity is intuitively compelling.

When care of the self is understood in this way, as a means by which to invent new modes of subjectivity, it is positioned as a strategy of antinormalization.[60] Arts of the self, that is, purposeful efforts to create and transform oneself, are seen as a potentially valuable contemporary strategy for challenging the conformist effects of discipline, theorized so effectively by Foucault in his earlier writings. Michael Schwartz, for example, says Foucault's aesthetics of existence amounts to a "tactic for denormalizing identity," and Johanna Oksala attests, "The way to contest normalizing power is by shaping oneself and one's lifestyle creatively."[61] This interpretation effectively posits two dueling forms of discipline. As Richard Flathman describes it, Foucault's work sets up a contrast between the self-discipline embodied in Greco-Roman techniques of the self and the "dominating disciplines" of disciplinary society.[62] It is as if ethics stands for a kind of good discipline that might oppose, or at least rework, bad discipline. In Flathman's terms, Foucault's late texts develop the idea of self-discipline as a "counter-discipline" that resists "cultural, social and political discipline."[63]

But if self-discipline and dominating discipline are both disciplines — forms of power that act locally and materially on the minute details of human existence to produce particular, ongoing effects — what exactly distinguishes one from the other? At first glance it would seem to be their respective sources. Self-discipline has a reflexive structure; it is imposed by the self on the self. On the other hand, the disciplinary power Foucault theorizes in *Discipline and Punish* and other works from that period seems to emanate from sites of institutional authority: schools, armies, prisons, factories. But this easy distinction between self- and externally imposed discipline cannot hold, since one of the characteristic features of disciplinary power of the dominating type is precisely its ability to be taken up and internalized by the subject. The disciplinary techniques Foucault chronicled in detail prior to his work on ethics are effective precisely because they are not simply exercised upon subjects from without but assumed by subjects who learn to regulate themselves even in the absence of any visible authority. If disciplinary power is a type of power that func-

*Crafting a Democratic Subject?*

—

tions by making the human subject "the principle of his own subjection," doesn't the distinction between good (self-imposed) discipline and bad (externally imposed) discipline become untenable?

When is ascetic self-care a practice of freedom and when is it the quiet, light operation of disciplinary power? Are those who would engage in reflexive acts of self-making today performing a kind of resistance or serving as "relays" for the reigning technologies of a given culture?[64] These difficulties are never addressed directly by Foucault, as Jean Grimshaw notes.[65] Foucault's language, however, hints at part of the problem: his discussions of ancient ethics refer repeatedly to the "self" as the source and object of ethical practice, whereas this term is nearly absent from his work on disciplinary power. In those texts, the "subject" is everywhere while the "self" hardly ever appears. This difference in language signals that the "self" is the name usually reserved for a form of being that predates disciplinary power and the processes of subjectification that attend it. (Foucault dates the origins of disciplinary power to the sixteenth century.) If the "self" and the "subject" are not synonymous, then it becomes necessary to ask, how is care of the self undertaken by a "self" who is a disciplinary subject? When is the deliberate fashioning of oneself a way of countering disciplinary normalization and surveillance, and when is it the recapitulation of those operations? These questions may express irresolvable dilemmas, yet I have argued elsewhere that there are good reasons to be skeptical about a resistance strategy that so closely mirrors the modality of power it seeks to contest.[66]

But Foucault also identifies another possible end of self-care. Here, emphasis lies on intersubjectivity rather than on subjectivity per se. The ethical practice of arts of the self, according to Foucault, is always a social endeavor that involves other selves and generates effects beyond the practitioner. There are at least two senses in which ancient care of the self is intersubjective, according to Foucault's account. On the one hand, although the aesthetics of existence is pursued by a self who is both its subject and object, this ethical actor should not be mistaken for a monadic or atomistic individual. The self is an embedded self, one whose action is shaped by social conditions of possibility as well as by the participation of others who help facilitate self-care. Yet the care of the self is intersubjective in another way as well. Not only is it a situated practice that may involve other selves, but, Foucault repeatedly suggests, care of the self is capable of generating effects beyond the self; indeed, it may be the pre-condition for caring for others and may help to shape broader social and political relations.[67]

The first sense in which care for the self is intersubjective is that the self who labors to craft himself never does so in isolation. His location in a particular historical and social context structures the pursuit of an aesthetics of existence. As noted above, Foucault maintains that practices of the self are never invented by an individual but are made available by "his culture, his society, his social group." By emphasizing the extent to which ancient self-care was understood and exercised in relation to a particular community, Foucault tries to show that the self's reflexive relation with itself never takes place in a vacuum; it is anchored to a cultural environment that is shared with others. This environment both provides and limits the techniques and resources available to any potential ethical subject. In addition, Foucault points out that Greco-Roman practices of self-care regularly involved the close participation of specific individuals who served as guides, masters, and teachers to those engaged in *epimeleia heautou*.[68]

The second way in which care of the self is intersubjective, on Foucault's account, is more significant. Here the point is not the context within which a situated self engages in arts of the self (often with assistance from others) but rather the effects that those arts can have on others and on one's community. Dispelling the negative associations that care of the self carries with it thanks to Christian traditions, in which "being concerned with oneself was denounced as a form of self-love, selfishness, or self-interest," Foucault maintains that for the ancients the meaning of self-care extended far beyond the individual self.[69] Speaking of the Greeks, he explains, "The care of the self . . . implies complex relations with others insofar as this *ethos* of freedom is also a way of caring for others. *Ethos* implies a relationship with others insofar as the care of the self enables one to occupy his rightful position in the city, the community, or interpersonal relations." The central claim here is that the relation the self has with itself—rapport à soi—is vitally connected to the relations one has with others. Caring for the self, on this view, serves a preparatory function, readying the individual for the complex, pluralistic relations that characterize communal and, specifically, political life. When Foucault characterizes self-care as intersubjective in this sense, he echoes the Socratic notion that "a person who took proper care of himself, would, by the same token, be able to conduct himself properly in relation to others and for others."[70]

Yet this characterization of the care of the self as being socially relevant is not exactly convincing. First, in articulating the Greek perspective, Foucault repeats, without interrogating, the assumption of a world in which humans' supposed rightful positions are given or at least unproblematic. But is this a plausible or desirable aim for an ethics of self-artistry undertaken in the present? And supposing one wants to grant that a certain kind of self-care can contribute to caring for others, why suppose that such care for others proceeds automatically from reflexive concern, as Foucault's language of implication suggests? Moreover, isn't it necessary to differentiate between the multiple kinds of relations that can exist between selves and others? If care for the self potentially assists in caring for others, this still leaves the meaning of caring for others open. Does self-care produce effects in intimate interpersonal relations; in social relations within a defined community such as a school, workplace, or neighborhood; or in political relations among citizens? Again, what is the value, the purpose, the *telos* of caring for oneself? What comes of it?

Foucault makes another provocative claim in this regard by explicitly linking the ethics of the care of the self to the problem of power. Specifically, he states that an ethics centered on an aesthetic and ascetic self-relation may serve as "a way of controlling and limiting power."[71] He even offers that there may be "no first or final point of resistance to political power other than in the relationship one has to oneself."[72] Foucault casts ethics in these terms not only in his commentary on Greco-Roman culture but also in relation to the present: "Power relations are not something that is bad in itself, that we have to break free of. I do not think that a society can exist without power relations, if by that one means the strategies by which individuals try to direct and control the conduct of others. The problem, then, is not to try to dissolve them in the utopia of completely transparent communication [referring to Habermas] but to acquire the rules of law, the management techniques, and also the morality, the *ethos*, the practice of the self, that will allow us to play these games of power with as little domination as possible."[73]

This passage relies on an important distinction Foucault makes between power relations, in which there is "necessarily the possibility of resistance," and what he calls "states of domination."[74] While power relations are "mobile, reversible and unstable," domination describes power relations that are "fixed in such a way that they are perpetually asymmetrical."[75] This distinction between power relations in which "there are always possibilities of changing the situation" and states of domination in which a field of power relations has been "blocked" is critical.[76] It underlies Foucault's repeated (and often misunderstood) claim that one cannot get outside of power relations, and it also makes legible the new problem he poses here: How might one "play these games of power with as little domination as possible"?

Ethics, defined as the kind of relationship you ought to have with yourself, rapport à soi, is presented as an integral part of the answer to this question. In connection with "rules of law" and "management techniques" (about which Foucault says almost nothing), the ethical self-relation is offered as one of the means by which power relations can be altered in the direction of greater flexibility and openness. This framing is crucial because it positions reflexive arts of the self as a tool in a distinctly political project: challenging sedimented patterns of inequality and promoting contestability and revisability.

Probing this insight in Foucault's work, however, is complicated by the fact that the primary models his texts offer for thinking about the sociopolitical effects of self-care remain those of the Greeks and Romans. Although Foucault attributes to them two distinct understandings of the connection between rapport à soi and broader social and political relations, neither of these understandings supports—indeed, each is at odds with—the claim that care of the self can help render power relations more open and symmetrical.

The ancient Greek view, exemplified by Plato's texts, was that care of the self took the form of self-rule and was a precondition for the effective rule of others.[77] As Foucault explains, "The exercise of political power required, as its own principle of internal regulation, power over oneself." Dominion over himself "qualified a man to exercise his mastery over others. The most kingly man was king over himself." This belief in the necessity of self-rule for political rule is illustrated by the figures of the tyrant and the good political leader, who appear throughout ancient political thought. The tyrant exemplifies the man who, "incapable of mastering his own passions," is prone to abuse his power and harm his subjects, while the ideal political ruler is one whose "self-rule moderated his rule over others."[78]

*Crafting a Democratic Subject?*

—

On Foucault's telling, the Greeks understood there to be a strong connection between the relationship one forged with oneself and how one interacted with others: "I think the postulate of this whole morality was that a person who took proper care of himself would, by the same token, be able to conduct himself properly in relation to others and for others."[79] This characterization is intriguing because it indicates that the care of the self should be understood as a socially and politically meaningful activity and not simply as an exercise in solipsism. The Greek interpretation of the intersubjective significance of the reflexive relation is troubled, however, by the fact that this connection is conceptualized through the category of rule, so that it is specifically rule over oneself that prepares one to rule others well. This formulation of the link between self-mastery and intersubjective relations is not particularly promising for those who, like Foucault, are interested in the contemporary problem of "how to play these games of power with as little domination as possible."

On the other hand, Foucault notes an important shift between Greek and Roman ethics that bears on the question of the purpose of self-care.[80] He explains that in the Hellenistic and Roman periods concern for the self became a "universal principle" that was "independent of political life."[81] While Plato consistently presented self-rule as a requirement for rule of the city, as exemplified in *Alcibiades*, "taking care of yourself for its own sake" emerges with the Epicureans, Foucault tells us, and "becomes something very general with Seneca, Pliny, and so on: everybody has to take care of himself."[82] As Foucault constructs it, when mastery over oneself becomes "something that is not primarily related to power over others," the "relation to the other" that this supposes is "much less non-reciprocal than before."[83] While the Greeks conceived of self-mastery as necessary in order to rule others well (a view that implies a "dissymmetrical relation to others"), the Romans effected "a dissociation . . . between power over oneself and power over others."[84] Flathman argues that this "dissociation" is the reason for Foucault's implicit endorsement of Roman, as compared to Greek, ethics. It is the separation of self-rule from the question of rule over others, he declares, that constitutes the appeal of Roman ethics for Foucault.[85]

If Flathman is correct, and Foucault finds the Roman divorce of self-mastery from mastery over others in some sense appealing, this does not so much resolve the question of the connection between the reflexive relation and self/other relations as deepen it. For, on Foucault's telling, the Roman version of care of the self understood that pursuit as something "done for its own sake," an undertaking relatively detached from one's relations with others. Here the self is "no longer a relay": the self is the definitive and only aim of the care of the self.[86] While this way of imagining the care of the self may have the merit of detaching the rule of oneself from rule over others, it does not offer an alternative framework for understanding how the relationship one constructs with oneself can guide, transform, or otherwise influence one's relationships with other selves. Foucault never provides his own argument for how an ethics of self-care might bear on interpersonal, social, or political relations, even as he maintains that such an ethics has a part to play in the transformation of power relations in the present. When Foucault comments, "Care for others should not be put before the care of oneself. The care of the self is ethically prior in that the relationship with oneself is ontologically prior," he only raises more questions about the possible interplay between care of oneself and care of others.[87]

Foucault's writings seem to produce a bind. Foucault contends that an ethics focused on the self's relation to itself bears the potential to transform relations with others by lessening domination, thereby gesturing toward its possible political significance. Yet the ancient models he analyzes approach the problem of the ethics-politics nexus in ways that do not provide many resources for such a conception, whether because reflexive, ethical relations and intersubjective, political relations are construed in terms of rule and mastery (as on the Greek conception) or, alternatively, because self-care is detached from the domain of political life altogether (as with the Romans). Foucault's work on ethics thereby persistently poses the question of politics without effectively addressing it.

### Linking Arts of the Self to Democratic Practice

Foucault gestures toward the possible contemporary political significance of aesthetic care for the self but does not fully conceptualize this dynamic, and the Greek and Roman traditions he interprets seem to offer little help in this regard. This underdeveloped but tantalizing aspect of his late work has captured considerable attention, however. Some readers tend to restate, without explicating, the claim that the ethics of the care of the self is politically salient. For example, Jon Simons writes, "Perhaps there is no more pressing political need than arts of the self through which people detach themselves from current subjectivities."[88] And Thomas Dumm de-

*Crafting a Democratic Subject?*

—

clares that Foucault "redefines politics as an activity of self-constitution."[89] These claims, however, do little more than assert that arts of the self are political. But in what sense is this so?

Connolly's work offers the most sustained and interesting effort to theorize the value of Foucauldian ethics for contemporary politics. Specifically, he elaborates a version of reflexive arts of the self that he believes is indispensable to an activist, pluralist democracy. In doing so, he responds to Foucault's invitation to reimagine the practice of self-care while also trying to show that particular ways of tending to oneself are democratically consequential. But how does he make this case? Is it persuasive? Does Connolly effectively show that we need a reflexive ethics today, for the sake of democratic politics and culture?

There are three main elements to Connolly's account: the guiding vision of pluralist democracy, the depiction of contemporary arts of the self, and, finally, the relationship he proposes between them. The ideal of public life Connolly advances resonates strongly with the conception of associative democracy laid out in the introduction. The pluralist democracy he advocates is characterized by citizen participation in shaping the conditions under which they live—through conventional mechanisms such as voting, campaigning, and running for office but also through collective self-organization, activism, and protest, as exemplified by past and present social movements in the United States. Such democracy is pluralist not only because multiple constituencies struggle to realize their collective goals, but because it also welcomes diverse and conflicting "fundamental orientations" into the political realm and aims not simply at the protection of existing plurality but toward deeper pluralization.[90]

It is with reference to this normative conception of democratic pluralism that the issue of reflexive arts of the self appears. Recognizing that the diverse and conflictual political culture he favors depends in part upon citizens' dispositions, lest it result in open hostility and aggression, Connolly points to "techniques of the self" as a means to develop the qualities of character suited to pluralist democracy.[91] Distinguishing between a creed and a sensibility, Connolly argues that the doctrine any believer, theistic or otherwise, holds is intertwined with the manner in which they hold it, the way in which they express and conduct themselves in light of that belief. This pairing is evident in the "bicameral orientation" he conceptualizes as being integral to pluralist democracy. It involves, first, "the faith, doctrine, creed, ideology or philosophy that you adopt as an engaged partisan in the world," and, second and most vitally, "the engrained sense that you should exercise presumptive receptivity toward others when drawing that faith, creed or philosophy into the public realm."[92] What is most central to the practice of democratic pluralism, therefore, is that participants, no matter what comprehensive views guide their political activities, be animated by a certain sort of sensibility. This sensibility, variously described as one of generosity, forbearance, and receptivity toward others, is meant to facilitate democratic engagement across differences and to guard against the demonization of those with whom one disagrees.

Arts of the self are fundamental, according to Connolly, because they can cultivate this sort of sensibility, thereby enabling citizens to approach one another with "agonistic respect" and "critical responsiveness"— central virtues of pluralist democracy. Tactics performed by the self upon itself serve as preparation for the challenges of political life marked by deep disagreement.[93] But what sort of tactics does Connolly have in mind? How does he conceptualize the practice of self-craftsmanship?

The reflexive relation Connolly theorizes entails a dynamic in which one part of the self works on other parts of the self, but he does not describe this as a relation of mastery; it is not a matter of establishing rule over oneself. Via arts of the self, one is able to "work tactically on gut feelings already sedimented in you." But how is this possible? What allows such desedimentation to occur? On Connolly's telling, it is "another voice in you"—an expression of inner plurality—that allows for this critical work to be undertaken.[94] The noncoherence of the self makes possible, although it does not ensure, tactical efforts that can culminate in "second-order correction," whereby hostile or defensive parts of the self can be re-crafted into something admirable.[95] A certain sort of discipline is involved in this dynamic insofar as self-artistry involves giving shape to oneself and, indeed, improving the self. But such self-crafting is not designed to result in a solid, permanent relation of rule. Rather, Connolly's arts of the self are intended partly to destabilize a person's sense of a unified self. When the self works upon itself, the point is not to achieve mastery but to dwell in, and in the process come to respect, the multiplicity that characterizes existence in every form.

So instead of linking the reflexive relation to intersubjective relations via the concept of rule, Connolly draws a connection on the basis of the plurality that he contends is alive within the self as well as in the socio-political world. The kind of relationship with oneself that Connolly celebrates is one in which the self recognizes and engages with inner discord and complexity. Experiencing intrasubjective plurality, Connolly argues, can help one to foster respect for intersubjective plurality. Actively engaging with diverse elements within the self, allowing different parts to challenge one another, can "desanctify" elements of one's identity.[96] This, in turn, serves to diminish "the drive to wholeness" that threatens to impose unitarian schemas upon plurality in its many guises.[97] In other words, Connolly suggests that appreciating the nonunity of oneself and acting upon the contingencies therein can help one generate a more generous, forbearing, and receptive attitude toward worldly plurality as well.[98]

By arguing that through self-intervention, or micropolitics, people can transform themselves in ways that ready them for macropolitics, Connolly endows Foucauldian aesthetics of existence with a strong, explicitly political aim: developing the sensibilities suitable to pluralist democratic politics. By thoughtfully and modestly working on oneself, Connolly claims, one can loosen the "vengeful, anxious, or stingy" elements of one's identity and thereby render oneself "more open to responsive engagement with alternative faiths, sensualities, gender practices, ethnicities and so on."[99] Connolly thus affirms Foucault's basic claim that techniques of the self can benefit intersubjective relations. But he specifies a practice of self-artistry that fosters qualities meant to facilitate passionate, yet respectful, encounters with fellow citizens, both potential allies and adversaries. By orienting self-care toward the cultivation of dispositions supportive of pluralist democratic culture, Connolly seems to provide what Foucault does not: a way of conceptualizing the link between care for the self and politics that is not premised on a dynamic of mastery. Perhaps Connolly articulates that "something new" that Foucault hinted might be generated out of the encounter staged with Greco-Roman ethics.

Yet vital questions remain in Connolly's theory. Most notably, what prompts someone to take up practices of self-intervention in the first place, and what ensures that such intervention will generate democratic effects? The puzzle is twofold, concerning both the impetus for self-care and the consequences of such reflexive activity. How does such activity, which Connolly presents as integral to democratic practice, get off the ground? What motivates this specific sort of reflexive relation, in which the self confronts diverse elements within itself and in the process becomes more forbearing and generous toward faiths other than one's own? Connolly does not devote as much attention to this matter as one might expect and at times seems simply to assume a subject who is predisposed to this kind of work upon the self. For example, in a discussion of the value of arts of the self, Connolly states, "If men first constitute 'women' as sources of nurturance from which to develop their own capacities for agency and then define them only as spectators and/or objects through which to confirm that agency, then any other sign of agency by women will be received as a threat to masculine integrity. Here work on established practices of masculinity becomes necessary."[100] Perhaps so, but this statement says nothing about what prompts or encourages that work. Reflexive labor may be necessary, but nothing assures that it will be exercised. Again, what is the catalyst for these arts of the self?

In addition, it is hard to know what ensures that self-intervention, if enacted, will result in dispositions that enhance, rather than endanger, democratic engagement. (The figure of Alcibiades, whom Foucault references often, is a potent reminder of the ways in which concern with the self can misfire.) Will the self who practices reflexive arts necessarily be more inclined to participate, passionately and respectfully, in collective action animated by a commitment to pluralization? Although Connolly is quick to remind readers that he is not counseling "self-indulgence," he never explains what protects care of the self from morphing into one of many unsavory alternatives — vanity, narcissism, selfishness, and so on — alternatives that are strongly encouraged by contemporary culture but which will hardly enrich the pluralist democracy Connolly advocates.[101] Why should one believe that focused attention on oneself will foster individuals who are interested in and especially capable of collaborative action to reshape social conditions? Why assume that the turn inward will give way to a turn outward?

At times Connolly posits a reciprocal relation between techniques of the self and collective political efforts, a formulation that may help to address these important questions regarding motivation (What sparks arts of the self?) and effects (What directs those arts toward democracy-enhancing results?). When Connolly conceptualizes self-intervention in this way, it seems to be both initiated and continually guided by existing political movements and their claims, which capture an individual's attention, prompting reflection, rethinking, and concerted work upon the self. For example, in a discussion concerning recent controversies regarding end-of-life treatment, Connolly describes the arts of the self through which an individual is able to unsettle her previously unquestioned assumptions about the nature of death. These arts of the self, through which the "nonnegotiable" becomes "rethinkable," Connolly says, can in turn prompt "public engagements" guided by the insights achieved through reflexive arts.[102] Yet Connolly notes that this process of self-intervention was also initially spurred by a new political movement claiming a right to die. This depiction is valuable because it helps to explain what prompts reflexive action and what makes this kind of self-care at least potentially supportive of democratic politics. That is, if Foucauldian-inspired tactics performed by the self upon itself are tied, from the very beginning, to collective political efforts (such as those articulating a right to die), then the ethical work undertaken by the individual is already shaped by and attentive to a specific public matter around which constituencies have organized.[103] Put somewhat differently, Connolly's account here implies that the care for the self capable of enriching democratic life is always-already bound up with care for shared conditions.

Unfortunately, Connolly is inconsistent in this regard, for he also positions Foucauldian self-artistry as an "essential preliminary to," and even the necessary "condition of," change at the macropolitical level.[104] That is, although Connolly claims that micropolitics and political movements work "in tandem," each producing effects on the other,[105] he sometimes privileges "action by the self on itself" as a starting point and necessary prelude to macropolitical change. This approach not only avoids the question of the genesis of such reflexive action and its possible harmful effects but also indicates that collective efforts to alter social conditions actually await proper techniques of the self. For example, in a rich discussion of criminal punishment in the United States, Connolly contends that "today the micropolitics of desire in the domain of criminal violence has become a *condition* for a macropolitics that reconfigures existing relations between class, race, crime and punishment."[106] Here and elsewhere in Connolly's writing the sequencing renders these activities primary and secondary rather than mutually inspiring and reinforcing.[107]

It is a mistake to grant chronological primacy to ethical self-intervention, however. How, after all, is such intervention, credited with producing salient effects at the macropolitical level, going to get off the ground, so to speak, or assuredly move in the direction of democratic engagement (rather than withdrawal, for example) if it is not tethered, from the beginning, to public claims that direct attention to a specific problem, defined as publicly significant and changeable? How and why would an individual take up reflexive work on the desire to punish if she were not already attuned, at least partially, to problems afflicting current criminal punishment practices? And that attunement is fostered, crucially, by the macropolitical efforts of democratic actors who define a public matter of concern and elicit the attention of other citizens.[108]

For reflexive self-care to be democratically significant, it must be inspired by and continually connected to larger political mobilizations. Connolly sometimes acknowledges that the arts of the self he celebrates are not themselves the starting point of collaborative action but instead exist in a dynamic, reciprocal relation with cooperative and antagonistic efforts to shape collective arrangements. Yet the self's relation with itself is also treated as a privileged site, the very source of democratic spirit and action.

This tendency to prioritize the self's reflexive relationship over other modes of relation defines the therapeutic ethics that ultimately emerges out of Foucault's and, to a lesser degree, Connolly's work. This ethics not only elides differences between caring for oneself and caring for conditions but also celebrates the former as primary or, as Foucault says, "ontologically prior." An ethics centered on the self's engagement with itself may have value, but it is not an ethics fit for democracy.

### Challenging Therapeutic Ethics

The claim that Foucauldian ethics amounts to a therapeutic ethics may sound surprising on the face of it, if therapy is thought of in modern psychological terms. Indeed, Foucault declares that people should "liberate [them]selves from the kind of subjectivity of which the psychoanalysts treat" and offers that "the art of living is the art of killing psychology."[109] In the same vein, Foucault stresses that the creative, productive reflexive relationship which fascinates him stands opposed to the idea of a self who bears a core truth in need of deciphering. And he rejects the suggestion that his interest in the arts of the self is anything like the "California cult of the self" and the quest for authenticity.[110] Connolly likewise stresses that the self engaged in reflexive care is actively shaping and reshaping itself rather than seeking a deep interiority. So in what sense do they articulate a therapeutic ethics?

I use this term to signify that the ethics in question, articulated in different ways by Foucault and Connolly, focuses squarely on the self as the primary site of engagement. The individual self is both the subject and object of ethical action, even if that self is seen as being situated, constructed, and malleable rather than as essential. The Greek term *thera-peuein*, Foucault tells us, had three related meanings: "to give medical care to oneself, to be one's own servant, and to devote oneself to oneself."[111] All three meanings involve a reflexive relationship. The label "therapeutic," as applied to Foucault's and Connolly's account of ethics, draws on this etymology and describes an ethics that consists of focused attention on oneself. This characterization applies to both Foucault and Connolly, despite the fact that the self is understood as a creative production and despite their shared belief that this ethics can generate effects beyond the self.

For even this latter claim reflects the therapeutic character of this ethics. The self's relation to itself is treated as fundamental, as the basis of other modes of relation, including democratic relations among citizens. The privilege granted to the individual reflexive relationship appears most clearly in Foucault's insistence that it is universally "prior to" one's relations with others and that alterations in intersubjective power relations follow from tending to the self in the proper way.[112] As Linda Zerilli argues, Foucault "takes for granted the idea that freedom would begin with changes in subjectivity that then bring about changes in the world."[113] The single self, though embedded in a particular cultural context and shaped rather than found, remains the locus of Foucault's ethics and the source of broader transformation.[114] And although Connolly claims that micropolitics and macropolitics mutually influence each other, self-care regularly appears in his work as a precondition of or a preliminary to engagement in collaborative democratic action. Therapeutic ethics is concerned above all with the relationship one has with oneself, which enjoys special status as the source of other relationships.

The therapeutic ethics advanced by Foucault and Connolly resonate strongly with dominant features of American culture. In particular, therapeutic ethics echoes a widely held popular belief, captured in this chapter's second epigraph, that working on oneself is the path to broader social change. This view is expressed quite clearly today in the doctrine of ethical consumerism, which holds that individuals should critically reflect on their consumption practices, making changes in themselves and in their personal conduct (namely, in what they buy) in order to generate collective change. In addition to expressing the striking and disturbing conviction that a primary way of shaping the self and becoming a better person is through purchasing commodities, this orientation rests on the belief that each individual's action will additively amount to something greater, producing transformation on a large scale. This is a more simplistic model than Connolly's in that it recognizes no difference between micropolitics and macropolitics, treating the latter as simply the cumulative result of the former. There are, nonetheless, real similarities between Foucauldian-inspired ethics and the more generalized conviction that transforming oneself is the most important and even the most politically significant project a person can undertake.

Even though Foucault's and Connolly's accounts of ethics may not intend to further the prevalent popular belief that you change the world by changing yourself, conceptualizing ethics primarily in terms of self-intervention is dangerous in the context of an American cultural environment that can fairly be described as narcissistic.[115] There is no doubt that the Foucauldian-inspired arts of the self Connolly advocates are meant to challenge reigning ways of being and to transform individuals in ways that enable them to engage more effectively in collective projects, including critical and oppositional endeavors that aim to alter status quo arrangements. Yet the massive popularity of self-help programs disseminating the view that worldly events are the direct result of one's personal thoughts, in conjunction with capitalist ideologies that tend to reduce the aesthetics of existence to the acquisition of a lifestyle through shopping, along with many other cultural influences that promote questionable techniques of the self, should make one hesitate before embracing an ethics that focuses so heavily on concern with oneself.[116] Even Connolly's version of therapeutic ethics, which he wants to demarcate from unappealing forms of self-indulgence, runs the risk of being captured by prevailing habits and beliefs that can render arts of the self nondemocratic, even antidemocratic.

Some of Connolly's own formulations bring this danger into relief. For example, Connolly sometimes uses the term *micropolitics* to refer not only to the self's reflexive tactics but also to small-scale intersubjective relations and projects that might not typically be recognized as political in nature but which Connolly maintains can support and enhance macropolitics.[117] Micropolitics of this sort are already "ubiquitous," but they can be developed, readers are told, in ways that are "more or less conducive to democratic politics."[118] This dimension of micropolitics is sometimes depicted by Connolly as a bridge connecting concentrated work on the self to organized forms of collective citizen action. But the concrete examples of micropolitical activity that he gives, even those that extend beyond the self's relation to itself, raise new doubts about how resistant or transformative such activity really is. Indeed, some of what Connolly has in mind seems depressingly adaptive to contemporary arrangements, considering how focused his examples are on individual lifestyle choices rather than on the admittedly more difficult problem of how to mobilize energies for more collaborative, oppositional, and inventive endeavors. Writing of micropolitics, Connolly counsels, "If you are in the middle class, buy a Prius or a Volt and explain to your friends and neighbors why you did; write in a blog; attend a pivotal rally; ride your bike to work more often; consider solar panels; introduce new topics at your church." While these things may be worth doing, it is not clear why one should believe they will foster an urge to "participate in larger political assemblages in more robust ways," as Connolly wagers.[119] Indeed, these recommendations seem to reinforce the belief that political change is a happy by-product of small decisions made by each individual. Despite Connolly's best intentions—and his ambitious calls for broad transformation in the direction of deepening pluralization, greater economic equality, and less vengeful foreign policy—the therapeutic ethics he endorses is too easily absorbed, even co-opted, by a dominant culture that rewards forms of preoccupation with the self that do little to facilitate associative democracy.

This point seems to be unwittingly made, in a slightly different context, by Cressida Heyes's *Self-Transformations: Foucault, Ethics, and Normalized Bodies*. Heyes's stated objective is to rescue Foucault's work on ethics from misreadings that liken self-care to self-indulgence, in order to defend the importance of "somaesthetics," in which the self strives to cultivate a body in ways that are resistant to normalization. Yet although Heyes is devoted to the idea that ethical self-discipline, performed by the self on the self, can be an "art of living with greater embodied freedom," the vast majority of the book is spent investigating, in great detail, case studies involving contemporary practices of askesis (sex reassignment surgery, Weight Watchers, and cosmetic surgery), which, Heyes convincingly argues, help to produce "docile bodies."[120] So although Heyes continues to hold out the hope that concentrated work on the self, and specifically on one's body, can serve as a site of resistance against normalizing power, the overwhelming sense conveyed by her research is how readily and thoroughly care for the self is promoted and practiced in conformist, "self-absorbed" ways.[121] There is little acknowledgment of the difficulty her examples pose to her celebration of a transgressive, liberating somaesthetics. What does it mean to endorse an ethics focused on rapport à soi and on "somatic askesis" in particular, in the context of a society that, by Heyes's own account, obsessively and successfully markets forms of self-care that produce compliant and often solipsistic selves? Why should one believe that Heyes's preferred example of good somatic self-discipline, yoga, is somehow safe from the normalizing influences so well documented in her treatments of sex reassignment surgery, organized weight loss, and cosmetic surgery? Like Connolly, Heyes seems to neglect the way in which even the best-intentioned calls for care of the self may still be too complicit with an American culture that celebrates and aggressively markets depoliticizing modes of self-care.

Still, the appeal of therapeutic ethics is undeniable. It soothes with the promise that one need not get tangled up in the messy, fraught world of intersubjective political struggle in order to engage in politically meaningful action. Whether tending to the self is seen as synonymous with politics, as in the popularized version of therapeutic ethics, or whether it is understood as a precursor to collective endeavors, as in Connolly's view, the suggestion that one ought to begin with focused attention on oneself is comforting. It spares one the challenges of attempting to address a public problem by acting in solidarity with and in opposition to other citizens, where there may be no assurance of success and when fatigue, disappointment, and frustration are likely. When the political landscape looks bleak—because there are few opportunities for ordinary citizens to govern themselves, because of growing corporate influence over politics at all levels, or because of any number of other depressing facts—therapeutic ethics reassures with the idea that one can be an engaged citizen all by oneself.

It is true that the arts of the self Connolly theorizes are meant to foster sensibilities that will, in turn, facilitate participation in public life rather than act as a substitute for it. And as I argued above, Connolly's inquiry into the ethics of self-care is most evocative and apt when such care is theorized as both inspired by and inspiring of collective democratic activity. Yet it is equally important not to exaggerate the connection between them. A genuine gap separates practices of self-artistry from collaborative efforts to shape the habitat in which people live, though Connolly's approach tends to cover it over, as his distinctive vocabulary indicates. "Action by the self on itself" is labeled micropolitics and paired with macropolitics, designating an array of large-scale institutional formations and shared practices, including efforts by social movements to disrupt hegemonic patterns of behavior and push for greater pluralization. Connolly's point is to insist on the political significance of arts of the self, and he marks this claim with the word *micropolitics*. The trouble with this representation, however, is that it designates the self-artistry undertaken by an individual to desanctify her identity and those collective struggles by which a constituency attempts to alter an element of shared conditions as two types of the same phenomenon. Indeed, the labels Connolly relies on imply that the individually practiced reflexive care of the self differs from the collectively pursued care of the world only in terms of scale: one is micro, the other is macro. This framing, I suggest, exaggerates the affinities between building a self and building a world.

By presenting arts of the self and collective citizen movements as variations on a single theme, Connolly's writings conceal the unique orientation that democratic politics entails, which sets it apart from any reflexive self-relation. Associative democratic endeavors are distinguished not only by the involvement of multiple actors but by the presence of a common object around which they organize. Thus any movement between the micropolitics of self-constitution and the macropolitics of transforming worldly habits, practices, laws, and norms is decidedly more complicated than Connolly's framing indicates, because it demands a turn away from oneself as the object of attention and toward a different and shared object of concern that serves as a site of mutual energy and advocacy.

This reorientation, I argue, is possible only if the self's reflexive relation with itself is initially activated by and remains tethered to a public matter of concern. If self-transformation is to move in a direction that enriches democratic subjectivity and readies one for participation in democratic contest, it must be guided from the start by the claims and actions of democratic constituencies. There is simply no reason to believe or hope that paying focused attention to oneself will enable rather than disable collective action unless the labors of self-constitution are set in motion by a publicly articulated claim regarding shared conditions that resonates with that individual, sparking reflection, examination, and transformation. For example, in the passage considered earlier in which Connolly describes the efforts undertaken by an individual who confronts disparate elements within herself that concern death and dying, this reflexive activity is potentially politically meaningful because it was initiated by the appearance of new movements claiming a right to die. For the work performed on the self to bear any democratic significance, the self must be able, at some point, to divest itself from the rapport à soi and refocus on a public matter as the primary object of concern. This divestment is made possible by the presence of a worldly problem that captures the attention of that individual from the start and allows the self to shift out of concentrated work on the self and into the pluralistic domain of democratic politics.

This insight sheds light on those problems afflicting Connolly's argument for arts of the self. In those places where Connolly—wrongly, as I have contended—presents a reflexive relationship as the starting point or origin of macropolitical endeavors, the questions of activation and effects loom large. What prompts someone to take up these all-important techniques of the self? Why would someone decide to engage in the strenuous arts of the self that, to Connolly, are indispensable to collective democratic undertakings? Moreover, under what circumstances can care for the self, if pursued, be counted on to generate democratic virtues rather than vices? What assures that self-intervention will result in styles of subjectivity that are especially well-suited to participation in associative projects? The answers to these queries, as demonstrated above, turn on the fact that any self-care that might matter for democracy is sparked by and remains bound to public efforts that bring "matters of fact" into view as common "matters of concern." Tending to oneself in the manner Connolly advocates cannot come out of nowhere; it is spurred into practice by publicly articulated claims that aim to elicit care, not primarily for a single self but for something defined as a public, contested matter worthy of citizen attention. Reflexive practices of self-transformation that might be able to nourish associative forms of democratic action are dependent on public processes of politicization for their activation and subsequent direction.

If we seek not just any ethics, but a democratic ethics, we are looking for an orientation or mode of being that can inspire participation in associative efforts to shape worldly conditions. Therapeutic ethics, focused as it is on the self's relationship to itself, cannot be the source of such a spirit. Showing concern for oneself and showing concern, in association with others, for a particular custom, norm, law, or practice are decidedly different enterprises. Collective action on behalf of a public matter does not simply follow from care of the self, as the therapeutic model sometimes suggests. Tending to the self can perhaps play a supportive role in readying people for the demands of democratic association and struggle. But to do so, arts of the self must be undertaken in response to and for the sake of collaborative arts that aim to make and remake features of the world. The task of a democratic ethos is to nourish this distinctive form of care among citizens.

# CHAPTER TWO

# LEVINASIAN ETHICS, CHARITY, AND DEMOCRACY

From the start, the encounter with the Other is my responsibility for him. That is the responsibility for my neighbor, which is, no doubt, the harsh name for what we call love of one's neighbor; love without Eros, charity.

— EMMANUEL LEVINAS

Compassion may itself be a substitute for justice. . . . Compassion already signifies inequality. The compassionate intend no justice, for justice might disrupt current power relationships.

— HANNAH ARENDT

If an ethics of self-care is unlikely to enrich democratic politics in the way its proponents suggest, is an explicitly intersubjective ethical approach needed? More specifically, might an ethics devoted to the self's relation to an Other—rather than centered on the self's relation to itself—provide sustenance and support for associative democratic activity?

Emmanuel Levinas's distinctive ethics, defined by an inescapable and infinite obligation to the Other, is often presented as an important alternative to the Foucauldian ethics of care of the self. If Foucault defended the "ontological priority" of the self's relation to itself, some find in Levinas's work a persuasive effort to "turn around Foucault's ontological order of primacy" by privileging the Other and its call to responsibility that summons the self.[1] Johanna Oksala, for example, argues that Levinas's ethical approach rightly regards the relation between the self and the Other as originary (and constitutive of the self), in contrast to Foucault's privileging of the reflexive relation as ontologically prior to all others. This reversal, Oksala contends, opens up a consideration of ethical relations between subjects. Barry Smart also questions the way in which "care for the self takes moral precedence over care for others" in Foucault's work. He claims that it is impossible for Foucault's ethics to imply care for others, as Foucault contends, unless "there is from the beginning . . . *already* a responsibility for the other," such as that articulated by Levinas.[2]

As is true in the case of Foucault, interest in Levinas's thought is often tied to the quest for a democratic ethos. This quest, as we have seen, is driven largely by the sense that American liberal democracy is afflicted by a "motivational deficit" and that this situation calls for an empowering ethics, however conceived, that can spark and sustain citizen action.[3] Could Levinasian ethics serve this vitalizing role? Perhaps an ethics defined by one's responsibility to the Other is what democracy needs.[4] Might the sense of absolute obligation to care for another remotivate citizens and draw them into collective democratic endeavors? Simon Critchley and Ewa Ziarek, among others, answer affirmatively. Critchley believes that Levinasian ethics can help deter the "nihilistic drift" of contemporary politics and potentially act as an impetus for collective democratic action to redress injustices.[5] Ziarek locates in Levinas's ethics a muchneeded "element of the unconditional," the sense of limitless obligation to the Other, that can help mitigate the dangers of unrestrained agonism by fostering democratic action oriented toward the fulfillment of this obligation.[6]

It is perhaps unsurprising that Levinas's ethics is invoked as a resource for democracy. The view of the self as being ultimately for the other seems to present a challenge to narrow self-interest, calling on people to concern themselves with the fate of others. The hope is that such concern, if deeply felt, can acquire a political form, encouraging individuals' involvement in democratic efforts that attempt to express the responsibility to care for other human beings. This chapter explores the possibilities of a Levinasian-inspired ethos for democracy. It ultimately argues that although Levinas's account of ethics is in many ways compelling, it is poorly suited to democratic politics because it revolves around a hierarchical, charitable relation that is focused on addressing immediate needs. Levinasian ethics is also routinely figured as a truth that exists prior to politics, a move which distracts from vital questions of how to inspire and sustain citizens' participation in associative democratic practices. Yet even if charitable ethics is not regarded as the absolute ground of politics, its features make it distinct from — even at odds with — associative democracy. A Levinasian ethics, though powerful in its incitement to personal responsibility, is not particularly supportive of collective projects seeking to shape worldly conditions.

I begin with a sketch of Levinas's unique and provocative ethics. Because it is impossible to provide an exegesis of his complex body of work here, my aim is to illuminate the contours of his ethics and to tend to those features taken up and developed by readers interested in linking Levinas's ethics to democratic life. A key part of this inquiry interrogates the notion of "the third" and questions whether this concept proves, as many readers claim it does, the political relevance of Levinas's ethics. Moving slightly away from Levinas's thought, I analyze the uses to which Levinas's ethics have been put by Critchley and Judith Butler, who in different ways seek to amplify its democratic potential. Both build on Levinas's work in suggestive ways, yet Critchley and Butler, like other advocates of Levinasian-inspired ethics, wrongly assume that a charitable model of ethics supports collective democratic projects. Butler at times grants even greater authority to Levinasian ethics, alleging that it reveals an uncontestable ontological truth that is external to but ought to govern the organization of political life.

This chapter contests this foundationalist gesture and, even more important, illuminates the gap separating charitable care for another's basic needs from collaborative care for shared conditions. While there is much to be admired in a Levinasian ethics of responsibility, a democratic ethos, as I argue throughout this book, depends upon something distinct from care for oneself or for an Other.

### Levinas's Singular Ethics

Levinas's dense, idiosyncratic, and intriguing writings on ethics are united by a powerful critical vision that indicts the Western tradition for its continuous attempts to "totalize" the world, to contain alterity, and "transmute" Otherness into the Same. This tendency to deny alterity, though evident in Heidegger no less than in Plato, is not confined to philosophical texts. Indeed, to Levinas, the devastating disasters of the twentieth century, with which he was intimately familiar, bear a secret affinity to Western philosophy: "The visage of being that shows itself in war is fixed in the concept of totality, which dominates Western philosophy."[7] He insists that the horror of Nazism must not be construed as anomalous or accidental but as essentially related to Western monism and the unrelenting desire for totality.

Human ways of thinking and being, according to Levinas, are afflicted by "an insurmountable allergy," "a horror of the Other which remains Other."[8] The task he pursues is nothing less than the disruption of this mode of relating to the world. Against reigning "egology," Levinas attempts to think the Other as Other. And he does so in the name of an unusual ethics that not only honors alterity but also calls for the self's profound responsibility for the Other.

At the heart of Levinas's ethics lies an encounter between self and Other, whose strangeness calls the I into question. This exposure to *Autrui*, or the human Other, interrupts the "imperialism and egoism" of the I or the Same.[9] In this encounter, the Other presents as a face—a presentation that always "exceeds the idea of the Other in me."[10] By *face*, Levinas does not mean a person's physical appearance, but that the Other "comes to me" in a way that escapes my cognitive powers and resists my attempts at containment or assimilation.[11] Although many responses to the face are in fact possible, including indifference and even violence, Levinas holds that the face of the Other cannot be fully possessed. It persists, "signifying in its uniqueness."[12] The face expresses beyond my attempts to evade or suppress it; it pleas, implores, and summons; it issues a demand that concerns me, even though I may fail to hear or heed it.

But what is this summons? What am I being called upon to do? The ethical "revelation" of the face, Levinas says, is itself a command, an incitement to responsibility.[13] In other words, the human Other not only puts into question the self's "naïve liberty," but also calls on the self to do something. From the "face of the other man" issues "a voice that commands, an order issued to me . . . to answer for the life of the other man."[14] When I am summoned, I am summoned to tend to the needs of a vulnerable Other, to concern myself with his well-being. Over and over again, the Other is described by Levinas as being needy, defenseless, precarious, miserable, vulnerable, destitute, suffering. As Michael Morgan explains, "The other person stands as other than the self, as a *no* to the I. But . . . the *no* is not one of hostility or anger or threat. It is . . . a *no* of need, of defenselessness, and of dependence."[15] Confronting such defenselessness and suffering, the self is obligated to respond generously. Levinas states, "In the relation to the other, the other appears to me as one to whom I owe something, toward whom I have a responsibility."[16]

The encounter with the Other, then, is marked by asymmetry; obligation runs in one direction.[17] The needy Other, figured as the "the stranger, the widow and the orphan," paradoxically commands the self from a position of "humility and height."[18] This is a relation not between equals but between one who is destitute and one who is not, he who is owed and he who owes. It is "the poor one," however, who occupies a superior position insofar as he issues a command which the self is called on to fulfill.[19] This nonreciprocal relation is the site of charity and altruism.[20]

What does the Other need? Throughout his texts, Levinas describes the suffering of the Other as well as its potential alleviation by the self in starkly material terms: hunger, bread, thirst, shelter, clothing, and so on. These descriptions cannot be taken as simply metaphorical since Levinas openly embraces materialism in relation to the responsibility one has to tend to the Other: "There is no bad materialism other than our own." Materialism itself, in the sense of the provision of the goods necessary for the sustenance of life, is equated with the highest spirituality.[21] Levinas writes, "The other concerns me in all his material misery. It is a matter, eventually, of nourishing him, of clothing him. It is exactly the biblical assertion: Feed the hungry, clothe the naked, give drink to the thirsty, give shelter to the shelterless. The material side of man, the material life of the other, concerns me, and, in the other, takes on an elevated signification and concerns my holiness."[22]

Levinas repeats this idea again and again, often in relation to the most basic of wants, hunger, and its simplest response, the provision of bread. In *Otherwise Than Being*, he talks often of tearing the bread from one's own mouth to give to the Other.[23] He also cites throughout his writings a scene from Vasily Grossman's epic novel about Nazism and Stalinism, *Life and Fate*, in which a Russian woman who "hates Germans" and is watching them remove the decomposing bodies of Russians from a building following the Battle of Stalingrad, gives a German officer a piece of bread from her pocket, saying, "There, have something to eat."[24] For Levinas, these actions—of going without food for the sake of a hungry other, of supplying bread even to one's enemy—express the fulfillment of an obligation to place the needs of an Other before one's own.[25] Indeed, at his most direct, Levinas declares that evil consists precisely in the failure to do so, in "the refusal of responsibility," the turning "away from the face of the other man," the denial of bread.[26]

The responsibility Levinas theorizes is distinct from dominant philosophical and practical conceptions, according to which responsibility is consciously and independently assumed by individual subjects or ascribed to them on the basis of their capacity for free action. Against this model in which human subjects bear responsibility for specific deeds that have been in some sense freely undertaken, Levinas describes a responsibility for the Other that is both unwilled and limitless. First, the responsibility of the self for the Other is not contracted or freely chosen. It is an unavoidable assignation: "To be a 'self' is to be responsible before having done anything."[27] Indeed, individuals have no say as to whether this responsibility binds them, though they may fail to enact it: the summons to respond, issued by the Other, is not a matter of "an obligation or a duty about which a decision could be made."[28] Second, the I is responsible from the start and furthermore "infinitely responsible."[29] "The word 'I' means to be answerable for everything and for everyone."[30] This extreme claim may seem nonsensical or even offensive, but it is worth considering the view that Levinas is trying to dislodge.[31] By means of this hyperbolic declaration he resists the idea that an individual has a specific, bounded set of responsibilities that could ultimately be fulfilled. The responsibility one has for the Other, he proclaims, is never finally accomplished; there is always something more to be done: "I am never in the clear toward the other man."[32]

The final piece of Levinas's account of unwilled and unlimited responsibility contends that the Other's summons to respond is the very source of subjectivity: the self exists because of the Other, with whom it cannot be reconciled. The exposure to *Autrui*, then, is not chronologically situated after the constitution of the self: "Being is not *first*, to give place afterwards by breaking up, to a diversity."[33] Although there are places in his work, most notably in the sequential narration of *Totality and Infinity*, where Levinas seems to describe a solitary subject in sole possession of the world, who only later encounters the Other, Levinas most often depicts the relationship with the Other as the very condition of possibility for subjectivity: "The relationship with the non-ego precedes any relationship of the ego with itself."[34] As Michael Morgan writes, for Levinas, "We are social before we are singular."[35]

Levinas is not making the now-familiar point that the self is constituted socially or through its myriad relations with others. He is claiming
that by virtue of being "preoriginally tied to the other" the self consists in
inescapable responsibility: "The I is, by its very position, responsibility
through and through."[36] To be an I at all is to be "straightaway for-the-
other, straightaway in obligation."[37] Through these sorts of formulations,
which appear frequently, Levinas is trying to do nothing less than over-
turn individualism in all its guises. The self, he maintains, is never for
itself, it is always and only for the Other. The origin, purpose, and meaning of the self's existence lie in its obligation to the fate of another. Levinas does not, however, claim this is a radically original idea or even an
unfamiliar one. The Bible, he says, affirms "a primordial responsibility 'for
the other,' such that, in an apparent paradox, concern for another may
precede concern for oneself."[38] The self is born from charity, defined by
"an unlimited obligation toward the other."[39]

But what kind of encounter between the self and the Other is Levinas talking about? At times he seems to be speaking of a direct, person-
to-person meeting, marked by the need for material assistance, while at
others, above all when he is speaking of the emergence of the self, he invokes a relation that is "originary" and "primordial." Is the relation that
Levinas labels *ethical* concrete or transcendental?[40] Does it occur in
everyday life or is it located in an "originary," "immemorial" past"?[41] In
Levinas's writings, it is consistently both. On the one hand, he speaks of
the face-to-face encounter in quite literal terms, as involving "the person
met on the street," and he says that the whole of his philosophy can be
summarized in the simple words, "Après vous, Monsieur," a claim which
identifies concern for the Other with everyday activities of "civility, hospitality, kindness and politeness."[42] At the same time, Levinas describes
the encounter with the face as prior to ontology and to being, preceding
the very emergence of the I. He writes, "The situation of the I in the face
of the Other is significant. It is a structure that illuminates, and conse-
quently its analysis is not the description of an empirical fact. . . . The
very principle of my enterprise—giving value to the relation of infinite
responsibility which goes from the I to the Other [*Autrui*] remains. Certainly I believe that this is our most valuable everyday experience, one that
allows us to resist a purely hierarchical world. But this is an illuminating
experience, metaempirical, as [Vladimir] Jankélévitch would say. This is
not pure empiricism."[43] Levinas claims that the encounter between the

self and the Other is "metaempirical" at the same time that it is "our most valuable everyday experience." The exposure to alterity can and does take the form of a concrete event, but it cannot be reduced to that. The asymmetrical relation in which one is called to respond by the Other is structural and primary in Levinas's account, persisting apart from any particular empirical instantiations of this structure.

The dual character of the ethical encounter helps explain how Levinas can simultaneously claim that responsibility for the Other is unavoidable and inescapable even as his work is guided by the reality of genocide, an event that signifies a devastating collapse of obligation to or concern for the Other. He simultaneously insists upon a responsibility "prior to freedom," about which one has no choice, while remaining only too aware of the ways in which human beings have failed to acknowledge or respond to the Other.[44] These two strains coexist without contradiction because the profound responsibility born of the originary encounter with the Other — to which one is hostage — cannot be evaded; it constitutes one's very existence as a self: "The I *is* responsibility." Yet at the same time, humans regularly and routinely do fail to respond to the "summons to respond" at the empirical level, in the social world, and thereby attempt to deny an alterity that can never be fully disavowed.[45]

If one accepts, with Levinas, that the self/Other encounter is both metaempirical and empirical, the question remains, in what sense is this relation ethical? *Ethics* is the central term and idea in Levinas's writings, but its meaning is far from self-evident. As Diane Perpich says, it is clear that Levinas provides a provocative, original philosophical outlook, "but is it an *ethics*?" It certainly is not in any typical sense. What Levinas calls ethics does not attempt to answer either the ancient question, "What is the best life for human beings?" or the Enlightenment question, "What ought I to do?"[46] He does not offer "general rules, principles, or procedures."[47] So what does *ethics* name? Levinasian ethics (usually appearing in the adjectival form in the original French) attempts to name a condition or situation rather than prescribe a set of actions. That is, the encounter between self and Other, whether in its primordial or everyday form, is itself ethical. As Critchley explains, "The ethical is an adjective that describes, *a posteriori*, as it were, a certain event of being in a relation to the other that is irreducible to comprehension. It is the relation which is ethical, not an ethics instantiated in relations."[48] Significantly, "the fact that the encounter with the Other is ethical does not mean that I will respond in an ethical way," as Colin Davis explains. That is, ethics, in the more conventional and "restricted sense of preferences, choices, and actions," is made possible by the ethical situation Levinas theorizes, but he does not focus on prescribing those particular choices or actions. Davis continues, "In keeping with his phenomenological background, he is descriptive rather than prescriptive, attempting to depict fundamental realities. And at this level, I am just as likely to respond to the non-violence of the Other with violence as with respect."[49]

Although ethics in Levinas's writings describes a circumstance or condition of people's lives rather than a set of instructions for conduct, the force of his work nonetheless arises from the normative implications of this apparently descriptive account. If one is persuaded by the claim that every individual is infinitely responsible to a human Other, whose demand for attention and response is so profound that it can never be fully evaded, this perspective would seem to radically challenge the way one thinks and acts in ordinary life.[50] Placing the Other rather than the self at the center of concern, Levinas calls his readers to account, despite the absence of any strong declarative statements centered on an *ought*. Levinas does not traffic in the most familiar sort of ethical theory, yet his work as a whole enunciates a "basic existential demand."[51] It is not difficult to locate in Levinas's thinking something close to a substantive ideal, defined by generosity, concern for others, and self-sacrifice.[52] In fact, in interviews, in which he speaks more directly and accessibly than in his formal writings, Levinas makes strong normative claims. For example, he states, "I am not afraid of the word *good*; the responsibility for the other is the good."[53] At another point he declares, "The only absolute value is the human possibility of giving the other priority over oneself."[54] Finally, Levinas regularly speaks of charity, or devotion to the care of another, as the very meaning of the human: "Our humanity consists in being able to recognize the priority of the other."[55] Most surprisingly, perhaps, Levinas embraces the term *humanism*, reappropriating it to signify "a humanism of the other man," defined by the awareness that "man is capable of putting the other's existence before his own."[56] Levinas's ethical outlook may be unconventional but it certainly does not abandon normativity altogether.

What might Levinas's unusual ethics, focused on a personal call to responsibility, offer the theory or practice of associative democracy? It would seem that deep concern for the needs of another could potentially, though not necessarily, motivate political engagement. Indeed, there are many powerful examples of associative democratic struggles—from the nineteenth-century abolitionist movement to campaigns for gay rights today—that cannot be explained on the basis of participants' self-interest alone. Might a sense of obligation to care for another be at work in such instances of solidarity among citizens? Is this an ethical orientation that, if fostered, can extend and invigorate associative democratic action?

Raising the question of the political, let alone democratic, implications of Levinasian ethics may seem a bit strange, since Levinas regularly professes what can only be called an antipolitical outlook. Aligning politics with the modern state and its bureaucratized, rational rule, Levinas often casts it as a totalizing force that does profound violence, both literal and otherwise, to the Other.[57] Politics, defined in part as "the art of foreseeing war and winning it by every means," is "opposed to morality."[58] It is not only the physical force exercised by the state that is of concern, however. Levinas figures the anonymity of administrative politics as a source of real harm, as the smooth functioning of the rule of law necessarily disregards the unique face of the Other in favor of that of an abstract individual: "There are, if you like, the tears that a civil servant cannot see: the tears of the Other."[59] Levinas's portrait of politics as totalizing raises the question, is ethics related to politics only as its interrogator?

Still, Levinas maintains that his focus on the "proximity and uniqueness of the other man is in no way a repudiation of politics."[60] And even as he paints a monistic, statist portrait of politics, callous to the singularity of human beings, he says that some sort of politics is necessary and indicates that it might actually serve as a complement to ethics. I investigate this prospect below, arguing that Levinas does little more than gesture toward the importance of an array of collective phenomena he labels politics, while continuing to privilege an unequal, dyadic model of charitable obligation as the very foundation of that underconceptualized politics. To make this case, I begin with a concept that has been held in abeyance until now: Levinas's notion of the third.

### More Than Two: From Ethics to Politics

In "Dialogue on Thinking-of-the-Other," Levinas asks, "But then what about humanity in its multiplicity? What about the one next to the other—the third, and along with him all the others? Can that responsibility toward the other who faces me, that response to the face of my fellow man ignore the third party who is also my other? Does he not also concern me?"[61] With these questions, Levinas challenges the simplicity of his ethics, focused so intently on the dyadic relation of self and other. Even if absolute responsibility to tend to the needs of another were exercisable in the intimacy of a relation-of-two, what becomes of this demand once it is recognized that no dyadic relation exists in isolation from the broader social world? It is not just you and me. What then? Levinas remarks, "If there were only two of us in the world, you and I, then there would be no question, then my system would work perfectly."[62] But of course this is not the case, a condition Levinas recognizes with the figure of the third.

The "proximity" of the ethical situation "becomes a problem when a third party enters."[63] That is, the structure of the ethical situation, marked by asymmetry, a unidirectional demand, and the experience of being hostage to the Other, is troubled by the third party. Difficulties arise from the recognition that there is not only a single Other to whom I owe response, but multiple Others: "How does this responsibility obligate if a third party troubles the exteriority of two?"[64]

The third party appears in slightly different guises in Levinas's writings. Often the third is presented as "another other" or a "fellowman," a third person who disrupts the charitable relation between self and other: "Human multiplicity does not allow the I—let us say does not allow me—to forget the third party . . . , fellowman of the fellowman."[65] The third "destroys the monopoly of one other's demands."[66] But Levinas also writes, "The third party looks at me in the eyes of the Other . . . the epiphany of the face *qua* face opens up humanity," which suggests that the third party appears through the face of the Other and reveals the "whole of humanity."[67] Here, the third party seems less like a concrete human other than an element of the face's "signifyingness," revealing "all the others."[68]

Notwithstanding the differences between these conceptualizations of the third, they share two striking features. First, the appearance of the third is not exceptional but constant, qualifying the absolutist character of the self's infinite responsibility to a single Other. Levinas warns that the self/Other relation and the appearance of the third are not "successive stages; in reality, they are inseparable and simultaneous, unless one is on a desert island, without humanity, without a third."[69] So the third is there all along: "The others"—in the plural—"concern me from the first."[70] But if this is so, doesn't this seriously qualify, if not undermine, Levinas's ethics? After all, the relation he places at the heart of the ethical is emphatically a relation-of-two, structured by a hierarchy in which one

*Levinasian Ethics and Democracy*

—

is absolutely, infinitely responsible for the fate of the Other. How can this stark and limitless obligation to one human Other obtain if it turns out that the I is in fact "responsible for the other *and* the third"?[71] Amid multiplicity, a permanent condition, the extremism of the charitable relation must falter. In place of a singular, unmistakable command, there are now competing demands, multiple needs. It is no longer enough to be completely devoted to a single other (supposing this is even possible or desirable): "I don't live in a world in which there is but one single 'first comer'; there is always a third party in the world: he or she is also my other, my fellow. Hence, it is important to me to know which of the two takes precedence. Is the one not the persecutor of the other? Must not human beings who are incomparable, be compared? . . . I must judge."[72]

If the dyad of self and Other, the site of the ethical for Levinas, never actually exists, that is, if this coupling can never be abstracted from the broader social environment and the many others that inhabit it, what sense does it make to build an ethics around it? Why define ethics in terms of an insular relation between self and Other if one's purported unlimited responsibility to the Other is always and necessarily limited by the reality of human multiplicity? This question is pressed further by Levinas's tendency to issue extreme statements about the total, self-sacrificing responsibility of the self for the Other and then quickly modify them with reference to what is true "in the concrete," in the world of plurality, where other considerations intervene, via the third, making the situation messier and the enactment of responsibility less clear.

What remains of absolute responsibility to the Other? How much force can this ethical demand, which Levinas articulates again and again, have once it is acknowledged that there is never simply me and you? The world of plurality contains complex webs of relationship, a cacophony of summons that exceed the self/Other dyad. Yet Levinas's fidelity to the dyadic self/Other relation and his insistence on "ethics as first philosophy" persist. The best way to understand this, I believe, is to recognize that Levinas posits the absolute, asymmetrical relation of obligation to a unique Other as the good even as it remains, finally, unrealizable. It continues to function as an indisputable ideal for Levinas, even in the presence of the third—and fourth, fifth, and sixth.[73] The call to full and uncompromised responsibility for the needs of one human Other remains and serves as a standard of judgment, even though it is a standard that cannot be finally, fully instantiated in practice.

This brings me to the second important feature of the third: the idea of justice. As Levinas describes it, the presence of the third, whether understood as another person or the invocation of humanity, marks the shift from charity to justice, or from ethics to politics. He writes, "I pass from the relation in which I am obligated to the other, responsible for the other, to one in which I ask myself which is first. I ask the question of justice: Which one, in that plurality, is the other par excellence? How can one judge? How to compare others—unique and incomparable?"[74] This captures one dimension of *justice*, a word Levinas uses very loosely to collect a number of ideas under a single term. Here and elsewhere, *justice* signifies the related problems of judgment, measurement, comparison, calculation, or, as Levinas often puts it, weighing. The I, Levinas says, must engage in these activities of discernment under conditions of plurality. They are unavoidable, thanks to the third: "A measure superimposes itself on the 'extravagant' generosity of the 'for the other.'"[75] While Levinas consistently identifies "the question of justice" with the third, itself emblematic of human multiplicity, he also attaches another set of meanings to justice, less directly related to adjudication. These include the following very broad concepts: the state, political authority, institutions, administration.[76] In these cases, which recur often, Levinas uses *justice* as a catchall for a range of political phenomena, all collective in nature. (On the contrary, when he speaks of the judgment and comparison required by the third, he often still describes these as undertakings of an I.) In a rather rudimentary way, *justice* is used by Levinas to refer to a whole range of problems related to political organization, problems that come into view once one accepts that the dyad of self/Other never actually exists as such. Yet he does little more than state that institutionalized politics in its many iterations is tied to the condition of plurality. In the absence of any specific theorizing of the related terms, such as *the state*, *institutions*, and so on, *justice* is little more than shorthand for an array of very general political terms.

Despite the vagueness of the term, it is important to consider Levinas's claim that the question of justice is unavoidable; charity cannot exist without it. Put somewhat differently but still accurately within the context of Levinas's work, ethics requires politics. That is, the total, unmitigated obligation embodied in the dyadic relation of self and Other is never sufficient; the reality of multiplicity means even selfless devotion to caring for another will not suffice because "I cannot neglect anyone." The charitable relation is incomplete because it answers the needs of only one. For this reason, "institutions and juridical procedures are necessary."[77] If ethics needs politics, this implies the possibility of a nontotalizing type of politics, that is, a form of political life that is something other than antithetical to ethics. Indeed, there are two vying politics in Levinas's thought, one a "horror," as discussed above, and the other a "promise."[78] There is the politics he associates with totalization, the suppression of alterity, and the Same, but also the politics that charitable ethics cannot do without. This insight is expressed well by Annabel Herzog, who argues that in Levinas's thought politics appears both as a source of misery and, paradoxically, as a solution. Levinas "says 'no' to politics . . . because of ethics" and simultaneously "says 'yes' to politics because my infinite generosity for the Other is not enough for all the others, because there is *more* to do."[79]

Does this mean that ethics and politics, in Levinas's eyes, are complements to one another or, as Robert Bernasconi puts it, are "two sides" of "the interhuman"?[80] Are they mutually supportive? Or is their complementarity of a different sort—are charity and justice, ethics and politics mutually disturbing, as Herzog writes, so that the perspective of each challenges the assumptions, occlusions, and limits of the other?[81] Although it is true, as we have seen, that Levinas says the third points toward the necessity of politics (in the very broad sense documented above), Herzog errs when she presents Levinasian ethics and politics as partners in a relationship of mutual support, or even of provocation. Ethics, the relation of obligation of the I to the Other, has a privileged foundational and normative status in Levinas's thought. It is the source of and the check on political life, which is or ought to be subordinate to it. As I suggested earlier, the dyadic model of unlimited responsibility to an Other serves as the standard in light of which all human relations should be judged. This is so despite the fact of plurality, which prevents the full realizability of this "supreme ethical principle."[82]

The relationship between ethics and politics, as conceptualized by Levinas, is one in which the ethical stands watch over the political, not the other way around. For example, Levinas states, "It is in terms of the relation to the Face or of me before the other that we can speak of the legitimacy or illegitimacy of the state."[83] The dyadic relation of unlimited responsibility, however impossible it may be to live out, remains the ideal with reference to which political practice ought to be shaped and assessed: the priority of the Other "remains the ethical measure of a necessary politics."[84] And "politics must be held in check by ethics."[85] In other words, if politics is not to become the totalizing, violent enterprise Levinas often depicts, it requires an influence beyond itself; a state cannot be "abandoned to its own necessity."[86] If "politics, left to itself, has its own determinism," then "love must watch over justice."[87] Although Levinas says that ethics needs politics and politics needs ethics, these claims do not mirror one another. If ethics needs politics, it is because the fact of human manyness renders even the deepest care for another inadequate; the sheer scope of human existence makes politics necessary. But politics needs ethics, according to Levinas, not for pragmatic reasons but because ethics properly reigns over politics, serving as foundation and guide. It is critical to see that ethics and politics are not simply complementary to one another. Ethics must regulate politics and serve as its standard; ethics remains primary. It, and nothing else, is first philosophy.

What, ultimately, is one to make of the third? Many of Levinas's readers believe this figure reveals the political significance of Levinasian ethics. C. Fred Alford, for example, declares that Levinas articulates a political theory through his conceptualization of the third and the recognition of an impossibility: "That I be responsible for all the others as I was for the one other."[88] The question of how to distribute one's infinite obligation to the Other in a world of Others is not answered by Levinas, Alford notes: "All Levinas will do is state that there is no solution, only a unique obligation to a multiplicity of others."[89] It is in the calculating and weighing of such limitless obligation, in the absence of clear directives or rules, that politics occurs. Similarly, William Simmons writes that Levinas is a "social and political thinker" because the third "universalizes" responsibility and points the way toward a politics that "serves ethics" by attempting to pursue this impossible task.[90] Ed Wingenbach says that Levinas presents an "imperative to political engagement," and Davis believes that the figure of the third shows the salience of Levinasian ethics for the "social and political domain."[91]

The tendency to point to the idea of the third to prove that Levinas's ethics are politically relevant is unsatisfying. As we have seen, when Levinas claims that the third marks the transition to justice or politics, he offers only the most general statements about what this means, stringing together a litany of broad political terms like the state, political authority, and institutions that are held to accompany the recognition that there are more than two of us. Levinas says nothing about what shape that politics might take or how the weighing of incomparables might be institutionalized or enacted at a collective level. Nor does he explain how the idea of personal, infinite responsibility can serve as a guide or standard for political arrangements. Indeed, all that the third divulges is that there are many selves and Others beyond the pair that Levinas puts at the center of his ethics. The third, as presented by Levinas, is a marker of human plurality. It reminds one of a basic fact about the world—that human beings are many, not one or two. But this still begs the question of how such plurality will be arranged, shaped, organized, lived out. The image of the third rightly points toward humans' basic existential condition—people live among multiple Others—but manyness is not yet a form of politics.

Suppose one were to push beyond Levinas's statements to ask what political response to plurality might be most faithful to Levinasian ethics. The answer is not necessarily those democratic forms of politics that readers like to connect to his thinking. Levinas's absolute responsibility to tend to the needs of another is, after all, a matter of charity. It requires the hierarchical provision of service to a suffering Other. Why suppose this imperative bears any special relationship to democracy? Nothing in this charitable model, which Levinas contends should reign over and regulate collective life, requires democratic organization or citizenship. A beneficent, paternal state offering few rights to self-government or association could provide for the material needs Levinas names.[92] Similarly, private philanthropy could pursue this charitable ethics. There is no reason to suppose that the ethical relation in which one cares for the needs of another will lead to democratic, rather than charitable, institutions and practices.

Critchley and Butler go beyond Levinas's thin conception of the third to develop original accounts of how Levinasian ethics might animate activist democracy. Yet their efforts fail to account for the difference between charity and democracy, wrongly supposing that concern for another's suffering can serve as the basis of cooperative and contentious democratic action.

### Critchley and the Elision of Charity and Democracy

We live in a time of sweeping political disappointment and face a reality of violent injustice, growing inequality, and reactionary and xenophobic movements that the institutions of liberal democracy appear ill-equipped to address. Under such circumstances, citizens are tempted by nihilism, whether in the form of passive withdrawal or violent destruction. This is the scene Critchley paints, which he says reveals our desperate need for ethics. More specifically, he declares that there is a "motivational deficit at the heart of secular liberal democracy" which must be addressed if nihilism is to be warded off: "What is lacking at the present time of massive political disappointment is a motivating, empowering conception of ethics that can face and face down the drift of the present, an ethics that is able to respond to and resist the political situation in which we find ourselves."[93] Political disappointment is the problem, and ethics is the solution. Over the course of several books Critchley has articulated a decidedly Levinasian ethical orientation that he believes can perform this motivating function, invigorating collective action among citizens in pursuit of greater justice.

In *Infinitely Demanding* Critchley presents an account of how "the ethical subject" is formed, which is the first piece of his argument for a Levinasian ethics that can help make up the motivational deficit he diagnoses. The model of the ethical subject provided here is characterized by "dividualism"; the subject in question is divided and sundered. Why? According to Critchley, one becomes an ethical subject by virtue of a demand or an address, through which the subject defines itself by binding itself to that demand. The Levinasian structure is clear, even as Critchley stresses the act of approval or affirmation that the subject undertakes, which seems to qualify Levinas's depiction of the demand as actual and binding regardless of one's personal approval.[94] The self who "commits itself" is committing to a "radical, one-sided, unfulfillable ethical demand of the other" to care for, even love, "the stranger, the foreigner, the adversary."[95] And this commitment gives rise to a split subject, split because it can never fulfill the exorbitant demand to become infinitely responsible for the fate of another: "The ethical subject is split between itself and a demand that it cannot meet."[96]

For Critchley, this division is not an injury to be healed. Indeed, the divided subject produced by commitment to an unfulfillable demand is the very site of conscience.[97] The internalization of such a demand results in a sense of discomfort that propels continued efforts to live up to an absolute but impossible responsibility. Most significant, "the infinitely demanding ethics of commitment," Critchley asserts, provides the motivational force for renewed democratic activity.

The "passage from ethics to politics" is presented by Critchley as both descriptive and normative. That is, he is articulating a recommendation, but one based on "contemporary activist politics"; it need not be invented. More precisely, he claims one can find the (always incomplete) enactment of responsibility to the Other in, for example, the plural and dispersed activities taking place under the name of anarchism, such as the protests against the World Trade Organization that have taken place around the globe since 1999.[98] Critchley claims that this anarchism and other recent instances of "direct democratic action" are motivated less by a quest for freedom than by a sense of "infinite responsibility."[99] Contemporary anarchism, Critchley wagers, is "about responsibility, whether sexual, ecological, or socio-economic." More pointedly still, it is Levinasian; this is "an anarchism of the other human being who places me under a heteronomous demand rather than the anarchism of the autonomous self."[100]

Jacques Rancière, commenting on Jacques Derrida's embrace of Levinasian ethics, sheds some critical light on Critchley's affirmation of a "passage" from ethics to politics. Rancière alleges that a focus on "infinite openness to otherness" cannot be anything other than depoliticizing. This is so because Levinas's model of ethics orients one toward a "transcendental horizon" that substitutes an ethical understanding of otherness for a political one. An orientation that centers on the figure of an absolute Other and on the notion of limitless responsibility, Rancière argues, is not a step on the way to collective political action, but a decisive move away from it: when Derrida and others contrast the problems of existing liberal democracy as a form of government with an ideal of infinite openness to the Other, what is lost is "democracy as a practice." This practice involves diverse, contestable figurations of otherness in which previously "uncounted" members of a polity interrupt normalized politics and position themselves as excluded but full political subjects. Ethical frameworks like Levinas's, taken up by Derrida, Critchley, and others, conceptualize "*one* infinite openness to otherness," bypassing the multiple, creative enactments of otherness that occur when newcomers on the political scene make themselves seen and heard, presenting "new objects" as "common concerns" in public. These diverse expressions of otherness, achieved in and through democratic agitation, are eclipsed entirely by an ethics that celebrates an abstract, already-given Other.[101]

Yet it is just this ethics of infinite responsibility to the Other that Critchley claims can nourish collective forms of democratic action and protest. Levinasian ethics is not just a useful support of direct democracy, moreover; it is the very source of it, on Critchley's telling. This is expressed repeatedly: the democratizing politics that interests Critchley alternately "arises from," "feeds from," and "flows from" the ethics of infinite responsibility to the Other.[102] Ethics and politics are not wholly separate activities or domains, nor is ethics only an interruption of the political.[103] Rather, ethics is actually requisite for true democracy because it supplies democracy with what it cannot provide itself: a "metapolitical moment."[104] It is exactly the "metapolitical" character of ethics—the sense in which it is above or beyond anything one might regard as political—that makes possible democratic "gathering, coalition or association," directed at the enactment of impossible responsibility.[105] Ethics and politics are not entirely separable since democratic action, for Critchley, is defined in terms of Levinasian responsibility. Yet ethics enjoys a special status relative to politics, acting as the guide and anchor of an otherwise suspect enterprise.

The trouble with Critchley's formulation lies in its elision of the difference between charitable ethics and associative democracy. In his view, the individual's acceptance of a radical demand to care for a singular Other leads rather seamlessly to participation in the collective, democratizing efforts he admires. But does the affirmation of a limitless responsibility to a needy Other really motivate engagement in associative struggles to remedy a public wrong, as Critchley claims? I believe it is mistaken to suppose such a connection because Levinasian charitable ethics is defined by characteristics that actually conflict with the practice of associative democracy. Moreover, the features of charity that restrict its ability to empower democratic action are not unique to Levinas. That is, the difficulties I identify should caution generally against mistaking acts of charity, however valuable, for democratic politics. Recognizing what Levinas's conception of charity shares with everyday understandings of the term helps to challenge the assumption that democracy is vitalized if one only cares more for others.

Three important elements of charity—in both the Levinasian and the more commonplace sense—warrant attention in relation to associative democracy. First, the charitable relation is characterized by hierarchy; there are benefactors and there are recipients. Levinas is adamant about this. The self/Other relationship is asymmetrical and nonreciprocal. It is a relation not of mutual support or care but one in which the self owes everything to the needy Other. One serves and the Other is served. Ordinary understandings of charity also presuppose inequality between those who give and those who receive. Whether one thinks of it in terms of individual charitable acts (donated money or time, for example) or of the efforts of an organization to provide services, hierarchy defines the relationship in which one party has access to resources that the other does not. As Janet Poppendieck has demonstrated in her fascinating study of the relatively recent rise of emergency food programs in the United States, the division between the administration and volunteers, on the one hand, and the recipients of aid, on the other, is stark: most emergency food clients "are left in the passive and dependent role that is so characteristic of charity, however kindly and gently it may be administered."[106]

However valuable charitable service may be—feeding the hungry, for example—it is difficult to see how the deeply unequal dynamic underlying that relationship could foster the relations of solidarity that associative democracy requires. Collective democratic activity is undertaken by ordinary citizens who join together in relations of mutual support and coaction. How are such coalitions encouraged, let alone motivated by, a charitable relation of extreme hierarchy? What allows for the division between benefactors and beneficiaries to be replaced by more equal relations of association between selves and others?

Charity is also concerned primarily with the direct fulfillment of basic needs. This is true of Levinas's ethics no less than of the Red Cross. The charitable relation Levinas conceptualizes centers on the provision of material support, such as shelter, food, and clothing. The self who answers the summons of the Other is figured, time and again, as the one who supplies bread. And perhaps the most popular image of charitable activity in the United States involves donating food, as in a canned food drive, and serving food to the hungry, as in a soup kitchen. Charitable relations are not only hierarchical, then, but marked by a specific end: the fulfillment of immediate material need.

It would be absurd, if not offensive, to deny the important role charitable giving can play in improving some recipients' quality of life. Yet the goal of addressing critical basic needs is not necessarily the same as or even consistent with collective democratic efforts to alter social conditions themselves. In other words, the urgent needs to which many charitable endeavors seek to respond may actually direct attention away from structural causes of deprivation, the potential objects of democratic organization and agitation. Poppendieck makes this argument in relation to emergency food, claiming that "the proliferation of charity *contributes* to our society's failure to grapple in meaningful ways with poverty. . . . This

massive charitable endeavor serves to relieve pressure for more fundamental solutions."[107] Indeed, Poppendieck contends that no amount of
charitable giving can substitute for political advocacy aimed at the causes
of hunger.[108]

Not every project undertaken by an association of democratic citizens is
directed at the sweeping transformation of social conditions. Many efforts
are less ambitious and more localized. Nonetheless, collective democratic
action, past and present, is focused on redressing features of the conditions under which people live. That is, rather than feeding the needy here
and now (no doubt a worthwhile endeavor), democratic organizing, unlike charitable giving, is inclined, for example, to make demands on behalf
of welfare reform, affordable housing, or unemployment benefits, issues
that are tied to structural conditions that affect the availability of food.
And the charitable outlook that supports day-to-day feeding efforts may
actually obscure broader questions concerning the "pathways that lead to
the food pantry door."[109] The second characteristic of charity, that is, the
delivery of immediate aid, does not directly support and may even detract
from collective struggles to change social conditions.

Finally, charity need not be a public phenomenon. It is often undertaken by private organizations and individuals who want to assist needy
individuals and groups. Such actors, though they may raise money or
"awareness" and offer direct services, do not typically aim to mobilize constituencies around a publicly articulated demand that calls for changes in
conditions. Democratic association, however, depends upon the recognition of a problem defined as a shared matter of concern, one that cannot
be adequately addressed by private actors and therefore requires public attention. By contrast, a charitable outlook invites one to see "personal generosity as a response to major social and economic dislocation."[110] That is,
charity's privatizing perspective on social wrongs locates remedies in the
goodwill of particular benefactors. Similarly, the assistance provided by
charities is usually understood as a gift rather than a right, a private offering rather than a public entitlement.[111] This too should raise doubts about
the compatibility of charitable ethics and democratic association.

These important features of charity are good reason to question the
extent to which secondary associations as such can be said to serve as
"schools of democracy."[112] There is a temptation to imagine that participation simply begets participation, à la Robert Putnam's view of "social capital," yet engagement in charitable endeavors may not foster the capacities

or practices that democratic politics requires.[113] Even the influential "resource model of political participation," which highlights the significance of "civic skills"—acquired partly through individuals' activities in nonpolitical organizations—for certain types of citizen participation, does not allay doubts about the likelihood that charitable work will foster democratic practices.[114] As Poppendieck's analysis of emergency food provision and Nina Eliasoph's ethnographic study of volunteer activity show, participation in charitable organizations, even when not restricted to making financial donations, usually takes the form of "lending a hand" to predetermined tasks directed at a "small circle of concern" rather than those initiative-taking and communicative "skill-acts" that Brady et al. argue can be transferred from nonpolitical to political settings.[115] As Eliasoph demonstrates through many compelling examples, contemporary forms of charitable volunteer work are often explicitly antipolitical, discouraging reflection and disagreement among participants in order to focus on "no-brainer," "indisputably good," small projects that do little to interrogate the sources of social problems.[116] (An especially perverse expression of this tendency was the routine depiction of Martin Luther King Jr. as a do-gooder volunteer by participants in Community House, an after-school program in the Midwest meant to empower disadvantaged youth. This representation, Eliasoph notes, completely ignores King's political positions concerning institutionalized racism, unions, foreign wars, and class inequality in order to render him an innocuous figure with whom no one could disagree.)[117] Indeed, the three features of charity specified above— unequal relations between providers and recipients, a focus on immediate need, and a basically privatized approach to social problems—may render charitable volunteerism an obstacle to rather than a support for collaborative democratic projects that engage in public contestation over worldly conditions. "Doing for" others may discourage "doing with" them.[118] The tendency of charitable volunteers to perform already-defined tasks related to immediate needs can occlude more expansive perspectives that interrogate the broader conditions that generate needs. And the provision of aid by private entities may distract participants' attention from the question of public, governmental responsibility. Charitable volunteerism may not be a training ground for democracy at all.

Critchley's argument, however, supposes a direct path from charity to democracy, from the self's Levinasian obligation to care for an Other to associative efforts to address injustice. He offers no account of how the inequality, for example, that marks the self/Other relation is transformed into a solidaristic bond among citizens acting in concert. Likewise, no explanation is given for the shift between personal concern for an Other's—or even others'—immediate material needs and mutual concern for broader social conditions. Critchley describes the radical democratic projects he aligns with Levinasian ethics as being motivated by "a shared experience of certain wrongs and a determination to right those wrongs." But how are those wrongs brought to light publicly? What facilitates the shared recognition of them and the desire to redress them collaboratively? Put somewhat differently, even if the self/Other encounter at the heart of Levinas's ethics is met by the self's desire to respond generously to its call (rather than by indifference, neglect, or violence), what directs that desire toward collective action with others? This is a question that concerns both agent and aim: how does the "unicity" of the I, called to account in the Levinasian scene, come to be replaced by a we? And how does the focus of intent shift from addressing the Other's immediate needs in their particularity to tending to wrongs understood as features of the social world that require collective advocacy? Rather than address these questions, Critchley wrongly assumes that charitable ethics generates democratic action.

The distinction between charitable and democratic forms of activity is crucial, yet it is something Critchley and others who advocate a Levinasian ethos for democracy overlook. Even more significant, however, is the acknowledgment that the charitable outlook, marked by the characteristics identified above, may actually serve as an obstacle to democratic mobilization. The charitable perspective leads one to see the solution to cases of suffering, deprivation, and need in the private provision of aid by the haves to the have-nots. Yet, as Poppendiek writes, "the joys and demands of personal charity divert us from the more fundamental solutions to the problems of deepening poverty and growing inequality." Charitable endeavors may replace rather than support politics.[119] This means that democratic action—collaborative, public, and directed at lasting conditions—may actually require overcoming the charitable orientation Levinasian ethics invites us to take up.

### Judith Butler and the False Promise of Precariousness

If Critchley assumes too seamless a movement from charity to democracy, perhaps what is needed is a more careful elaboration of how Levinasian ethics might be reworked or transformed in ways that could animate associative democratic projects. Butler's recent work posits less of a direct link between the charitable self/Other relation and democratic politics, even as she makes Levinas central to her theorizing about democratic ethos. Can this more circuitous route from charity to democracy reveal the value of Levinasian ethics for politics?

Whether Butler's recent work, which is the focus here, performs an "ethical turn" of its own is the subject of some debate. Although Butler once worried that the fascination with ethics might displace politics, some readers identify a turn toward ethics in her writings since 2000.[120] Other interpreters maintain that despite the adoption of a more explicitly ethical idiom, these texts are actually continuous with rather than a departure from her previous writings. Moya Lloyd as well as Samuel Chambers and Terrell Carver hold that Butler's most recent work, namely, *Precarious Life*, *Giving an Account of Oneself*, and *Frames of War*, are of a piece with her previous books.[121] On this reading, supported by Butler's own remarks on the tenth anniversary of the publication of *Gender Trouble*, all of her writing has a common concern and aim: to expose the workings of "normative violence" and to explore the possibilities of more "livable" lives for all human beings.[122] This interpretation defines Butler's work by its sustained attention to how "culturally particular norms define who is recognizable as a subject capable of living a life that counts."[123] Without disputing the thematic coherence this reading locates in Butler's work or insisting upon a definitive rupture in her writings, I find it nonetheless undeniable that the category of ethics assumes new prominence in Butler's recent books. While it may be reasonable to group all of Butler's writings (so far) in terms of the problems of social intelligibility and livability, it is also the case that her last few books pursue these problems in a new way: by dwelling on precariousness as an ethically significant fact that Levinas helps bring to light and by suggesting that awareness of such vulnerability can and should reinvigorate democratic politics today.[124]

In *Precarious Life* and *Giving an Account of Oneself*, Butler, like Critchley, dwells on Levinas's scene of the encounter between self and Other. Yet what she finds in that scene is not mainly the sense of unlimited responsibility that Critchley argues can and should invigorate collective citizen action. Instead, it is the sense of precariousness that is expressed through the "face of the other." Having quoted Levinas's reference to "the face as the extreme precariousness of the other," Butler explains that to respond to the face "means to be awake to what is precarious in another life or, rather, the precariousness of life itself."[125] What is most significant about the Levinasian dyad is its potential to reveal a common precariousness; the vulnerability of the needy Other, in its utter particularity, makes visible or intelligible the vulnerability of all human beings. It is this universal precariousness that lies at the heart of Butler's ethics and that she claims can support new forms of democratic association and guide the "political tasks" they undertake.[126]

Precariousness means that humans are "all subject to each other, vulnerable to destruction by the other and in need of protection."[127] Butler's ethical approach centers on acknowledging this "fundamental dependency" that cannot be willed away, avowing rather than denying humanity's state of shared "injurability."[128] But how is such an ethics of precariousness democratically significant? Butler offers two answers. First, she claims that this ethical perspective can inaugurate new collectivities that are rooted in an affirmation of "common human vulnerability."[129] A sense of solidarity can emerge, she proposes, on the basis of such universal insecurity: a "we" born of shared dependency and vulnerability.[130] In other words, the experience of "helplessness and need" is not necessarily privatizing; it may actually help constitute a "political community."[131] Most striking about this line of Butler's thought is the way in which the formation of community is tied to the recognition of an indisputable fact about human experience, in all times and places. As Antonio Y. Vásquez-Arroyo puts it, Butler elevates vulnerability to the "plane of ontology." This maneuver is important because it aims to "anchor responsibility . . . in advance of the scene of power in which encounters with others occur."[132] The very fact of vulnerability and dependency, evinced in the Levinasian scene of address, can serve as a bond, Butler suggests, a new basis for social relations. As George Shulman notes, what Butler calls on to be acknowledged here, in order to refound community, is not "concrete others," "a constitution," or "a problematic history," but a "truth about human life as such."[133]

Building upon this understanding of the importance of "avowing injurability," Butler argues in *Frames of War* that although precariousness itself is universal, is an existential condition, one must be alert to the ways in which precariousness is differentially distributed, rendering some lives much more vulnerable and injurable than others. The second link between Butler's ethics and democracy lies here. Butler says that while precariousness is a feature of human life as such, "precarity" designates

a "politically induced condition in which certain populations . . . are differentially exposed to injury, violence, and death."[134] And she contends
that minimizing this unequal distribution of precariousness is a pressing
"political task," one that follows from the ethical truth Butler presents
under the names of precariousness, vulnerability, dependency, and injurability. Precariousness, as evinced by the Levinasian face, assigns humankind to a political project: organizing precariousness in more egalitarian
ways. Indeed, according to Butler, the acknowledgment of precariousness
imposes obligations. If one grasps that precariousness is "not a feature
of *this* or *that* life" but a shared condition, then one cannot avoid taking
on the task of redistribution: "The injunction to think precariousness in
terms of equality emerges precisely from the irrefutable generalizability
of this condition."[135] Butler maintains that because vulnerability characterizes human existence as such, is "coextensive with birth itself," full affirmation of this fact necessitates concern for the egalitarian distribution
of vulnerability among all people and populations.[136] Shared precariousness, then, if it is only recognized, can serve both as the bond that unites
a political community and also as the source of a normative commitment
to create social arrangements that distribute precariousness more fairly.

There are two notable problems with Butler's attempt to connect Levinas's ethics to democratic politics. The first directly concerns her appropriation of Levinas. Significantly, what Butler takes from Levinas's depiction of the encounter with a singular Other in its alterity is a universal
truth: the vulnerability of all human beings. It is strange that in the several
books that develop this idea, Butler does not address the extent to which
this marks a departure from Levinas, who never describes the neediness
or dependency of the Other in universal terms. (In fact, he does not even
describe any particular self and Other as having this in common.) Indeed,
the very idea of the face of the Other revealing "the precariousness of
life itself" seems to run the risk of denying the radical alterity, the singularity, of the particular Other in favor of a thematizing, even totalizing concept of precariousness. Butler's reading of the Levinasian scene
effectively erases particularity, turning the Other into a representative of
a general case. The unique, vulnerable Other is immediately rendered as
an instance of vulnerable being itself. At the same time, the hierarchy that
characterizes the Levinasian ethical encounter, in which the self is summoned to respond to the needs of a suffering, defenseless Other, is also
erased. When Butler draws out of Levinas's ethics a generalized vulnera-

bility that is thought to serve as a point of identification, she covers over the decidedly nonreciprocal dynamic in which the Other commands the self from a paradoxical position of "humility and height." The hierarchy that marks the Levinasian ethical relation and defines charitable ethics more broadly vanishes in Butler's hands. It is fair to ask whether Butler's ethics of universal precariousness is in the end Levinasian in any meaningful sense.

Even if one answers this question no, this does not yet determine whether Butler's ethics of precariousness is a promising resource for democracy. Perhaps Butler has rightly diverged from Levinas by privileging a conception of universal vulnerability. But here a second difficulty emerges. Butler declares that the fact of precariousness brings with it not only the potential for new forms of community but an obligation of redistribution. How is this possible? Supposing for the moment that the recognition and affirmation of vulnerability as an unavoidable existential truth were somehow achieved, why would this acknowledgment entail an "injunction" to pursue equality, as Butler insists? The idea of universal precariousness could perhaps become mobilizing, if enunciated as a public claim and tied to a demand for the redistribution of vulnerability across populations—a claim and demand that would most likely center on charging a specific, concrete program, policy, or practice with wrongly rendering certain groups especially and unnecessarily vulnerable. But this is not what Butler says when she claims that because precariousness is true, we must pursue a politics committed to its reorganization. The objection here is not simply logical, though Butler can fairly be charged with succumbing to the classic is–ought problem. Butler's contention that the ethics of precariousness is politically salient depends on the unjustified assertion that a specific truth about the world compels the pursuit of a particular normative end; injurability "imposes an obligation upon us."[137] (In some ways, this move between descriptive and normative registers mirrors a slippage in Levinas's own writings, in which *responsibility* names both an unavoidable situation of the self's indebtedness to the Other and the desirable action through which the self answers the call issued by the Other.) Butler's ethics are most relevant to what she calls "radical democracy" if one accepts, as she does, that human precariousness is not only a fact but also inherently prescriptive, mandating a specific response on the part of the "political communities" to which it is thought to give rise.

This tendency to position a certain (commendable) politics as the product of an ethical realization strains against another element of Butler's thought. In the same texts in which Butler highlights the Levinasian dyad as the source of a profound ethical truth that can guide politics, she seems to challenge Levinas's portrait of the ethical self/Other relation by continually reminding readers of the broader—what I would call worldly— contexts in which actual dyadic encounters occur. That is, Butler stresses the social conditions that shape relations between subjects: "If the claim of the other upon me is to reach me, it must be mediated in some way." And: "Our very capacity to respond with non-violence . . . depends upon the frames by which the world is given and by which the domain of appearance is circumscribed."[138] Butler tends to present "conditions" in fairly abstract, even cognitive terms, namely as "frames" and "norms" that govern intelligibility, and thus misses the full complexity of those worldly conditions I theorize in the next two chapters. Nonetheless, Butler's persistent invocation of "conditions" serves to redirect attention away from the intimacy of the dyad and toward collective arrangements. In so doing, she issues a direct challenge to Levinas: "It is not enough to say, in a Levinasian vein, that the claim is made upon me prior to my knowing and as an inaugurating instance of my coming into being. That may be formally true, but its truth is of no use to me if I lack the conditions for responsiveness that allow me to apprehend it in the midst of this social and political life."[139]

"Social and political life," that is, the specific policies, habits, laws, vocabularies, and traditions that characterize a particular context, has everything to do with whether I will hear the call of the Other and with whether a life will even register as a life, as injurable and hence grievable. In these places and others, Butler complicates the Levinasian scene of self and Other—which, as we have seen, she also presents as revelatory of universal precariousness—by foregrounding the extent to which such a scene can never be counted on to function as the origin of an absolute ethical truth, governed as it is by complex institutional arrangements that, for example, humanize some subjects while "derealizing" others.[140] Although Butler mobilizes a distinction between precariousness and precarity to insist that the recognition of precariousness's generalizability leads to an injunction to equalize existing precarity, her orientation toward conditions gives reason to question this argument, particularly the sequencing it advances.[141] Is it even possible to access "precariousness as such"? If precarity—the particular configurations of power that render some

groups especially insecure and even unreal, while protecting and bene-
fiting others—shapes every encounter, then why not locate democratic
struggle on just this terrain? Why imagine such struggle as a consequence
of an absolute truth contained in the Other's face? Perhaps the critical
task is not to see and avow "primary human vulnerability" as an uncontestable and universal ethical truth (a possibility that Butler's emphasis on
enabling and restraining conditions throws into question) but to engage in
the risky business of democratic contestation, publicizing and casting as
changeable those specific harms that are systematically and unnecessarily
wrought on some human beings and not others.

Butler's distinction between precariousness and precarity and her
understanding of precarity as a "politically induced condition" brings her
close to tethering "an ethical demand to political analysis," as Shulman
writes.[142] Her further specification that "our obligations" are actually to
conditions, to institutions and environments, lends credence to Lloyd's
claim that Butler aims to reconcile ethics and politics.[143] According to
Lloyd, by focusing so much on norms Butler effectively politicizes Levinas's ethics, identifying the factors that "inhibit . . . an ethical encounter."
Lloyd continues, "Her exploration of ethics is thus embedded in an account of the politics—or power relations—involved in producing the
human." This implies that "political struggles against the norm are a way
of securing the possibility of ethical relations."[144] This reading attributes
to Butler a view which prioritizes political action directed at common
conditions, conditions that can make possible nonviolent ethical relations
between selves and others. Yet, as Lloyd points out in a subsequent essay,
Butler's approach actually wavers on this key point. At the same time that
Butler explores "how power circumscribes" ethical encounters, she "takes
for granted the ethical imperative itself," which mandates the equalization
of vulnerability. Thus Butler argues both as though "the ethical imperative
is *apolitical* (because it is presented as prediscursive and thus, as not predi-
cated on power relations)" and as though "ethical encounters in determi-
nate contexts are political (because they operate through power relations
and normative violence)."[145] These two lines of thinking persist in Butler's
recent writings and cannot be easily reconciled. Rather than simply deny
the former, as Lloyd's earlier reading suggests, one might want to consider
why the notion of an ethical imperative beyond politics holds such appeal,
even for a thinker like Butler, who is otherwise so attuned to the workings of power and to the importance of democratic contestation aimed

at reshaping power relations. Might it be, as Shulman has provocatively suggested, that the romance with ethical absolutes betrays a cynicism or despair about the possibilities of democratic mobilization?[146] Could it be that quiescence, the absence of political dissent in the form of "bodies joined in protest, generating power by acting in concert," has driven theorists, including Butler, to "imagine founding community on acknowledgement of an extra-political truth?"[147]

### Parting Ways with Levinas

In the end, a common problem afflicts Critchley's and Butler's efforts to deploy Levinas for explicitly democratic purposes. In each case, the movement from Levinasian ethics to democratic activity, from individual concern for the Other to shared concern for worldly conditions, is glossed over, assumed rather than accounted for. More pointedly, both approaches rely on an *if, then* structure, according to which democratic activity follows from the recognition of an ethical truth (credited to Levinas). The trouble is twofold. First, the *if* in both cases is a rather large *if*. Neither Critchley nor Butler focuses on how their central ethical truths, infinite responsibility and universal precariousness, respectively, come to light and become objects of belief or affirmation. They are merely alluring *if*'s. Critchley's all-important moment of the self's commitment to an unfulfillable obligation is assumed without explanation of how or why such a demand is heard, felt, and taken up (or not). His analysis does not address how a self "binds itself" to Levinasian obligation.[148] Even Butler, who is more attuned to the "frames" that affect one's ability to perceive the vulnerability of the Other, still posits the fact of universal vulnerability with very little consideration of how such a supposed truth comes to be formulated, articulated, or accepted in particular worldly contexts.

The *if* becomes a more pressing problem in both cases because it is coupled with an unwarranted *then*, which ushers in democratic activity. Collective mobilization, in Critchley's and Butler's texts, often appears as a consequence of a prior, ethical truth. As we have seen, Critchley credits the existence of an inescapable demand with the appearance of collaborative citizen projects that challenge perceived injustices. He does not address why or how this obligation finds expression in democratic action rather than in charitable direct aid. He simply states that admirable attempts at democratization follow from the fact of infinite responsibility. Although Butler sometimes presents that ethical insight as being itself dependent on alterable sociopolitical conditions, she repeatedly claims that if universal vulnerability is accepted, then an egalitarian political project follows. As Shulman argues, Butler effectively ignores how such a truth is "politically generated" and instead treats universal injurability as a revelatory fact that, if only accepted and affirmed, leads to desirable political outcomes.[149]

The remedy is not to be found by filling in missing pieces of Critchley's and Butler's efforts to wed Levinasian ethics to democratic politics. It is not a matter of fleshing out details that their accounts move over too quickly. This is because, as I have been suggesting, it is a mistake to look to Levinas for a democratic ethics. Contemporary liberal democracy might indeed benefit from a motivating, empowering ethical spirit, but it is not to be found in Levinas's ethics of limitless personal responsibility to the Other. The Levinasian model fixes attention on a dyadic relation, obscuring the worldly contexts that serve as the sites and objects of democratic action. As in the case of the therapeutic ethics I analyzed in chapter 1, a real gap separates charitable ethics from associative democratic practice, in which citizens act publicly and collaboratively in order to shape the world in which they live.[150] This distance between charity and democracy is one that even Critchley's and Butler's creative modifications cannot overcome.

One might suppose at this point that the very quest for ethics is in doubt. If neither Foucauldian nor Levinasian ethics holds great promise for the elaboration of a democratic ethos, should we question the aspiration itself? This is surely too hasty, for the ethics of self-care and of care for the Other, despite their influence, do not exhaust the field of possibilities. Indeed, there is a distinctive form of care, neither therapeutic nor charitable, that is uniquely capable of nourishing associative democracy. It is to this alternative ethics that we now turn.

CHAPTER THREE

≡

# THE DEMOCRATIC ETHICS OF CARE FOR WORLDLY THINGS

*Res* means what concerns men.
— MARTIN HEIDEGGER

Each object gathers around itself a different assembly of relevant parties.
— BRUNO LATOUR

To question Foucauldian and Levinasian ethics is not to reject the quest for a democratic ethos. The critique offered in
the preceding chapters does not now culminate in a call for a
return to more universal and absolute modes of morality that
would somehow overcome the limitations of care for the self
and care for the Other. Nor are the doubts I have raised meant
to divorce democracy from ethos, in the name of a rationalist-
institutionalist vision of politics or the autonomy of the political. Theorists such as Connolly, Critchley, and Butler are
right to insist that democratic practice is irreducible to formal
structures of government; it is always shaped by the dispositions, habits of mind, affective comportments, and felt commitments of its participants (and nonparticipants). The exploration and elaboration of a democratic ethos is a meaningful
endeavor. The problem lies not with the desire to articulate an
ethics for democracy but with the mistaken supposition that
therapeutic and charitable models are suitable to the task.

In this chapter I lay the groundwork for an alternative

democratic ethos, one centered on the notion of care for the world, a subject I will continue to elaborate in chapter 4. This conception, prefigured in earlier chapters but not yet fully presented, captures a spirit which already animates associative democratic projects but which deserves to be explicitly thematized and purposefully cultivated. Care for the world, distinct from concern for oneself or for an Other, is an ethos uniquely fit for democratic life.[1]

Like the ethical orientations that take inspiration from Foucault and Levinas, the democratic ethos I posit privileges relations of care: expressions of regard and concern and active tending to. Yet such care involves different agents and recipients than those assumed by therapeutic and charitable models. Democratic care is collaborative, expressed in joint action by plural participants. The practitioner of such care is never a self but always an association of selves. Even more important, the recipient of care is not another person or even persons, but the world, understood as the array of material and immaterial conditions under which human beings live — both with one another and with a rich variety of nonhumans, organic and technological. More specifically still, coaction among citizens is directed not at the world per se but at particular worldly things that become objects of shared attention and concern. This thing, a concept that, like world, awaits full theorization, is crucial to every democratic undertaking. It is the third term — a practice, place, law, habit, or event — around which people gather, both in solidarity and division.

Yet it is precisely the world with its many potential objects of concern that is absent from the Foucauldian and Levinasian ethical scenes. The relations of self/self and self/Other tend to suppose that it is a single human being rather than a collectivity who exercises care, and in addition the intimacy of those dyadic relations threatens to eclipse worldly conditions altogether. There is little room in these accounts for anything other than human selves and others. This is true even of Levinas's much-celebrated third, which evokes the presence of another human being but not the milieu inhabited by plural human beings. Both ethical approaches neglect something vital to democratic politics, and that is the central role played by things. These are matters of concern that serve as the focal points of collective democratic activity, both cooperative and antagonistic. A viable democratic ethos, I argue, is one that supports and inspires mutual care for worldly conditions.

## Practicing Care

To attest to care about something is, at the most basic level, to indicate that the something in question has a claim on our attention; if we care in this sense, we are interested, not indifferent. This meaning of the word is most evident in the negative expression, "I don't care." Care for worldly things, which I place at the center of democratic ethics, certainly requires, in the first instance, this giving of attention, yet it also entails a second, stronger and more deeply felt sentiment which is expressed in action. The difference between these modalities of care is evinced by the distinction between caring about and caring for something. In the second, more demanding sense, to care is to feel and show concern, solicitude, or regard for something. It implies not merely an attitude but a form of engagement or activity consisting in enduring dispositional conduct. Care for the world is meant to invoke this richer notion of care, which involves not only paying attention but active tending to and looking after.

Care for the world, as an ethical concept, draws on ordinary definitions of what it means to care, but it also marks a departure from conventional usage, where the implied object of care is another human being. Similarly, it challenges the intra- and intersubjective portraits of care presented by Foucauldian therapeutic ethics and Levinasian charitable ethics. Despite the rigor of their work, the view of the caring activity each advances corresponds to familiar ways of thinking about care, which in both cases is identified with nurturance of a specific human being. Care for the world as a democratic ethos is distinctive because it departs from this commonplace understanding to specify a mode of collaborative caretaking that is directed not at a person or even persons but at the conditions of their lives.

Care for the world, conceptualized as a distinctively democratic ethos, is partly inspired by Hannah Arendt's notion of *amor mundi*, or love of the world. *Amor Mundi* is the title Arendt originally intended to give to her landmark book *The Human Condition*, and it is an idea that arguably informs all of her work, though references to it are scattered.[2] As I read it, the phrase is meant to describe an emotional investment in and deep affection for something other than human selves, namely, for the complex, extrasubjective "web" that constitutes the conditions of our lives. The worldly ethics I elaborate builds on Arendt's insight into the distinctive regard and concern, even love, that is expressed through action in concert, when people combine together to tend not to themselves but to the world in which they live.[3] A key example of such amor mundi in action, according to Arendt, was the antiwar practices of civil disobedience of the 1960s and 1970s, in which participants effectively "took sides for the world's sake."[4] In what follows, I take up the invitation posed by Arendt's evocative but underdeveloped notion of amor mundi, which expresses a special kind of care enacted by citizens in association, in order to fully conceptualize and advocate what Arendt does not: a worldly ethics for democracy.[5]

The language of care that I draw on in defense of this specific ethos features prominently in the literature of care ethics. Some advocates of care ethics have challenged the tendency to privatize, if not denigrate, caring activities and to cast care as incompatible with the public pursuit of impartial, universalist justice. The field of feminist care ethics began with work that treated maternal care for a child as paradigmatic, thereby retaining a very traditional and feminized conception of care, albeit revalued as morally worthy.[6] But while early contributions focused on a dyadic, usually familial relation in which an individual cares for a particular vulnerable Other, more recent writings have developed an expansive notion of care that is explicitly linked to political life.[7] Joan Tronto's "political theory of care" is especially intriguing because she challenges the tendency to think of care as intimate, suggesting both that care can be undertaken collectively by an association of actors and also that care can at times mean caring for objects and environments as well as people.[8] She offers examples of caring activities that are neither individualist nor dyadic, such as the collective creation of new institutions like Gay Men's Health Crisis, Project Open Hand, and the Shanti Project that successfully transformed the circumstances faced by HIV/AIDS patients.[9]

The argument I make for a democratic ethics focused on care for the world resonates in some respects with Tronto's. I agree that the notion of care, freed from its privatized and gendered connotations and tethered to the practice of citizenship, has the potential to "change the terms of political debate and discussion."[10] Yet Tronto's tendency to collapse many disparate kinds of care together (people, she says, "spend most of their lives" caring) makes it difficult to recognize and appreciate what I argue is a specifically democratic mode of care, associative in character and oriented toward worldly things. Tronto's important effort to expand the notion of care unfortunately results in a fairly generic definition—providing for people's needs—which does not facilitate differentiation among diverse forms of caregiving.[11] Democratic care for the world, for example, though not unrelated to the fulfillment of people's needs, may involve, paradoxically, displacing immediately vulnerable people from the center of analysis in order to bring into view and work to transform the complex environment out of which their needs arise.

Tronto believes that if people were to become more adept at caring in a general sense, that is, by developing qualities of "attentiveness, responsibility, competence, responsiveness," they would become better citizens. Yet I want to insist on a certain discontinuity among modes of caregiving. That is, although caring for oneself, others, and the world have something in common—signaled by the presence of the term *care*—they are far from identical or even mutually supportive activities. Indeed, if they were, the turn to Foucault and Levinas for a democratic ethos would be more persuasive than I am willing to grant. Democratic care is not simply an extension or expansion of caring for oneself or caring for another. As I have suggested, those practices of care, while valuable, may impede participation in action in concert that aims to shape worldly conditions because they either direct people's focus inward as they "work on" themselves or, alternatively, turn toward answering the immediate needs of vulnerable Others. Neither activity, however worthy, can be counted on to encourage coordinated action by citizens who aim to affect an aspect of public life. One may personally tend very effectively to a child or an ailing parent, but such care may never translate into coaction with others that aims to address, say, the availability of low-cost quality child care or the social marginalization of the elderly. Quite simply, democratic politics depends on a style and practice of care that are distinct from those of other, more familiar forms. The difference lies in the identity of both those who care and those who are cared for.

## The World and Its Things

What does it mean to say that the world is at the center of associative democratic politics or to claim, further, that caring for this entity amounts to a democratic ethos? I want to elaborate here an understanding of *world*, thinking both with and against Arendt's conceptualization of the term, and defend its significance to a uniquely democratic ethical sensibility.

The world is both material and nonmaterial. In Arendt's political theory, it names both a "physical . . . in-between" and a "second, subjective in-between" that is constituted by "deeds and words."[12] The world is not strictly tangible. Its materiality, what can be seen and touched, is never isolated from languages, relationships, norms, habits, and traditions, the more intangible elements of existence that overlie the physical. Yet Arendt's conception, which I selectively draw upon, also demarcates *world* from *earth* and *nature*, reserving *world* for what is man-made.[13] Indeed, *world*, in both its tangible and intangible dimensions, is synonymous with *human artifice* to Arendt. As Hanna Pitkin explains, it is "the material culture of humanly made or altered objects and the nonmaterial culture of humanly sustained relationships, institutions, customs, mores, concepts, and civilization in general."[14] In other words, *world* stands for culture, or that which is humanly made, whether an object or a practice, in opposition to nature, which is given. This division, however, is hard to maintain, insofar as humanly produced customs, institutions, relations, and objects are inevitably bound up with the natural. A particularly dramatic example is the British Petroleum oil spill in the Gulf of Mexico in 2010, which may be regarded as a site of the dense entanglement of man-made objects (an oil rig, dispersants, cameras, caps, saws, valves, and so on), natural entities (human beings, water, salt, tides, oil, animals), and cultural artifacts (corporations, regulations, the commercial fishing industry, legal claims, protests, media coverage, and so on). It is impossible to isolate the cultural from the natural without doing violence to reality. Even much simpler activities reveal this to be so. When I sit down to have lunch, where I eat, what I eat, and how I eat it are never simply worldly (cultural) or earthly (natural) in character but always and necessarily an amalgamation of both. The concept of world that I forward builds on Arendt's insight into the entanglement of the tangible and the intangible but rejects the line she tries to draw between world and earth. The world, as conceptualized here, denies that culture/nature opposition and instead aims to capture the total interplay between elements falsely assigned to either side of this division.

*World* here does not refer only to what is man-made. Nonetheless, much of the world is created and all of it affected by human beings, a fact that is integral to the democratic ethos I advocate. Indeed, as Arendt points out, politics itself depends on the belief that "man can act in and change and build a common world together with others."[15] To affirm this world-building capacity is not to deny to nonhumans the ability to affect the world nor should it be mistaken for a claim to absolute mastery. But it is certainly the case that human beings possess an especially potent as well as self-reflexive capacity to shape the complex environment of which they are a part. The world, in short, should be understood as highly susceptible to human decision making and activity.

At the same time, the world—both tangible and intangible, organic and inorganic—shapes the human beings who are uniquely powerful in its construction. As Arendt points out, even the conditions of our existence that are clearly humanly made and variable have a "conditioning effect" on us: "The things that owe their existence exclusively to men nonetheless constantly condition their human makers."[16] There is a reciprocal relation of mutual influence between human beings, who help build the world, and the world itself. This is especially evident in the realm of technology. Arendt's famous example of this phenomenon is the invention of the telescope and its effects on human subjectivity. On her telling, the realization that human senses were fallible and less reliable than manufactured instruments in ascertaining reality gave rise to profound doubt and distrust in human perception, motivating a fateful turn inward; this was the advent of modern subjectivism.[17] A current example can be found in the incredibly swift invention and adoption of new devices and practices of communication: cell phones, social networking, wireless Internet, texting, smart phones, and so on. Recent studies have found that the widespread use of such technology, the ingenious creations of human beings, may alter the human beings who use them, reshaping the neural networks in the brain in ways that affect concentration, the ability to prioritize, and short-term memory.[18] In other words, these "things that owe their existence exclusively to men," in Arendt's phrase, have cognitive and emotional effects on their human makers. This means that the human capacity to shape the world is never the end of the story.

To what extent can one describe the world as a conditioned and conditioning habitat for human beings (though not for them alone)? Does it make sense to think of it as an overall environment or setting? On the one hand, this representation, by casting the world as a mere background or container, runs the risk of exaggerating the separation between it and human actors.[19] This depiction seems to obscure that human beings are of the world and not just in it, while also minimizing the vitality and activity of nonhuman existence. There is more enmeshment and reciprocal influence between human beings and "everything else" included in the concept *world* than the language of habitat or context might imply. On the other hand, part of the value of the concept of world, both in Arendt's understanding and my own, lies in its broadly anti-anthropocentric character. World displaces human beings from the center of analysis and brings into view a complex material and immaterial assemblage that is irreducible to human beings themselves. Although the world is never simply an inert background, it is the site and context of human action, among many other things. And worldly conditions, many of them produced, sustained, and altered by human actors, are nonetheless distinguishable from those actors themselves.[20] Naming the world is important because it brings into focus a complex, heterogeneous entity that is distinct from any human being or collection of human beings.

The world is the stuff of associative democratic politics. It is not only the site or space of collaborative democratic practice but also its very object. As Tocqueville noted, when citizens participate in public affairs they "take a look at something other than themselves."[21] The focus of their attention, that "something" else, is a feature of the world. And, as Arendt points out, the world is "that about which we speak" when we address one another as citizens.[22] The world, or rather some element of it, is the reason citizens struggle with and against each other. When democratic constituencies organize themselves, they do so with reference to a specific worldly matter, whether it has a relatively concrete, physical character (the polar ice caps, the U.S.-Mexico border, a local development project) or is somewhat less so (a constitutional amendment banning gay marriage, the Geneva Conventions, media representations of women of color). To say, with Arendt, that the world is "at stake" in politics means that although the specific motivations and sentiments that inspire collective democratic action vary widely and produce outcomes that are uncertain, an underlying impulse, the "wish to change the world," is shared by even the most divergent democratic actors.[23]

Yet, as the above references hint, it is not so much the world at large that serves as the third term around which democratic actors associate as some specific feature of that world: a thing. I use this term purposefully, not in reference to a generic object but in recognition of the fact that *thing*, as Heidegger noted, originally meant "a gathering, and specifically a gathering to deliberate a matter under discussion, a contested matter."[24] *Thing* designated precisely an associative activity by which participants collectively addressed a matter of importance. Subsequently, the term shifted, so that rather than referencing the assembly itself, *thing* signified the "affair or matter of pertinence" that drew people together in deliberation, denoting what concerned human beings and was therefore a "matter for discourse." The original meaning of *thing* as assembly and its later naming of a "matter of pertinence" are a reminder that whether citizens are acting cooperatively on behalf of a shared goal or struggling against one another in pursuit of competing projects, their relations are mediated by the presence of a third term, a feature of the world that concerns or "bears upon" them.[25]

Worldly things, the objects of associative democratic action, are defined by three principal features: they are multiple, fluctuating, and contested. First, rather than thinking of the world as the focal point of democratic efforts, it is illuminating to consider the vast array of worldly things that have been and can become objects of political attention and advocacy. In place of Arendt's famous description of the world as akin to a table around which citizen-actors gather, we might envision a democratic scene involving multiple tables, each serving as a site of interaction and contention.[26] The contemporary political environment in the United States, for example, is marked by ongoing struggles over energy policy, health care, immigration, the war in Afghanistan, and financial regulation, among many other issues. It may make some sense to say, with Arendt, that the world is at stake in debates over these issues, insofar as each pertains to the conditions under which human beings live; but this framing may prevent us from appreciating the many, varied things or matters of pertinence that draw people into democratic politics and serve as third terms between them. It is not so much the world per se that motivates citizens to participate in democratic activity (a characterization which can sound overly grand), but some particular feature of that world that becomes a site of mobilization.

Second, emphasizing things rather than the world in general prompts us to consider how a particular matter becomes a political thing, the focus of concerted attention and activity. Recalling that *thing* originally named not a generic object but an affair or matter of importance, a contested matter prompting discussion and deliberation, we can then ask, how does an entity, practice, habit, or policy become such a thing? In other words, recognizing plural worldly things as the objects of democratic action invites us to tend to processes of politicization. While Arendt's table metaphor tends to depict the common world as something that is there, mediating relations among individuals, or not there, like the disappearing table at a séance, this portrait should be challenged by Romand Coles's more dynamic notion of "tabling."[27] Coles's conception draws attention to the process by which some feature of the world is constituted as a thing. These things, the many tables around which citizens act, whether cooperatively or oppositionally, are not simply present or absent; they are called into existence through strategies of politicization.

Bruno Latour captures such a process of transformation in his distinction between a "matter of fact" and a "matter of concern."[28] The emergence of a worldly thing as an object around which people associate requires that what was previously regarded as a matter of fact—a relatively unproblematic feature of existence—is reconfigured as important, changeable, and demanding of public attention, that is, a matter of concern. Something is politicized once it is, in Nancy Fraser's words, "contested across a range of different discursive arenas and among a range of different publics," in contrast with what is not contested in public at all or what is contested only in specialized enclaves. A matter of concern in this political sense is publicly recognizable as an object of attention and dispute. As Hanna Pitkin has pointed out, "A social condition becomes a public issue only when it is widely perceived as a problem, and as remediable through public action."[29] Consider how various matters of fact, for example, the widespread consumption of meat, use of fur and leather, and medical experimentation upon animals, have been transformed into matters of concern calling for attention and action, thanks in large part to the efforts of People for the Ethical Treatment of Animals. The emergence of a discourse around animal rights in the late twentieth century exemplifies the degree to which political things are created rather than discovered. The tabling process is one in which a feature of existence, a taken-for-granted practice, policy, or custom, is reframed so that it becomes legible as a problem warranting collective advocacy and action.

Jacques Rancière's distinctive theory of democracy contains a powerful account of politicization that further enriches one's understanding of the process whereby a particular matter of fact is constituted as a matter of concern. For my purposes—exposing the critical role played by worldly things in associative practices of democracy—two insights are especially significant. First, Rancière portrays collective organizing by ordinary citizens who seek to challenge existing arrangements as involving the "assertion of a common world."[30] What is being asserted here is not the world in the broadest possible sense (the entire assemblage that constitutes earthly

Chapter 3

—

94

reality, about which I spoke earlier) but, more specifically, a mutual context within which a dispute is possible. Democratic actors must establish that a common world of this sort exists, one that is shared with those they address. It is a question of "creating a stage" on which a "specific conflict" can occur.[31] As Rancière notes, when those who are presently "uncounted" within a polity aim to publicly articulate a wrong to be redressed, they attempt to make themselves "of some account" by enacting a radical equality the social order denies (a scenario that, to Rancière, is definitive of democracy as such). These democratic actors are in the demanding position of having to behave "*as though* such a stage existed, as though there were a common world of argument" already in place, in the hopes of bringing it into being.[32] The task here is to set up a context for dispute, and this is done by way of the public presentation of a particular object, what I am calling a worldly thing.[33] The attempt to constitute a "common/litigious" object and thereby a stage upon which a conflict can occur is bound up, Rancière notes, with the status of those who posit this object.[34] This leads to his second major insight: the ability to "present a common object" turns upon whether those doing the presenting are regarded as subjects at all: Are they "speaking or just making noise"?[35] Whether the object they designate is acknowledged as an object of conflict has everything to do with whether they are "counted as arguers" at all.[36] The achievement of political subjectivity and the ability to present a common object are co-constitutive. Neither precedes the other. Rancière helps reveal just how pivotal worldly things are when he says that agency itself is the "capacity to put something in the middle as an object of argumentation."[37]

In his analysis of the work it takes to "make an object political," Andrew Barry draws on the dual meaning of *demonstration* to emphasize that a central goal of any democratic constituency is to define and render visible an object of potential intervention to a broader public audience. *Demonstration* historically referred to a practice in which a demonstrator in an anatomy lecture theater "pointed out the feature of the body which was being shown and about which the lecturer was speaking." Barry holds that contemporary political protests, or demonstrations, can also be understood as an attempt to show something to others, that is, a specific matter requiring attention and action. For example, antiroad protests in the United Kingdom and elsewhere in Europe in the 1990s occurred not in places of public administration but in the very areas in which roads were being built, amidst their construction. The protests were "something like a demonstration in the technical sense: an act of *pointing out*" a particular site, one marked by obvious signs of environmental destruction such as downed trees, noise, and dead animals. By "directing attention to" a particular object, the protests were demonstrations in a double sense: they were collective, public actions designed to bring into focus an object worthy of attention and concern.[38] Rancière likewise emphasizes the revelatory dimensions of political demonstration, stressing that "the demonstration proper to politics is always both argument and opening up the world." The collective articulation of demands in public exemplifies, in Rancière's view, that "politics is aesthetic in principle": to demonstrate is not only to forward an argument but also to participate in making visible what was once invisible. More precisely, democratic action involves "opening up the world" so that "new objects"—what I call worldly things—can appear.[39]

Finally, the things that serve as the focal points of democratic activity are disputed; they do not admit of a single identity or meaning. The antiroad protesters Barry describes attempted to define and illuminate an object, a new road, in a way very different from that of the proponents of construction, who depicted it as an important instrument of economic development. The object is the same only in the most basic sense; its signification is not. Emilie Gomart and Maarten Hajer provide a similar example in their analysis of a struggle over land use on the Hoeksche Waard, an island south of Rotterdam. The conflict in this case was complex; the debate could not be reduced to pro- and antidevelopment measures, as multiple visions of the island vied with one another. While the object was in some sense common in that all participants understood themselves to be engaged in the question of land use on Hoeksche Waard, each constituency actually "created their own Hoeksche Waard."[40] Even objects less concrete than roads and land masses are subject to competing constructions. Noortje Marres, for example, has shown how the Extractive Industries Review (EIR) of 2000, commissioned by the World Bank to evaluate fossil fuel projects funded by the bank and their effects on "poverty reduction," became "an object of contention," subject to competing "framing" practices, some of which were "urgency-creating" and others "urgency-deflating." Most notably, certain actors struggled to constitute the EIR as a referendum on climate change generally and on the bank's institutional responsibility to address it in particular. The EIR was a "hairy object," a complex entity subject to competing efforts at definition, Marres shows.[41] Worldly things, then, are not only plural and dynamic but also disputed.

Latour's reflections on the possibility of what he calls *Dingpolitik*, or "object-oriented democracy," presents the worldly thing as discordant. Latour poses the question, "What is the *res* of *respublica*?" and envisions democracy as a contentious practice of assembly that is directed toward "divisive matters of concern." Latour's remarks on the meaning of Dingpolitik are notable because he resists the urge to position the matter of concern, or worldly thing, as the site of communitarian unity. Rather, drawing on the etymology of *thing*, cited earlier, Latour conceptualizes the *Ding* of Dingpolitik as that which "brings people together *because* it divides them." A worldly thing may serve as a shared object of concern for a particular collective, helping to produce a bond among them, but in addition it is always a disputed object, a third term that divides as well as unites. That it is never secure in its meaning, marked by a single name, is not, however, evidence against commonality. Rather, it accentuates that in politics what is common in the sense of connecting people is also that which divides them.[42]

This last point is crucial. An object need not be the "same" for all parties in order for it to be "common" to them. Worldly things are objects of deep, ongoing disagreement, yet they serve as third terms that link human subjects to one another, not in spite of being disputed but because they are disputed. This formulation, which is meant to capture a distinctively contentious form of commonality, pushes against Arendt's characterization of politics as an activity that involves multiple perspectives on the same object. While the emphasis on varied perspectives rightly points to an absence of unity among plural participants, the reference to the object's sameness exaggerates its stability and consistency. A particular organized constituency may act to collectively affect a worldly thing whose name and meaning are roughly the same to its members, but the label and concept they use will always vie with those offered by other constituencies who are seeking to produce effects of their own. Strict sameness is not possible here, but mediation does not require it. A litigious matter is common in the sense of serving as a shared site of attention and struggle, though that matter is subject to competing characterizations, interpretations, and calls to action.

The naming and renaming of worldly things by competing actors illustrates how contentious commonality works. For example, recent debates in the United States concerning immigration policy are characterized by struggle over the very terms of discussion: Does the central issue lie in the treatment of illegal immigrants or undocumented workers? To take another example, when and how is the call for universal health care recast as a question of socialized medicine? And what is at stake in speaking of a fetus as opposed to a baby in debates over abortion? These examples demonstrate that political contestation entails more than the expression of multiple perspectives on the same object: it involves struggle over what the object itself is.

The shift from world to worldly things calls attention to the diversity, dynamism, and contentiousness of the targets of democratic activity. There is no single, unitary focal point of associative activity among citizens. Instead, particular elements of the world, things, come in and out of focus as the result of collective action, as new claims are articulated and objects move from the margins of attention to the center and back again.

That state of flux means there is never one table that mediates between democratic actors but many, appearing, disappearing, and reappearing. New political things, around which citizens associate, come into being, and previously active sites of engagement recede. Still other, future political things, not yet having appeared on the horizon of intelligibility, may at present be unimaginable. Finally, the objects at the center of democratic struggles are not the same for all relevant actors; (re)naming and (re)defining them are crucial tools of persuasion and mobilization by competing constituencies. Still, such disputed objects serve as common terms, both relating and separating those who associate around them. Appreciating the pivotal role played by such third terms moves us closer to an ethics of democratic care, in which care is enacted neither for a self nor selves but for worldly things.

### Subject Verb Object? Questioning the Relationship between Humans and Things

Does the outlook articulated above, which highlights the importance of worldly things in associative democratic action, reinscribe a problematic subject/object divide? Does this account posit human actors alone as agents who collectively organize, both with and against one another, in order to act upon mere matter? Are activity and passivity assigned oppositionally and absolutely? Is there a danger that the worldly perspective offered here celebrates the human capacity to shape conditions in ways that may deny efficacy to other entities or potentially collude with fantasies of human mastery?

The work of Latour and Jane Bennett raises the question of "thing-power" and suggests that "things — edibles, commodities, storms, metals" — regularly act as "quasi-agents or forces."[43] In their respective writings, Latour and Bennett call for acknowledgment of a "wider distribution of agency" than is usually recognized.[44] Human beings do not have a monopoly on agency; a more accurate picture of agency is a "distributive" one in which effects are produced by a "human-nonhuman working group," never by humans alone.[45] *Actants* is the term Latour introduces to break up the subject/object dichotomy and name the coparticipants, both human and nonhuman, in a collective responsible for generating effects.[46]

Both Latour and Bennett offer an array of examples to support their claims that agency is diffuse and shared among an "association of actants."[47] Latour writes that one should see the act of a person shooting a gun as the doing of a "hybrid actor comprising gun and gunman." According to Latour, "It is neither people nor guns that kill. Responsibility for action must be shared among the various actants."[48] Bennett cites many instances, both ordinary and extraordinary, of assemblages of humans and nonhumans producing effects. The very process of writing reveals, she says, that agency is "distributed across an ontologically heterogenous field, rather than being a capacity localized in a human body or in a collective produced (only) by human efforts." The book Bennett wrote "emerged from the confederate agency of . . . memories, intentions, contentions, intestinal bacteria, eyeglasses and blood sugar, as well as from the plastic computer keyboard, the bird song from the open window, or the air and particulates in the room, to name only a few of the participants."[49] Bennett offers an extended analysis of the blackout that occurred in North America in 2003 as a highly illustrative example of the agency of an assemblage: "The elements of this assemblage, while they include humans and their (social, legal, linguistic) constructions, also include some very active and powerful nonhumans: electrons, trees, wind, fire, electromagnetic fields."[50]

The assemblage approach to agency challenges the tendency to see human beings alone as agents who act upon an externalized material environment.[51] In place of this traditional subject/object division, Latour and Bennett encourage people to embrace a messier, more entangled view of human and nonhuman interaction, one in which agency is shared among an array of entities. This view is especially provocative when it comes to thinking about politics. What would it mean to envision democratic activity from the perspective opened up by Latour and Bennett? Bennett articulates what is at stake: "The appropriate unit of analysis for democratic theory is neither the individual human nor an exclusively human collective but the (ontologically heterogenous) 'public' coalescing around a problem." In other words, to think meaningfully about agency in the context of contemporary democracy requires taking seriously the "interactions between human, viral, animal and technological bodies."[52] One must relinquish the view that humans alone are agents who impose their designs on inert objects.

How does Latour's and Bennett's perspective bear on the account I have given of worldly things as the focal points of associative democratic action? Does the idea of a democratic ethos centered on care for the world align with their efforts to challenge anthropocentrism? Or does the view I am articulating rely on a conception of agency—or an understanding of the relationship between human beings and things—that the notion of a generative assemblage is meant to challenge?

There are at least two ways in which Latour's and Bennett's writings complement and converge with my thinking here. First, although they would likely challenge my conceptual vocabulary, namely, the distinction between an association of human beings and the worldly things they seek to affect, their arguments do lend support to the conception of world I advance here. World, as I have imagined it, involves a vast array of relations, places, practices, organisms, material goods, and so on that coexist with one another in complex webs, defying any neat nature/culture divide and exceeding the category of human being. *World* refers to the sum total of conditions of life on earth. The rich heterogeneity I ascribe to world resonates with Latour's and Bennett's interest in assemblages, the diverse, interactive entities that collaboratively produce effects. One might even say that world is the meta-assemblage out of which any particular assemblage can emerge.

The critical perspective offered by Latour and Bennett helps illuminate something that remains too concealed in the account I have given so far of worldly things. Although they emphasize what Bennett calls "thing-power," that is, the capacity of nonhumans to produce effects, their work stresses that no actant, thing or otherwise, ever exists in isolation or acts alone. This insight implies that what I have been calling a worldly thing—the focal point of democratic organizing—is never a truly singular object. Indeed, it is always a more complex, heterogenous entity than this.[53] In the examples mentioned earlier, the worldly things at issue—new road construction in the United Kingdom, land use on Hoeksche Waard, and the evaluation of fossil fuel projects contained in the EIR—are themselves far from simple, involving diverse human and nonhuman, organic and nonorganic forces. It is important to recognize *worldly thing* as shorthand for what is actually a constellation rather than a unitary object. It is useful shorthand for thinking about democratic politics, however, because *worldly thing* helps denote that a particular issue has been successfully politicized, has been named and identified as a focal point of attention, transformed from a matter of fact into a matter of concern.

On the other hand, I do not embrace Latour's and Bennett's shift to ascribing agency to actants. This move expands the conception of agency but also runs the risk of erasing distinctions between the entities that participate in an effect-generating assemblage. As my terminology indicates, I retain a focus on the ways in which human beings collectively affect the world of which they are a part.[54] While it is true, as Latour and Bennett insist, that the power to build the world does not belong to humans alone, it would be a mistake for this insight to cover over meaningful differences in the agentic capacities of entities. For this reason I do not take up the vocabulary of actants and assemblages, preferring to mark a distinction between the human power to shape existential conditions, whether for good or ill, and the contributions made by other bodies, matter, or energy.

Latour and Bennett believe that seeing and thinking in terms of actants and assemblages is a necessary corollary to acknowledging interdependence between humans and nonhumans. They maintain that the acknowledgment of coexistentialism—deep interconnectedness between all living and nonliving things—requires letting go of conventional notions of agency.[55] Attributing effects to assemblages rather than to human subjects, they claim, honors the basic truth of coexistence while also undermining dangerous norms of instrumentality and fantasies of mastery. They contend that if humans see actants all around them, they will be less inclined to assume a controlling posture toward nonhuman entities and more interested in nourishing the relational webs and ecosystems in which they participate.

It is possible, however, indeed, desirable, to achieve awareness of and respect for complex interdependency without leveling distinctions between actants. One can acknowledge, for example, that human beings never truly act alone: whatever effects they produce always depend upon the involvement of multiple nonhumans, and humans themselves are vulnerable to forces and processes they cannot control. Yet one can simultaneously acknowledge the special capacities and responsibilities of human beings in particular.

Refusing to equalize all actants need not mean attributing potency to humans alone or sanctioning a settled hierarchy of being. Singling out the human capacity to collaboratively shape the world is valid and important because humans are capable of exercising care in ways that other actants are not. They are able to coordinate with one another through joint action that strives to shape social conditions. This capacity is integral to democratic citizenship. That this ability to engage in reflective, purposeful collective projects can lead to disaster is no reason to deny the specifically human capacity to shape the world by collapsing it into the generic category of actant. Indeed, doing so may unintentionally diminish humans' sense of responsibility for worldly conditions.

There is real value in an intervention like Bennett's that draws attention to the powerful influence, for example, that worms have had on human history. Quoting Darwin, Bennett writes that worms make history by producing "vegetable mold, which makes possible 'seedlings of all kinds,' which makes possible an earth hospitable to humans, which makes possible the cultural artifacts, rituals, plans, and endeavors of human history."[56] Bennett's account challenges the tendency to see human beings alone as the actors on history's stage and alerts us to the ways in which our doings are never ours alone. At the same time, it would be absurd to say that humans and worms are both actants and leave it at that.[57] Both creatures make vital contributions to the world in which humans and worms live. But they do not do so *in the same way*. To ignore the unique power and corresponding responsibility of human actants is as unrealistic as believing in the dream of human mastery over brute matter that Bennett and Latour challenge.

Acknowledging the fact of coexistence should not rule out recognition of human beings' potent effect-producing capacities. Human beings are agents in a special sense. They may be fallible, nonsovereign, and regularly unable to predict or even adequately respond to the results of their actions. But that does not mean they are simply one participant among many in an assemblage. While it is true, for example, as I pointed out earlier, that the British Petroleum oil spill illustrates the complicated interplay of material and immaterial, natural and cultural, human and nonhuman factors, it would be absurd to deny that human beings played a role in that devastating event unlike the role played by other actants. While the leak was impossible in the absence of the actant, oil, for example, it makes no sense to ignore that human beings, with their world-building capacities, are the most significant contributing actants involved.

Bennett states that her account of "vibrant matter" is not an argument for the "radical equalization" of all matter, yet there is no concept within her actant/assemblage framework that specifies the human capacity to produce effects, especially by acting in concert.[58] Nonetheless, there are at least two ways in which Bennett, I think, acknowledges a special standing for humans among actants, granting a basic distinction between specifically human associations and the worldly things they aim to affect. First, in a discussion of why it is important to perceive actions as the results of assemblages, she says that by doing so people are better able to interrogate the assemblages in which they participate. This implies that human beings are able to reflect upon the contributions they make to assemblages of which they are a part in ways that, say, worms or steel cannot. If this is so, why resort to an overly broad notion of actant that detracts from this important human capacity to make judgments about our conduct? Second, Bennett states that becoming aware of the power of nonhumans can contribute to human survival and happiness. More specifically, she says that if we pay attention to the effects of vibrant matter, we are able to ask, "How is this food or worm or aluminum contributing to a problem affecting me? How might these nonhumans contribute to its solution?"[59] The perspective Bennett articulates here is one in which human beings are able to shape their world better by understanding the workings of certain nonhuman entities. Though not strictly instrumentalist, since it is rooted in attentiveness to the liveliness of these nonhumans, the vantage point Bennett invites us to occupy is nonetheless one in which human beings are in a position of trying to collectively solve a worldly problem. All actants are not equal here because it is human beings, not food or worms or aluminum, who are in the position of trying to solve problems they face, many of which they are specially responsible for.

## The Art of Association: Solidarities and Publics

If democratic politics involves a distinctive object of care, who is it that cares for this worldly thing? I have stressed that an association of individuals, not a single actor, strives to address what was once a matter of fact and now appears as a contentious matter of concern. Two clarifications are crucial. First, the associations that coalesce around a worldly thing do not necessarily exist in advance; they emerge in relation to that third term. There is a specific, limited kind of commonality at work here, a commonality not of identity but of a shared object. Second, *association* is a term that broadly captures both relations among those working together on behalf of a project and the antagonistic struggles that take place between constituencies who aim to define and treat worldly things in divergent ways. Association takes the form of both solidaristic groups and conflictual publics.

On this first point, John Dewey's treatment of what he calls the public contains an insightful description of how communities come into being in relation to specific worldly things. By the end of *The Public and Its Problems* Dewey seems to embrace a communitarian and statist conception of the public, but the earlier part of this famous text speaks of publics in the plural and traces their origins not to any organic sense of unity among a people but to a problem that prompts a contingent collective formation. As Marres points out, before the "U Turn" toward the "Great Community" that Dewey makes in the text, he provides a very different and distinctive conceptualization of the public as emerging in response to a problem, defined as a transaction that not only has "extensive and enduring indirect consequences" that "affect the welfare of many" but also requires attention and action of some kind.[60] According to this account, a public comes into being by virtue of a specific matter; "the *source* of a public" is a set of consequences brought about by "conjoint action" of one kind or another, consequences whose effects are so critical and widespread as to give rise to a new collectivity, a public, made up of those affected.[61] Most striking about Dewey's account, apart from the importance he grants, albeit inconsistently, to the worldly things that serve to generate a public, is the vocabulary of care he uses to describe the emergent public's activity. According to Dewey, the public that "comes into existence" around a pressing problem does so because the "indirect consequences" to which they are subject must be "systematically cared for."[62] It is in response to perceived neglect that the public forms, seeking to institute "measures and means of caring for these consequences."[63]

Dewey's suggestive account of the formation of "caring" publics in response to specific, mutually recognized problems seems to imply, however, that such formation is inevitable. Yet the constitution of organized collectivities seeking to address a perceived common concern is far from automatic. Indeed, in some political science circles it is a matter of consensus that citizens' participation in collective action, not their apparent apathy or inaction, amounts to the mystery standing in need of explanation.[64] While it is true that associations do not form easily or readily around the sorts of issues Dewey labels problems, they nonetheless do form. And substantial research shows that it is a mistake to dismiss these forms of collective action as being irrational, given the multiple, complex factors that seem to play a role in motivating citizens' participation.[65] Despite the narrow model of self-interest and cost-benefit calculation made famous by Mancur Olson, people who take part in associative democratic politics appear to be motivated by an array of incentives, some of which are "purposive," that is, related to a commitment to "suprapersonal" organizational goals, understood as collective goods, and some "solidary," or related to the pleasure derived from coming together to work on behalf of a shared project.[66]

When democratic associations form, against considerable odds, they take shape around objects of mutual attention. Following Patchen Markell, one might accurately cast such associative action as a "*second* step rather than a first," in recognition of the worldly phenomena that "occasion, provoke or summons" the collective response. Though such responsiveness is never assured, Markell notes that, *pace* Arendt, "if we can never quite lose our capacity to act altogether, this is because there never ceases to be a fund of doings and happenings—beginnings—to which we might respond." Worldly phenomena are the "points of departure" for associative democratic endeavors.[67] Interpreted as publicly consequential and worthy of organized response, specific worldly matters lie at the center of both solidaristic associations among plural individuals acting on behalf of shared ends and antagonistic associations involving diverse solidaristic communities who advocate competing ends. Third terms, worldly things, mediate relations between democratic actors in both cooperation and struggle.

When democratic association takes the form of solidarity among individuals, a worldly thing serves as a bond among participants. Members of a solidaristic group are connected to one another by this thing and by the action they seek to undertake on its behalf. This portrait of solidarity resembles what Sally Scholz has designated as "political solidarity" and distinguished from "social solidarity," in which group members are united by a shared characteristic or identity. Here what makes solidarity possible is less a common identity than a "common goal."[68] The linchpin of political solidarity is a singular project directed at worldly conditions. Therefore membership in solidaristic forms of association is open to those who are most directly affected by a specific practice, law, or custom as well as to those who are less so. As Scholz puts it, political solidarity involves oppressed and nonoppressed people working collaboratively.[69] What connects members are not exclusively shared identity markers or similar experiences but common commitment to a goal—a goal, I would add, that concerns a worldly thing. Recent prominent examples of such project-related solidarity are the many coalitions of lesbian, gay, bisexual, and transgender people and their allies working on behalf of antidiscrimination measures in localities throughout the United States.[70]

An extraordinary example of solidarity enacted by "advantaged" and "disadvantaged" people connected by a common goal can be found in Danish resistance to Nazism during the Second World War. Amy Allen, writing about what she calls "Arendtian solidarity," cites this example from Arendt's writings as a paradigmatic case in which citizens' action in concert is rooted not in shared identity but in a shared object of concern. While Danish people resisted "in terms of the Jewish identity under attack," such solidarity did not require being a "*member* of that group." For example, when the Nazis approached Danish officials about distributing the yellow star to be worn by Jews, the king of Denmark announced that he would be the first to wear it, although he was not a Jew. As Allen shows, the varied strategies undertaken by the Danish resistance illuminates Arendt's view that "collective political movements are held together not by a shared identity, but by the shared commitment of distinct individuals to work together for the attainment of a common goal."[71]

This concept, however, is missing from many accounts of solidarity. Jodi Dean's work, for example, posits two primary types of solidarity that she aims to challenge. "Affectional solidarity" refers to bonds of friendship and love among individuals while "conventional solidarity" extends "beyond those to whom we are immediately connected through our mutual feelings to include those to whom we are mediately connected . . . to something standing beyond us to construct us as a group." While the reference to "something beyond us" is evocative, what Dean is actually referring to is an identity category, for example, women or African Americans.[72] The typology Dean constructs misses a form of solidaristic association in which "mutual feelings" are not about love and friendship among members, as they are in her definition of "affectional solidarity," but about collective feelings of concern for shared conditions.[73] Dean's model of conventional solidarity further assumes that the mediating force connecting participants is always an identity category. Dean's work does not acknowledge a form of solidarity that is defined not by identity but by identification with a project.[74]

The conception of solidarity advanced here also departs from the "universal solidarity" that Dean defends as an alternative model of association. She praises this third approach to solidarity as one that overcomes the us/them distinctions at work in affectional and conventional solidarity. Yet project-oriented solidarity, which revolves around a worldly thing that binds individuals together, is never universal; it does not envisage an all-inclusive we. Solidarities are plural and vie with one another over the worldly things they aim to affect. The second form of democratic association, therefore, is more contentious than cooperative. Here, too, a worldly thing is pivotal, but rather than acting as a bond among coactors organized in solidarity with one another, it divides citizens, serving as a disputed object between them. Solidarity, in other words, exists within a broader context of democratic association, one marked by disagreement and contest.

*Public* refers to the expansive mode of association that takes place in relation to a specific, contested worldly thing. This type of association, like the solidarity discussed above, is oriented toward a particular object, what Marres calls an issue. But unlike the solidaristic pursuit of a common goal, a public is defined by competing, antagonistic perspectives on the issue. Borrowing from Dewey, Marres contends that "issues call publics into being"; a public emerges, if and when it does, only in relation to a practical problem that has been successfully "public-ised."[75] Such a public, however, bears no resemblance to the Public that Dewey invokes in his most communitarian vein. Though a particular issue lies at the center of Marres's public, it is always an "object of contention."[76] There is no "shared interest" among members of a public, only "joint and antagonistic attachments" to the object in question.[77] By "joint," Marres means to high-light that the relevant constituencies are connected to each other by a spe-cific issue without sharing a common perspective or agenda. Indeed, the public is defined by "irreconcilable attachments"; actors "come together in controversy."[78]

This view of a public as connected by a divisive object complements my earlier description of worldly things as being unsettled. As I argued, worldly things are never fixed, unitary objects; they are dynamic entities, subject to competing constructions and significations. Though they are contentious and unstable, worldly things nonetheless mediate relations among the competing constituencies that constitute a public; they act as third terms, joining adversaries in disagreement. Marres's analysis of the "near-public" that developed around the EIR demonstrates a distinc-tive mode of association in which diverse actors, from nongovernmental organizations focused on the environment to international banks, were "bound together by mutual exclusivities between their various attach-ments."[79] As Latour suggested with the notion of Dingpolitik, a public is, paradoxically, constituted as a collective by what divides them.

Worldly things, then, play a critical role in democratic politics, serving as the focal points of both cooperative and competitive modes of associa-tion. In solidarity with one another, democratic citizens work on behalf of a common goal, attempting to tend to a worldly thing in a particular way. At the same time, such solidarities exist within broader publics whose participants struggle to define and shape worldly things in incompatible ways. Worldly things, in their capacity both to unite and to divide, are in-dispensable to democratic politics.

### An Ethos for Democracy?

I offer here a world-centered account of associative democratic politics and begin to make the case for a distinctive ethics centered on collabo-rative care for worldly things. Rather than accept the false choice some-times offered between traditional, universalist morality, on the one hand, and an ethics focused on the self or the Other, my book explores com-peting *ethe* and draws attention to the limits of Foucauldian and Levinas-ian approaches to democratic theory and practice.[80] The worldly ethics advocated in this chapter and the next centers on a relation of care, yet, as I have shown, such care involves agents—associations, in the form of

solidarities and publics—and recipients of care—public matters of concern—that differ from those that define therapeutic and charitable ethics.

An example will help to illustrate what distinguishes democratic care
for the world from other practices of care. The problem of hunger is a
widely recognized (which is not to say, adequately addressed) problem,
both domestically and globally.[81] Supposing that a contemporary U.S. citizen is alert to this problem, that is, already cares *about* it, what kind of response, what kind of active caring *for* might follow? A certain intrasubjective strategy or care for the self is one possibility. The person might work
on herself with the aim of cultivating new personal habits that embody
her concern. She might, through so-called arts of the self, strive to diminish her desire to eat meat or to cultivate pleasure in a vegetarian diet, in
recognition of the extent to which animal-based food production contributes to the problem of global hunger.[82] On the other hand, responding to
the fact of hunger might take the form of caring for the immediate hunger
of an Other, directly addressing her material need.[83] Here, the concerned
actor may become more alert and responsive to those she encounters in
everyday life, providing for them rather than turning away. Caring for the
needy, singular Other is one admirable way of taking up the problem of
hunger. But what might it mean to approach the phenomenon of hunger
from the perspective of caring for the world? To address the phenomenon of hunger in this way means something different. It requires tending,
together with others, to the conditions that helped to produce hunger in
its many forms in the first place.

Caring for the world, which is to say, tending to a specific worldly thing
together with others, requires a shift in perspective, one which involves
decentering both oneself and suffering Other(s) in order to bring into
view the collective conditions, including worldly practices, habits, and
laws, out of which hunger is born. There are many contributing conditions
that might become specific matters of concern, among them inequitable
international trade policies, patterns of uncompensated resource extrac-
tion in developing countries, agricultural subsidies, wasteful consumption among the world's most well-off, paltry social services in the United
States, and so on. And there are a range of possible contestations that
could be pursued, such as campaigning for debt relief in developing countries, promoting new microfinancing initiatives, organizing on behalf of
domestic food programs or subsidy reform, and many others. Yet what

distinguishes these pursuits from other laudable forms of care is a shared orientation toward a third term, that is, a feature of the world in which we live, and a collective effort to shape it. Such care is integral to a democratic ethos.

How compelling is the account given so far of this ethical sensibility? Is care for the world a meaningful alternative ethos, potentially invigorating of democratic association? Or is care for the world too open-ended of a notion to carry ethical weight? If care for worldly things refers to associative efforts to tend to a specific matter of fact reconstituted as a matter of concern, can one say that every time citizens organize themselves collectively to affect social conditions they are enacting such care? Surely this is too broad. But if one wants to say that care for the world, in its fullest ethical sense, characterizes some efforts but not others, on what basis can this distinction be made? A democratic ethos centered on care for worldly things is not only descriptive but normative; not every collaborative citizen project embodies this spirit. What, then, supplies the critical vantage point for identifying those democratic endeavors that aim not only to build a world but also to care for it?

≡

# CHAPTER FOUR

# PARTISANSHIP FOR THE WORLD

## Tending to the World as Home and In-Between

Admire the world for never ending on you as you would admire an opponent, without taking your eyes off him, or walking away.
—ANNIE DILLARD

I've begun so late, really only in recent years, to truly love the world.
—HANNAH ARENDT

I have examined the central role played by worldly things in practices of democratic association. In both solidarities and publics, a contentious object of concern serves as the focal point of relations among citizens, relations ranging from co-operative to antagonistic. This third term, obscured by both Foucauldian and Levinasian ethical dyads, is integral to democratic politics and to its animating ethos. Indeed, I have argued that care for the world, expressed as collaborative care for a specific worldly thing, is definitive of democratic ethics.

One might wonder, however, whether the account of care for the world I have given is too thin to carry ethical force. After all, the thing-centered portrait of associative democratic politics presented in chapter 3 is largely (re)descriptive; it makes a claim about the structure of collective action rather than prescribing action of a certain kind. Does this mean that care for the world is enacted whenever democratic citizens organize collectively to address a matter of concern, regardless of the specific goals or ends they seek? Surely not. From the perspective of an impassioned democratic ethics, all associative activity is not equal. But if care for the world in its fullest sense characterizes some citizen efforts but not others, more needs to be said about its substantive aims.

Put differently, one must ask, what is the difference between building the world and caring for it? Building the world is open-ended; human beings cannot help but shape the world of which they are a part, purposefully as well as unintentionally, with consequences ranging from the benign to the glorious to the disastrous. But what special kinds of action exhibit democratic care of the world? What normative ends are specific to it? If human action and speech as such are world-constituting and if all forms of association aspire to affect worldly things in some way, what does it mean to truly care for the world? Which kinds of action express *amor mundi* and which do not?

This chapter develops the normative valence of care for the world by refining it to mean care for the world *as* world. This move relies upon a more substantive conception of world than has been advanced so far, one which stresses the world's status as common.[1] In what follows I explain that the claim to commonality should be understood as prescriptive rather than descriptive, and I specify two dimensions of the world's commonality: the world as a shared home for human beings and the world as a mediating entity that connects and also separates individuals.[2] Democratic care for the world involves coordinated coaction by citizens that tends to the world both as a collective home and as an in-between. These ends are integral to the democratic ethos I advocate here.

### The World as a Shared Home

Arendt's notion of world has served as a touchstone in this project, even as it has been challenged and reworked. I have affirmed her placement of the tangible and intangible world, irreducible to human beings, at the center of politics even as I have refused her boundary between world and earth. And in place of her tendency to depict the world as either present or absent, I have emphasized a multitude of dynamic, contested, and slippery worldly things acting as third terms among democratic constituencies.

A central attribute of the Arendtian world is its commonality. Arendt's references to the world are often modified by the word *common*, and she describes the world as being "common to all people" and "common to all of us."[3] I think there are two important dimensions to commonality that, taken together, specify what it means to care for the world as world and thereby imbue democratic ethos with its particular normative aims. In one sense, for the world to be common means that it mediates between us, both connecting and separating individuals. (This sense of commonality was introduced in chapter 3's theorization of worldly things.) But to describe the world as common means something else too, something distinct from its potential status as an in-between. To say that the world is "common to all of us" indicates that the world is our shared home.

To claim that the world is a shared home is not to make the unsupportable assertion that the world is shared at all equitably. Rather, it is to say that the world, conceptualized as a tangible and intangible, organic and inorganic web, partially given to human beings and partially made by them, ought to provide hospitable conditions for all, not just some, human beings. The world's commonality, both as a mediating presence and as a collective home, is something to be achieved or sought after; it is far from assured.

I want to defend a normative conception of the world as common in the sense of being a home for all people.[4] More specifically, I argue that in order for humans to be at home in the world, certain of their basic needs must be met. Collaborative pursuit of this aim of universal provision of basic needs is part of what it means to care for the world as world. This approach to the world's commonality may seem like a considerable departure from Arendt, whose apparent hostility toward material needs and desire to empty political life of the so-called social question have been targets of substantial criticism. It is true that my construction of the world as home and of the corresponding importance of basic needs should not be attributed to Arendt. Yet her work, as we will see, alerts one to the profound harms wrought by poverty and gives reason to believe that its alleviation is of great importance, even as she mistakenly identifies that project as prepolitical. Far more than is usually recognized, Arendt makes clear that material deprivation inflicts more than bodily injury. If read in conversation with contemporary advocates of economic and social rights and human capabilities, Arendt's work encourages one to think about how material conditions affect personhood in general and democratic citizenship in particular. This insight in turn affirms the importance of a democratic ethos that involves struggling to make the world a better home for all human beings.

Activists, theorists, and state actors have counted economic and social rights among the human rights demanded, conceptualized, and ratified over the past several decades. Linking basic needs to the concept of human rights is unmistakably powerful. To speak of a right not to be hungry challenges the limits of more conventional conceptions of human rights (such as the eighteenth-century rights of man to personal liberty and political freedom), but it also redefines hunger to be not merely a problem or a pity but a fundamental violation. Still, as in the case of any human rights claim, the very definition of welfare rights, let alone the question of their institutionalization and enforcement, is a matter of ongoing debate. Even among those who endorse the existence of such rights it can be difficult to render them "clearly specifiable."[5] Amartya Sen's capabilities approach, for example, includes what others would label economic rights among the "substantive opportunities" people are held to require to be really, and not only formally, free. Sen acknowledges that there is no fixed, absolute list of these requirements. He does not see this absence as cause for lament, however, and maintains that the question of rights or capabilities must remain open to democratic discussion and contestation. What is necessary for real freedom cannot be delineated and settled once and for all. This point—that no set of rights or capabilities is beyond "the reach of democracy"—is critically important, especially in light of the dangers of paternalistic, hierarchical care (see chapter 2).[6]

Nonetheless, it is also the case that those marshaling the language of economic rights and human capabilities, including Sen, regularly identify some specific provisions with those concepts, and there is considerable overlap between working definitions. A minimum set of material needs—adequate nutritional food, clean water and sanitation, shelter, clothing, basic medical care, and at least primary education—forms the basis of the majority of economic rights claims and also constitutes what Sen calls "elementary capabilities."[7] This list, while imperfect and debatable, captures the basic needs that I argue must be satisfied if the world is to be a collective home for human beings.

The capabilities approach, as developed by Sen and Martha Nussbaum, proffers two ways of thinking about why the fulfillment of basic needs matters.[8] These insights contribute to the account I develop here, in conversation with Arendt, of what it means to care for the world by tending to it as a home for all people. First, capabilities, though spelled out with varying specificity by Sen and Nussbaum, is a concept meant to name the range of "substantive opportunities" that people require to live a fully human life: not only familiar civil and political liberties, for example, but also access to adequate nutrition and health care.[9] Some measure of subsistence, on this view, is necessary though not sufficient for persons to live with human dignity at all. Their very status as persons depends on certain of their basic needs being fulfilled.

Material needs are vitally important, according to the capabilities perspective, for a second reason as well: their fulfillment makes possible certain other, widely recognized rights and liberties.[10] Because the capabilities framework emphasizes "what people are actually able to do or be," it interrogates whether certain freedoms are in fact exercisable.[11] From this vantage point, unless basic needs are met, conventional political rights, for example, rights against government interference and rights to political participation, are merely nominal. Nussbaum explains, "In short, liberty is not just a matter of having rights on paper, it requires being in a position to exercise those rights." Without certain "material preconditions," there is only a "simulacrum" of "liberties of choice."[12] The distinction between formal freedom and real freedom, central to capabilities theory though not unique to it, captures this insight. In this spirit, none other than Isaiah Berlin was at pains to point out that certain "minimum conditions" are required so that "any degree of significant 'negative' liberty can be exercised . . . without which it is of little or no value to those who may theoretically possess it."[13]

What does this all mean with regard to a democratic ethos of care for the world? I am suggesting that one way of honoring the world's commonality, of tending to it properly, as common, is by working with others to make the world or, more accurately, certain places, laws, customs, and practices within it, more hospitable for every human being. The arguments I sketch above are valuable because they direct attention toward the basic human needs that must be addressed if the world is to be a home. Arendt's work can potentially further heighten awareness of what is materially required for the world to be a place in which human beings are able to live as persons and citizens. I read with and against Arendt in order to argue that the alleviation of poverty, through the collective transformation of existential conditions, is essential if the world is to be a home for all human beings.

Arendt's writings often convey indifference at best and disdain at worst for "the predicament of poverty."[14] Most notably, *The Human Condition* and *On Revolution* depict human bodily needs as a perpetual threat to free political life. According to Arendt, a hallmark of modernity is the invasion of the public realm, the site of free self-government among citizens, by the demands of necessity or humanly bodily needs, the management of which was once assigned to the private household. The story Arendt tells is one of the creation of "nationwide administration of housekeeping," which destroyed the Greek boundaries between the private sphere, in which men were "driven by wants and needs," and the political sphere, "the sphere of freedom."[15] The Greeks, Arendt says, understood there to be a special connection between the household, where "necessity ruled over all activities," and the polis, where citizens engaged in the two highest human capacities, action and speech: "It was a matter of course that the mastering of the necessities of life in the household was the condition for freedom in the polis."[16] Arendt's account acknowledges the profound costs of such arrangements. The logic that served to justify slavery and eliminate "life's burden" for citizens was more than a "violent injustice" for the enslaved. It constituted a deprivation for citizens as well, who, by ridding themselves almost completely of responsibility for their bodily needs, substituted "vicarious life for real life."[17] Yet when Arendt explains that the Greeks understood necessity as "a prepolitical phenomenon," it is hard not to hear her affirming this insight, especially when read together with her depictions of a modern, ravenous society that admits housekeeping activities into public. In the face of the social realm's "irresistible tendency to grow, to devour," Arendt warns, "the private and the intimate, on the one hand, and the political, on the other, have proved incapable of defending themselves."[18]

This dramatic scene, part invasion, part infection, reappears in Arendt's narrative of the French Revolution. Here, too, the politics of freedom is threatened by "the social question," or "what we may better and more simply call the existence of poverty."[19] As Arendt describes it, "When the poor, driven by the needs of their bodies, burst on to the scene of the French Revolution," freedom "had to be surrendered to necessity." In other words, the "urgent needs of the people . . . unleashed the terror and sent the Revolution to its doom."[20] Mark Reinhardt explains that Arendt's account "offers a cautionary tale about the consequences of modern, radical struggles that take up inappropriate objects."[21] *The Human Condition*, Reinhardt notes, does not identify the precise reason for the inappropriateness of human needs. But two central worries are clear. In both texts, human bodily needs are represented as threats to plurality and freedom, themselves arguably definitive of the political for Arendt. On the one hand, needs are homogeneous because the "life process which permeates our bodies" is the same for all human animals: "In so far as we all need bread, we are indeed all the same, and may as well unite into one body."[22] This is a dilemma for pluralistic politics because "the public preoccupation with matters that . . . cannot account for difference" stands in the way of speech and action among individuals who disclose to one another "who" they are, which is never "the same as anyone who has ever lived, lives, or will live."[23] On the other hand, Arendt continues to oppose necessity to freedom. When it comes to basic life processes, humans are subject to them; life is a "driving force" that rules over them. All men experience the "absolute dictate of necessity," and, though universal and unavoidable, this dictate is so powerful, Arendt implies, that it undermines the freedom-as-spontaneity which she identifies with politics.[24] As Reinhardt observes, in Arendt's view the French peasants who made the problem of basic needs a matter of political concern, "brought coercion into the one sphere in which the experience of freedom is possible."[25]

Arendt's well-known response to the threats she associates with the entry of the life process into public is to defend a politics that seems to be emptied of the social question altogether. This puzzling image of a "purified" politics is so striking and exasperating that it is easy to misread Arendt as being unconcerned with the plight of impoverished people and the provision of basic needs. She is not. Arendt does continually locate the social question in a category that she regards as nonpolitical, whether "the private" (ancient) or "administration" (modern), but she never dismisses the importance of material conditions.

In fact, Arendt theorizes poverty as deeply harmful in ways that exceed the physical. The pain and deprivation caused by unfulfilled basic needs go beyond the agony experienced by a hungry body or the suffering wrought by untreated disease. Poverty, Arendt suggests, inflicts grave injuries, both to personhood and to citizenship. In *On Revolution*, just after describing the needs of the French peasants as having brought the Revolution to ruin, Arendt cites at some length the words of John Adams, words that capture the devastating effects that poverty has on personhood, on one's sense of being seen, heard, and recognized as a fellow human being by others. What Adams understood, Arendt says, is that "darkness rather than want is the curse of poverty." That is, poverty entails "the insult of oblivion" and occasions the "crippling consequences of obscurity." Writing of "the poor man," Adams observed, "He feels himself out of the sight of others, groping in the dark. Mankind takes no notice of him. . . . In the midst of a crowd, at church, in the market . . . he is in as much obscurity as he would be in a garret or a cellar. He is not disapproved, censured or reproached; *he is only not seen.*" These harms are less obvious than the "obvious ruin" of physical want, but they are no less significant.[26] As Cristina Beltrán notes, Arendt understands, like Adams, that "the poor lack more than bread—they lack voice and visibility."[27]

In addition to the grave consequences poverty has on personhood as such, Arendt points to its meaning for citizenship in particular. In a late speech she describes citizenship as a "kind of second life" that a person can experience in addition to her personal, private life. This "second life in the common," however, which Arendt sees as especially imperiled in 1975, depends upon the satisfaction of basic needs. As she explains, "Indeed, freedom, political life, the life of the citizen—this 'public happiness' I've been speaking of—*is* a luxury, it is an *additional* happiness that one is made capable of only after the requirements of life process have been fulfilled." Lest one wonder whether the "luxury" of political life is something to be enjoyed only by those with adequate means, Arendt continues, "How much have we to change the lives of the poor? In other words, how much money do we have to give them to make them capable of enjoying public happiness? Education is very nice, but the real thing is money. Only when they can enjoy the public will they be willing and able to make sacrifices for the public good. To ask sacrifices of individuals who are not yet citizens is to ask them for an idealism which they do not have and cannot have in view of the urgency of the life process. Before we ask the poor for idealism, we must first make them citizens: and this involves so changing the circumstances of their private lives that they become capable of enjoying the 'public.'"[28]

This passage posits that poverty effectively denies citizenship to those who suffer it. Indeed, Arendt says that poor people must be made citizens and that this requires access to enough money to ensure that they are not consumed by the struggle for survival. Although Arendt's remarks are of a general nature and do not specify how such a financial remedy might be instituted, there is no question that she believes the practices of citizenship have as their condition of possibility the elimination of poverty.

Arendt's thinking about the consequences of poverty echoes the arguments made by others in support of social and economic rights. The provision of basic needs, she implies, is required for personhood, or what Nussbaum refers to as human dignity. In addition, material conditions are of special importance to the practices of citizenship; if there is any hope that the notion of "public happiness" through political participation might be revived, it requires, among other things, that all people be "made capable," as Arendt says, of its pursuit, namely, by ensuring that their basic needs are met. Arendt's stress on capability here is not unusual. Throughout her writings she endorses an understanding of freedom that is a "predicate of ability rather than volition," a matter of the I-can.[29] Like Sen's and Nussbaum's capabilities approach, Arendt invites one to think about how poverty affects what people are actually "able to do or be," both as persons and as citizens.

What is troubling about Arendt's thinking on the subject of material need is not that she discounts its significance or is oblivious to the harms of poverty—far from it. Rather, the difficulty lies with Arendt's repeated efforts to assign the social question to a domain marked nonpolitical. For the ancients, Arendt says, the "maintenance of life" was confined, for better or worse, to the private realm; in modernity, the social has assumed this task through practices of administration. Although Arendt worries about the increasing presence of bureaucratic management and its normalizing effects, she believes that in the modern era there is no going back to the prior public–private division. The provision of basic needs, she thinks, should be handled by administration, which Arendt identifies with technical expertise and instrumental reason. Why? According to Arendt, "There are things where right measures can be figured out. These things can really be administered and are not then subject to public debate. Public debate can only deal with things which—if we want to put it negatively—we cannot figure out with certainty. Otherwise, if we can figure it out with certainty, why do we all need to get together?" Tellingly, Arendt cites the provision of adequate housing as just such a matter: it can be "figure[d] out with certainty" and therefore ought to be subject to administrative decision making, not to political debate and contestation. Indeed, she distinguishes the social problem of adequate housing from the political problem of whether housing should be integrated, the former standing for what is nondebatable. She asserts, "There shouldn't be any debate about the question that everybody should have decent housing."[30] This statement makes plain that Arendt believes both that there is a public obligation to provide for basic needs and that this obligation is so self-evident that it ought not to be subject to political debate but merely administered effectively.

The problem is not that Arendt does not care about human needs, but that she mistakenly (wishfully?) supposes that such needs enjoy a status akin to universally agreed upon rights. She believes that poverty deprives people of more than food, clothing, shelter, and health care. It plunges them into a painful obscurity and effectively robs them of citizenship. Yet she somehow imagines that the declaration "Everybody should have decent housing" is not a political claim.

Arendt's rather sanguine attitude about the self-evidence of human needs and their related assignment to the practice of administration must be countered by a view which instead regards needs as objects of ongoing political struggle. Nancy Fraser argues convincingly that "needs talk," that is, discussion and dispute over what various people need and how those needs should be fulfilled, is precisely a "medium for the making and contesting of political claims."[31] Needs, including the basic needs invoked here, are "irreducibly interpretive," never simply given ends that await technical means.[32]

Arendt illuminates the harms wrought by poverty and encourages us to think about how people become materially capable of participating in political life. One should take these insights seriously, yet one need not accept Arendt's indefensible supposition that all-important basic needs are recognized and secure and somehow beyond public contestation. It is all too easy to see that in fact no agreement about the need for adequate housing or its provision by government exists. Instead there is what Fraser describes as a "struggle where groups with unequal discursive (and non-discursive) resources compete to establish as hegemonic their respective interpretations of legitimate social needs."[33] If we follow Arendt in appreciating the enabling and disabling effects of material conditions, then we ought to express that appreciation by engaging in just this struggle.

When members of the Chicago Anti-Eviction Campaign (AEC) organize to "stop all economically-motivated evictions in Chicago" they participate in this kind of political contest over needs. Their efforts, some of which have been quite successful, center on halting evictions in the city as well as defending the right of homeless people to live in "people-less" foreclosed properties.[34] Their ongoing political action is rooted in the conviction that "housing is a human right," a declaration that echoes Arendt's statement that "everybody should have decent housing."[35] Yet the actions undertaken by AEC, including public pressure campaigns, human blockades, and legal support, should also remind one that democratic care for the world, in the form of making the world a better home for all people, takes place in relation to particular, identifiable matters of concern. The assertion of a general human right to housing is usually not articulated in the abstract but is tethered to specific worldly things, such as those around which members of AEC associate. They have mobilized to defend, both legally and publicly, specific persons and families in Chicago who are threatened with eviction, whether from homes they own, rent (public and private), or occupy (which would otherwise be "people-less"). In mobilizing on behalf of these residents, AEC tries to persuade its fellow Chicagoans that these incidents are not isolated but shaped by changeable worldly practices, including a systemic pattern of unchecked racialized gentrification in Chicago and local and national economic policies favoring the well-off. The group's rallying cry is, "The rich got bailed out, we will not be put out!"[36] These activists have done an impressive job of building a solidaristic association across racial and class lines, in part by articulating the harms that forced eviction and displacement create, not just for certain individuals but for entire communities and neighborhoods made up of public and private renters, homeowners, and the homeless. They have worked to define foreclosures and displacements as a shared problem, an object of common concern. Although I suggested above that Arendt's assertion that everybody should have decent housing ought to be understood, contra Arendt herself, as a political claim, rather than as the expression of an incontrovertible fact, it is more accurate to describe it as a partial or incomplete political claim, one which can come fully to life only if it is connected to a specific demand about how particular worldly arrangements need to be transformed. This is the kind of claim AEC makes when it declares, "The Chicago Anti-Eviction Campaign will continue struggling to stop all economically-motivated evictions in Chicago. We are no longer willing to wait for any authority to institute our human right to housing."[37]

Care for the world—a democratic ethos—is enacted in part through collaborative efforts directed at creating material conditions that make the world a home to all people. Minimally, such home making requires transforming collective arrangements so as to secure basic needs.[38] These needs, defined and sought on the shaky ground of politics, affect both personhood and citizenship and are integral to the experience of being at home on this planet. This account of caring for the world as a collective home overlaps with arguments made on behalf of economic rights and capabilities. Yet the emphasis placed on tending to the world by seeking to collectively affect a specific thing in order to create more hospitable circumstances rightly puts conditions and contexts at the center of concern. Privileging the world—the complex assemblage within which human beings exist but which is irreducible to them—instead of focusing strictly on humans' rights or capabilities orients one toward features of milieus rather than characteristics of persons. The capabilities approach, by directing one toward substantive opportunities, does raise the problem of enabling conditions, but, as a glance at the growing literature in this area shows, the emphasis on human capabilities also invites fixation on identifying and cataloging the capabilities themselves. This distracts from the vital question of how to transform worldly environments to actualize capabilities, however defined.[39] While the task of caring for the world necessarily involves thinking and arguing about what needs must be met for the world to become a genuine home, it nonetheless makes a difference whether political thought and action are focused on the capacities of human beings or on the world in which they live. It is crucially important, as I have tried to show, that a democratic ethos be animated by a specific kind of care: not for oneself or an Other or even for many others, but for the world in which those many selves and others live.

Tending to the world as a collective home does not exhaust the meaning of a world-centered democratic ethos, however. It is not enough, from the perspective of caring for the world, that one strives, together with others, to ensure people's basic needs are met. Caring for the world involves paying attention to and being concerned about another dimension of the world's commonality: its mediating power. As we will see, caring for the world in this respect entails creating and protecting opportunities for the world to serve as an in-between, connecting and separating people.

### The World as In-Between

If the first element of the world's commonality concerns its status as a home for all people, the second element pertains to its role as an intermediary between individuals. Earlier I theorized that the world was the sum total of the conditions of life on earth (see chapter 3), consisting of a cultural artifice, intangible webs of relation, and natural phenomena, the last of which Arendt excludes from her conception. I argued that associative democratic politics always revolves around worldly things, features of this dense, complex entity that are constituted as matters of concern. This prior account provides a basis for thinking about the second dimension of the world's commonality, namely, its capacity to serve as an in-between. But more still needs to be said. What does it mean to say that the world should be tended to, or fostered and cultivated, as an intermediary? What is involved in properly caring for the world as an "interspace"?[40]

Although human beings are in and of the world and never wholly apart from it, Arendt's persistent attention to the world's mediating properties is nonetheless apt. Without assuming a radical separation between human beings and other worldly phenomena, one can appreciate how the world, as a sum total of conditions, exists around and between humans, potentially establishing distance between selves as well as a bond between them.[41] To Arendt, the world is common by virtue of performing a critical task: it "gathers us together and yet prevents us from falling over each other."[42] The world mediates between people in this double sense: it establishes a connection that preserves distinction; it is the simultaneous antidote to isolation and massification. As Reinhardt notes, this emphasis on the world as in-between is striking in its claim to a form of political commonality that is not subject centered; what is common here is extra-subjective, between us, not in us.[43]

Such mediation is by no means assured, however, as any reader of Arendt knows; the threat of worldlessness looms large.[44] The seemingly solid table between people, Arendt warns, may vanish. This does not signify for Arendt that the world has literally ended but that it has lost "its *power* to gather them together, to relate and separate them."[45] But what is the source of this power? What allows the world to perform this gathering, to simultaneously assure distance and connection between people?

As I have suggested, such gathering occurs by way of specific, politicized worldly things, objects of debate and dispute that link citizens to one another in both agreement and controversy (see chapter 3). Such objects are shared, even though, contra Arendt, they are not precisely the same for all involved. Worldly things are fluctuating, contested third terms. They are called by different names, tied to incompatible projects, rejected by some as insignificant. Yet these slippery, inconstant matters of concern nonetheless mediate relations between people, enabling both their separation from and connection to one another. The public expression of "innumerable perspectives" preserves distinction while the fact that divergent voices refer to and speak about—even disagree about—a specific, identifiable object of dispute fosters a sense of connection. For the world to be felt as a mediating presence, Arendt contends, depends upon "our speaking with one another" in "public political space," where "things can first be recognized in their many-sidedness."[46] It is when citizens engage with each other in this way, voicing and hearing a "plurality of standpoints" on a particular, contested thing, that "the world thrusts itself between them."[47]

Arendt believes that democratic politics, characterized by the exchange of opinions and ideas among diverse citizens, is the primary activity that generates the world's power to relate and separate.[48] Why is this? According to Arendt, when people participate in associative politics with their peers, they engage in an exchange of opinions that is about the world at present, about the action to be taken, and about how the world will look in the future.[49] The world is, quite simply, "that about which we speak" as citizens. And it is through our "speaking with one another about it" that the world can appear as something common, in the specific sense of existing between us.[50]

The world-as-intermediary is, to a large extent, produced through this exchange; it is not simply there prior to it. As Arendt explains, "The world *comes into being only if* there are perspectives; it exists as the order of worldly things only if it is viewed this way, now that, at a given time."[51] The world can *inter-est* only if it is "talked about by human beings" who make it a shared "object of discourse."[52] More specifically, it is in political space, "an area where there are many voices" discussing "affairs of the world," that this special kind of commonality is forged.[53] To express one's *doxa* in the presence of other citizens is to reveal "the world as it opens itself to me." This revelation affirms distance, on the one hand, because the world "opens itself" differently to every individual. At the same time, the expression of "what appears to me" also affirms the existence of a world which "opens to everyone" and thus links us together.[54] For the world to act as an intermediary requires "the presence of others in a politically organized sphere," something which cannot be taken for granted.[55] It is on a "meeting ground" of citizens, of "men in all their variety" who "see and hear" from different positions, that the world can emerge, however briefly, as something common, in the specific sense of lying between people.[56]

Returning to the account I presented in chapter 3, one can appreciate that when citizens associate with one another in relation to a specific worldly thing, whether in cooperative solidarities or antagonistic publics, the world's mediating qualities are thereby intensified. Public discussion and contestation over a particular matter, which has a mutual claim on participants' attention, heightens awareness of an in-between. Indeed, the world appears as an intermediary by way of many particular things or matters of concern that serve as third terms, connecting and dividing citizens. This means that although democratic action in concert is motivated in the first place by the desire to affect the conditions under which humans live, it is also through association with others that the world's status as an in-between is elicited and reinforced.

Now an answer to the question, What does it mean to care for the world *as* an in-between?, becomes clearer. What, in connection with caring for the world as a collective home, does a democratic ethos entail? Caring for the world as a potential intermediary means fostering practices and building institutions that provide as many citizens as possible with meaningful opportunities to articulate their innumerable perspectives in the presence of one another and to influence the conditions under which they live. This is the way that "commonness of the world" is cultivated and realized. Put plainly, this dimension of care for the world calls for broad efforts of democratization: the expansion of the power of ordinary citizens to participate in their own government through multiple and accessible sites for the exchange of opinions and decision making.

This project involves creating sources of citizen power that are as inclusive as possible, for the absence or marginalization of any individual counts as a loss to the world itself, the "manifold" character of which is compromised if it is not subject to a broad range of viewpoints.[57] The world's richness and complexity are diminished in the absence of opportunities for it to become an "object of discourse" among diverse equals. As Kimberley Curtis has written, it is critically important that the "being-in-the-world" of those who have been left out of public affairs be illuminated: "They must be seen, noticed and taken account of."[58] Expansive and accessible practices of self-government are vital to the full inclusion of all democratic citizens; they are also essential if the world is to be common at all, if it is to acquire mediating power. Caring for the world, then, is expressed in part by creating opportunities for citizens to interact with one another in ways that allow aspects of the world to come into focus as shared, disputed objects between them, sites of contentious commonality. Arendt's beloved council system exemplifies the style of democratization that is central to this ethos, but, as we will see later in this chapter, there are many possible forms this democratizing care for the world can take.

Stated negatively, in the absence of regular opportunities for citizens to gather as equals and to debate and decide upon matters of concern, the common world may be eclipsed. As Arendt warns in her assessment of American political culture, "The booth in which we deposit our ballots is much too small, for this booth has only room for one."[59] It is too small because it precludes the kind of exchange among plural individuals that would allow for the mutual recognition of an intermediary, not necessarily the world writ large but a worldly thing, a third term that both links and separates. The lack of democratic spaces and practices that enable the articulation of diverse perspectives on a shared, yet disputed, matter of concern means people's experience of the world as common, in the sense of lying between them, may be lost.

I have been outlining two kinds of commonality that inform the normative aims integral to the democratic ethos advocated here. The first concerns the world's status as a home for all people, while the second concerns the world's mediating power. If the ethos of democracy entails caring for the world as world, such a spirit is exemplified by associative projects that respect and foster the world's commonality. Care for the world involves specific normative aspirations, intertwined with a caring, regardful affect: making the world a better home by ensuring that basic needs are met and creating and sustaining democratic practices that enable the world to emerge as an in-between.

### Interlude: Self-Interested Care?

If caring for the world means caring for the world as humans' collective home and caring for the world as a mediating force between human beings, is this ethos susceptible to the charge of anthropocentrism? Does it imply that the world is for humans and humans alone? If so, does this ethics too readily tolerate or even promote harm to nonhuman elements of the world?

Although "anthropocentrism" carries multiple meanings, most relevant here is the term's reference to a myopic outlook focused on human interests at the expense of all other possible interests.[60] The worry lies with a sort of "human chauvinism," "speciesism," or egocentrism that shows insufficient concern for nonhumans.[61] In particular, critics of anthropocentrism object to the tendency to ascribe only instrumental, not intrinsic, value to nonhumans, which in turn supports a dominating stance toward nonhuman life.

Is the ethos of care for the world — refined to mean care for the world as home and as in-between — guilty of promoting such anthropocentrism? Since both normative ends discussed above direct attention to human beings' relation to the world, this is surely a legitimate question. Yet the ethos developed here does not reflect an anthropocentric outlook, if by that is meant a view that licenses exploitation of nonhuman elements of the world on the grounds that human interests, whatever they may be, trump all others.[62] At the same time, however, the ethos of care for the world does not, as the notions of home and in-between attest, disavow concern for the fates of human beings in particular. What is at stake, then, is the possibility of enlightened anthropocentrism, of transformed self-interest that heeds the insights of coexistentialism.

Coexistentialism refers to an ecological perspective that takes the interconnectedness of all worldly entities, humans and nonhumans, organic and inorganic matter, as its starting point (see chapter 3). Latour's and Bennett's work helped reveal the interdependent webs of relation that characterize what I call world but that are obscured by traditional dichotomies between human agents, who are exalted, and inert matter, which is denigrated. Coexistentialism locates human beings within this worldly "mesh" rather than above it.[63] Such an ecological awareness challenges fantasies of mastery by reminding people of the extent to which they are affected by the doings of nonhumans.

Our understandings of human well-being and self-interest are susceptible to transformation by the coexistentialist perspective. The choice is not between the domineering, shortsighted pursuit of human interests, on the one hand, and the rejection of self-interest altogether, on the other. Indeed, the recognition of deep interconnectedness can shape and nurture "new self-interest," as Bennett suggests.[64] Although *Vibrant Matter* aims to question conventional human/nonhuman hierarchies, the book, Bennett explains, is motivated by a self-interested "concern for *human* survival and happiness."[65] In place of "fantasies of conquest and consumption" Bennett encourages a chastened form of self-interest. It is in people's own interest, she argues, to understand the ways in which nonhumans and humans are bound to one another, generating effects in parliament rather than in isolation from one another. The purpose of the coexistentialist view is not to reject self-interest as hopelessly chauvinistic or destructive but to foster "new self-interest" that is guided by an ecological sensibility.

Bennett's reimagined self-interest resonates with notions of enlightened, weak, or broad anthropocentrism in the field of environmental ethics, which emerged originally as a challenge to anthropocentrism and the tendency to assign only instrumental value to nonhuman entities. Indeed, the enterprise of environmental ethics was initially defined as an attempt to develop a thoroughly nonanthropocentric worldview that renders nonhumans morally considerable. A strand of recent environmental thought, however, is concerned not with forgoing anthropocentrism altogether, a project it questions on both metaphysical and practical grounds, but with transforming the understanding of human interest so that it is enlightened.[66]

This broad form of anthropocentrism does not accept dominant economistic notions of human well-being but instead redefines well-being to include a fuller range of values, for example, aesthetic and spiritual, that reflect and further an ecological sensibility. Andrew Light and Bryan Norton advocate this approach from a pragmatist-pluralist perspective. Light argues that if contemporary environmental ethicists wish to take on environmental problems in policy contexts, this is best accomplished not by attempting to "overcome" human interests but by "redirecting them toward environmental concerns."[67] He contends that if we are concerned with the "moral motivation of humans to respond to environmental issues," focusing on reconstructing the sense of what is in our own interest is more likely to succeed than an attempt to reject anthropocentrism wholesale.[68] Light's pragmatic approach counsels that in many situations anthropocentric values are best suited to motivate nonenvironmentalists. For example, studies show that concern for future human generations is a highly significant value that encourages efforts to protect nonhuman entities.[69] In other situations, "nonanthropocentric claims will be more appealing." Light writes that "what appeals best is an empirical question," and he links this pragmatic outlook to a "pluralist ethic" that accepts a range of arguments, anthropocentric and nonanthropocentric and involving instrumental and intrinsic values claims, against doing harm to ecosystems.[70] Philosophical purity matters less than ethico-political resonance.

Where does this leave the democratic ethos I advance here? Care for the world *is* a way of caring for human beings; it is neither neutral nor disinterested. It is an ethos meant to generate benefits for people. But these benefits are linked to self-interest properly understood, that is, they are born of the coexistentialist insight. Caring for the world involves not owning, ruling, or enjoying dominion over but collaboratively tending to the world, an entity that is bigger, richer, and more varied and lively than human life alone. Such care should be guided by awareness of the webs of relation that link human beings across borders and time not only to one another, but also to other "vibrant matter" as well. Such awareness does not, however, require that one attempt (in vain?) to thoroughly equalize one's concern for humans with concern for nonhumans. Genuinely ecologically minded self-interest is enough to aspire to.

Political struggles to fulfill basic needs, which, I have argued, express care for the world as a collective home for human beings, must be continually informed by this sense of interdependency. Making the world a home for human beings cannot be a matter of blind chauvinism that treats human interests, enlightened or not, as unquestionably the highest good. Rather, coexistentialism will sometimes require skepticism about needs claims, especially in the context of capitalist materialism, where they may mask problematic and grossly unequal consumption practices. More demanding still, claims about needs provision, even worthwhile basic needs, that minimize or ignore interdependencies must be challenged and supplanted with more soundly ecological arguments and strategies. For example, the widespread use of pesticides, monocultural farming methods, and genetic engineering in agriculture are often defended as ways of addressing unmet basic needs by increasing the global supply of inexpensive food but are now thought to contribute to global colony collapse disorders among bees.[71] The potentially catastrophic harms associated with the decline of bee populations, including but not limited to the human food supply, should warn against policies that fail to consider human needs in the context of ecological complexity. This example, though cautionary, also points toward the possibility of a reimagined form of self-interest, one that begins with recognition of human dependency on the pollination practices of bees.

Caring for the world as a collective human home and as a mediating power between human beings is not a cover for domination of all that is nonhuman. If we humans come to know the world for the dense interplay that it is, we can appreciate the extent to which our fates are bound up with the doings of all sorts of matter. A coexistentialist perspective can and should guide the way we care for the world, as both home and in-between.

### Pursuing the Dual Ends of Care for the World

The democratic ethos of care for the world centers on two normative ends. But what is the relationship between them? To what extent does making the world a home, through the struggle to provide basic human needs for all, converge with the project of increasing opportunities for democratic discussion and decision making and thereby fostering the world's status as an in-between? Are these aims compatible? Put somewhat differently, can a democratic ethos meaningfully combine concern for distribution with concern with procedure?

From a certain perspective, these ends can be seen as mutually reinforcing, or at least potentially so. As we have seen, advocates of economic and social rights, unexpectedly allied with Arendt, alert us to the ways in which adequate material conditions may be prerequisites for democratic citizenship. Making the world a home in the sense of providing for basic needs may be bound up with the expansion of democratic practice to those presently disenfranchised. Additionally, creating more sites and opportunities for democratic self-governance by ordinary people may contribute to the creation of policies that are better at addressing the needs of nonelites as they come to have a greater voice in decision making.[72]

Yet making the world a better home is not the same as helping the world to emerge as an in-between. Neither end entails the other, nor is there any guarantee that they will support one another. Material outcomes can be achieved nondemocratically, as when the needy are objects of hierarchical and private charity (see chapter 3), and the democratic structure of decision making does not, on its own, assure that basic needs will be met. Critiques of welfare paternalism, such as Julie Anne White's *Democracy, Justice and the Welfare State*, point to the ways in which citizens' basic needs are often managed in ways that position recipients of welfare as objects rather than subjects. Rather than participating in "needs interpretation," they are administered to. In the United States the meeting of needs is usually regarded as "a domain of expertise rather than [of] politics" and in practice is largely divided between professionals and recipients, a dynamic that replicates the hierarchical authority structure of the traditional family.[73] While welfare provision of this sort may meet some basic needs, it typically does so in a nondemocratic way. This example makes clear the fact that addressing basic needs, a central component of caring for the world, is not identical with the other element of this ethos, namely, supporting the expansion of democratic power.

Similarly, democratization may or may not cohere with the aim of providing for basic needs. It is a well-recognized and oft-lamented truth of democratic politics that democratic structures and procedures, however inclusive and accessible, do not assure that particular substantive decisions will be arrived at. The classic illustration of this problem in the context of the United States is the fact that democratic majorities fairly regularly decide matters in ways that contradict established constitutional protections. For example, democratically elected state legislatures in Virginia and Texas passed laws prohibiting, respectively, interracial marriage and consensual homosexual activity. Yet in the landmark cases *Loving v. Virginia* (1967) and *Lawrence v. Texas* (2003) the U.S. Supreme Court struck down those laws on the grounds that they violated constitutional guarantees of substantive due process and equal protection. The Committee on Economic, Social and Cultural Rights at the United Nations has recognized this dilemma as well, explaining that "there is no basis whatsoever to assume that the realization of economic, social, and cultural rights will *necessarily* result from the achievement of civil and political rights."[74]

One response to this persistent difficulty is to sacrifice either the commitment to material outcomes or democratic decision making, a step that would resolve the dilemma. Nussbaum, for example, asserts that the capabilities she outlines, which require the provision of certain material needs, are so important that their realization ought not to be left to democratic procedures of debate and decision. Indeed, she maintains that people's desires are often so distorted that they cannot be counted on to even want the capabilities she identifies. Because of this, the creation of just institutional arrangements cannot be entrusted to them: "A habituated preference not to have any one of the items on the [capabilities] list will not count in the social choice function." Philosophers thus have a special part to play in constitutional design; only the properly "*informed* desire" of affected citizens will be permitted to play a role in this endeavor and even then only a "limited and ancillary" one.[75] Nussbaum tries to mitigate the paternalism of this view by conceptually dividing the task of constitution creation from subsequent decision making that takes place within that order. It is mistaken, she says, to rely on peoples' actual desires when establishing a constitution that protects the capabilities. Here what is needed is a "normative basis that desire reliably fails to provide."[76] But within this rightly ordered society, which does not yet exist anywhere, "spheres of choice" are protected so that citizens can "pursue their own desires" and participate in self-government, activities that are included in Nussbaum's list of protected capabilities.[77]

Sen, the originator of the capabilities approach, rejects this view wholeheartedly, refusing even to compose a definitive list of the capabilities, as Nussbaum does, because he believes such a task should be undertaken democratically, through deliberation and debate, rather than by a theorist.[78] The same is true when it comes to the question of how to create more just, that is, capabilities enhancing, political orders. As David A. Crocker has noted, "The role that Nussbaum gives to the philosopher and the constitution, Sen gives to the society or group itself."[79] From Sen's perspective Nussbaum effectively bypasses those people her theory is meant to apply to in practice.[80] Indeed, for Nussbaum, the goal of providing for human capabilities effectively trumps Sen's commitment to "plurality, agency and choice."[81] But Sen is especially attuned, and rightly so, to the dangers of charitable paternalism, something Nussbaum seems unfazed by. Sen is alert to the sizable costs of treating the satisfaction of basic needs as the highest good: social arrangements, he maintains, should be evaluated in terms of their contribution to enhancing and guaranteeing the capabilities of "individuals seen as agents of change, rather than passive recipients of benefits."[82] This statement folds together concern for the enrichment of capabilities with concern for people's standing as full participants in decision making. Sen can be understood to defend the importance of democratic practices of, in Fraser's words, "needs interpretation." Although imperfect and indeterminate, Sen's view reflects a compelling dual commitment that Nussbaum's theory evades by regarding needs as being largely predetermined and allowing for their provision to be orchestrated from above by those who know best. Nussbaum's approach aims to avoid the dilemma posed by the simultaneous concern for improved material conditions and insistence on democratic forms of authority. But that avoidance comes at a price: some subjects are regarded as objects, a move that threatens to undermine even the circumscribed role Nussbaum grants to democratic politics (after a constitution has been correctly designed so that people are equipped with "informed desire"). Unlike Nussbaum, who restricts democratic decision making to those who enjoy a proper constitution created by experts, Sen maintains a commitment to two coequal and tensely related aims: the fulfillment of human capabilities and the protection and expansion of democratic power.

The general dilemma to which both Sen and Nussbaum respond, albeit in very different ways, is usually framed by political theorists in terms of a vexed relationship between process and outcome or between procedural and substantive rights. In the United States this problem often has to do with the dynamic between legislatures and courts and the so-called counter-majoritarian difficulty. Most thinkers working within the liberal-democratic tradition broadly construed regard both process and outcome, procedure and substance, as vital to political legitimacy, even as they strongly dispute which procedural and substantive guarantees are desirable and how best to address conflicts between them. Often this duality is expressed as a commitment to democracy, on the one hand, which is aligned with certain procedures or processes, and a commitment to liberalism, constitutionalism, or individual rights, on the other, any of which serve as shorthand for a set of substantive goods or outcomes. The sense that both sides are integral to the legitimacy of a political order is widely shared, and potential differences between the two are often depicted as conflicts between democracy and something else that is also valuable but is not itself held to be part and parcel of democracy.

My argument identifies the pursuit both of substantive ends and of democratic processes as integral to a specifically democratic ethos. This ethos is committed to making the world a better home by creating conditions that fulfill everyone's basic needs and to increasing the chances for the world to serve, via practices of the exchange of opinions and decision making by ordinary citizens, as a mediating presence. Worldly ethics combines substantive and procedural ends, which together define what it means to actively and democratically care for the world. These two aims, though neither entails the other, are nonetheless equally important to the democratic spirit I envision and endorse.

The pairing of the two kinds of aims within a democratic ethos resonates with Corey Brettschneider's position that one should understand democracy to involve a dual commitment to procedures and outcomes.[83] I do not aim to present a definitive, analytical account of democracy as such, and my book is quite different from Brettschneider's project. Nonetheless, Brettschneider's approach invites one to consider the possibility that plural and sometimes conflicting commitments lie at the heart of democracy itself, an insight that is important to the democratic ethos I advocate.

Although Brettschneider's book, in the end, tends to cover over the tragic dimensions of democracy that his theory opens up, it contains two kernels of insight that are relevant to my argument for democratic ethos.[84] In relation to the worldly ethics I elaborate here, Brettschneider's conception of democracy is suggestive because it recognizes, first, that procedural and substantive goods alike are vital dimensions of democracy, as both an ideal and an ongoing practice. This conception is perhaps less contrarian than it appears to be; as Brettschneider notes, people ordinarily understand democracy to involve both rule by and rule for the people, a formulation that places a dual commitment and also a potential conflict at the very center of democratic politics.[85] Such a dual commitment, I submit, is enacted by constituencies who strive to care for the world as world. Second, Brettschneider's view aims to "embrace the tension" between these two kinds of ends.[86] That is, he affirms a complex picture of democracy, according to which there may be friction between the goods it involves, friction that cannot be resolved without remainder. This does not mean there will always be a contradiction between procedural and substantive rights in practice, as they may very well align, but that there sometimes will be. And in these cases, a "loss to democracy" is unavoidable.[87] Extending this insight in order to reflect on the ethos envisioned here, I note that the pursuit of either of its two primary ends at the expense of the other entails a genuine loss: a loss to democracy and to its distinctive spirit of care for the world.

The democratizing aim that is integral to the democratic ethos of care for the world is not necessarily enabling of—and indeed, in practice, could undermine—the ethos's other normative aim: the establishment of material conditions that support the lives of all, not just some, human beings. One need only consider some of the results of the California initiative and referendum system—in particular Proposition 13 in 1978 and the since-overruled Proposition 187 in 1994—to appreciate how citizens' majoritarian decision making can fail to address the problem of basic needs and, even more problematically, may institute measures that make it more, not less, difficult for people to access public education, health care, and other vital provisions like food stamps and housing assistance. (It is arguable whether the referendum system fosters the kind of exchange of opinions and interaction that encourages the apprehension of common but contentious worldly things between participants.) This example is a reminder that expanding the sites in which democratic power is exercised cannot, in and of itself, assure that the world will be made a more hospitable place. At the same time, many charitable initiatives meant to address human needs do so in ways that are unlikely to foster democratic forms of exchange in which worldly things can come into view as objects of shared attention, controversy, and action (see chapter 3). Organizations like food banks are defined by hierarchical relations between citizens and by predefined, relatively narrow tasks executed by those at the top. These features tend to divert attention from the broader, worldly arrangements that contribute to widespread hunger and that could serve potential objects of criticism and transformation by coactors in association together. Efforts to respond to the "needy" do not necessarily advance and may even limit democratic relations in which citizens aim to collectively define and address worldly matters of concern.

In the end the democratic ethos advanced in this book directs us toward two important but distinct modalities of care for the world. Tending to the world as a collective home and as an in-between are not interchangeable activities, and one of these aims may be sought in the absence of the other, as the examples above reveal. Yet acknowledging the tension that can exist between outcome-related goals and process-related goals does not require people to choose one aspect of care for the world over the other. Indeed, the best examples of associative care for the world reveal that these normative ends, though they do not entail one another, can be sought simultaneously. The most compelling expressions of democratic ethos aspire to make the world a better home for all people by addressing basic needs at the same time that they endeavor to extend democratic forms of governance that allow the world to acquire its mediating power.

Various efforts have been undertaken to reorganize social services in the United States in ways that provide for people's needs through processes called community needs assessment that include not only policymakers and direct providers but also those in need. Attempts to create alternative institutions that include the voices of the needy, as White shows, pose a "fundamental challenge to the professional-client relationship" that dominates institutions of public care at present. Organizations such as the Beacons project in New York City, a network of school-based community centers, model mutual rather than paternalistic relations in their approach to meeting needs. Beacons programs are located in public schools throughout the city and offer a range of important services to both adults and children, including adult education classes in computer literacy and English conversational skills, safe youth after-school activities, counseling services, and tutoring. Although the programs are funded by the city, they are designed, implemented, and maintained by community organizations geographically located in the areas of the Beacons schools. This unusual structure "broke down any permanent distinction between caregivers and those cared for," as those who organize and run the programs use the facilities, live in the community, and have family members who use the programs. The Beacons programs have explicitly "rejected a division of labor in which governance of services was done by one class of providers for a separate class of recipients."[88] Most significant, the Beacons do not assume "that those unable to meet their own material needs in the marketplace are also unable to be democratic citizens."[89] In light of this commitment, the programs enact a "more participatory politics of needs interpretation" and a more egalitarian distribution of the work of caretaking.[90] Efforts like this enact collaborative care for the world in a double sense, endeavoring to address people's basic needs (for education and safety especially) while democratizing conventionally hierarchical relations.

A very different form of democratic association, No More Deaths, or No Más Muertes, enacts care for the world in ways that pursue its dual normative aims. This organization, formed as a coalition of social activist as well as diverse faith-based groups, including Catholic, Jewish, and Unitarian, in 2004, works to prevent the deaths of migrants on the Mexico–Arizona border. Participants model solidaristic association, as they are bound together not by a shared identity but by a common goal: no more deaths. Various strategies are used in pursuit of this goal: direct provision of water, food, and medical aid in the Arizona desert through the use of a fixed base camp and mobile camps, monitoring of U.S. border control operations, advocating a change in U.S. immigration policies that use the language of militarizing and criminalizing, and publicizing the plight of migrants. The efforts of No Más Muertes, which now has chapters in Tucson, Flagstaff, and Phoenix, are informed by the idea of civil initiative, which was central to the Sanctuary movement of the 1980s and is defined as the community practice of acting together on behalf of human rights, even when such action conflicts with local law.[91] No Más Muertes offers a striking example of care for the world in practice. Working to make the world a more hospitable place for human beings, members struggle to ensure that no undocumented persons trying to cross the U.S.-Mexico border die because of a lack of water, food, or medical care. In addition to addressing basic needs, the organization, through weekly open meetings, relies on forms of democratic discussion and decision making in its own governance and works to build a grass-roots movement in Arizonan communities through coordinated house-by-house and business outreach to organize public resistance to S.B. 1070, an Arizona bill that at the time of its passage was the most restrictive immigration law in the country.[92] Members of No Más Muertes exhibit their love for the world by simultaneously seeking to transform the material conditions faced by people in the border region and by generating new forms of democratic power.

A final example of care for the world can be found in the burgeoning Right to the City movement, which was initiated in 2007 in Los Angeles and consists of the activities of allied community organizations in eight urban regions of the United States. The Right to the City takes its name from Henry Lefebvre's book of 1967, which stipulated the right of all city inhabitants to a fair distribution of such urban resources as transportation, housing, and public parks as well as control over the decision-making processes that shape cities.[93] From the beginning the right to the city has been understood in a way that combines concern for material needs with concern for democratic governance. When David Harvey, the critical geographer, began reviving the term in 2003, he defined it as "not merely a right of access to what the property speculators and state planners define, but an active right to make the city different, to shape it more in accord with our desires, and to re-make ourselves thereby in a different image."[94] While the Right to the City struggles to secure housing, health care, and public space, it also aims to increase the power of city residents, especially the disenfranchised, to engage in the design and development of cities. Participants aim at the equitable distribution of urban resources together with the empowerment of a city's inhabitants to determine the conditions under which they live. For example, Right to the City initiated a campaign titled We Call These Projects Home: Solving the Housing Crisis from the Ground Up. As part of this program, the organization published a report that foregrounded the voices of public housing residents in seven cities across the United States in an effort to draw attention to the importance of available, safe public housing. The purpose of the report was twofold:

to advocate the expansion and maintenance of public housing that is inadequate and greater resident participation, that is, opportunities for residents to be decision makers in the public housing communities in which they live. The Right to the City advocates "the right for all people to produce the living conditions that meet their needs."[95] In so doing, participants in the movement exhibit care for the world as both home and in-between.

A democratic ethos centered on caring for the world is not a formula. It does not spell out exactly how to proceed or prescribe a program for enacting such care. It does, however, reframe the question of ethics and democracy, urging us to think differently about the spirit of democratic citizenship. It privileges a form of care undertaken by associations whose participants actively tend to specific features of their material and immaterial environment. An ethos that animates democratic engagement is one which orients citizens' attention and concern toward conditions rather than particular individuals. The ethos I have been advancing departs from the approaches taken by Foucault, Levinas, and their interpreters, because it involves a particular modality of care that is not intra- or intersubjective but extrasubjective.

Care for the world as world is explicitly affective and normative in character. This ethos is dispositional insofar as it involves feelings and activities of care directed toward worldly things. But it also incorporates a normative perspective, specifying that such care respects the world's status as common, in the dual sense of home and in-between. The ethos of democracy, as I formulate it, is expressed in and fostered by some movements and not others; not every collective endeavor aiming to affect a worldly thing embodies its spirit.

Care for the world as world provides a perspective from which to think and act. It is a democratic-ethical vantage point that encourages us to question the meaning of our activities and those of others. The ethical vision presented here invites the question, To what extent am I participating in associative projects that exhibit care for a worldly thing, a feature of existential conditions? Do my efforts, together with those of others, aim to make the world in some way more hospitable to all? Do they strive to create democratic spaces in which the world can emerge, however fleetingly, as something between us?

# SELF/OTHER/WORLD

Forging Connections and Fostering Democratic Care

The preceding pages have conceptualized and advocated a democratic ethos focused on collaborative care for the world. This argument was developed largely by distinguishing care for the world from the sorts of dyadic care relations—care for the self and care for the Other—that define Foucauldian and Levinasian ethics. In particular, I have contended that this democratic modality of care involves unique practitioners, recipients, and aims, all of which set care for the world apart from even the most admirable forms of self-care or active concern for another. Indeed, the claim has been one not only of distinction but also of tension: the orientations encouraged by Foucauldian and Levinasian ethics, the most prominent in the turn to ethics, may need to be resisted, even overcome, if democratic care is to be enacted.

Without abandoning this claim, I want to muddy these lines a bit. If the earlier analysis often sought to keep care for the self, Other, and world separate in order to illuminate the contours of a world-centered democratic ethos, this depiction runs the risk of overdrawing those distinctions, suggesting that an unbridgeable divide separates different ethical practices of care from one another. It is wrong, I have argued, to collapse these modes of care, to conflate therapeutic, charitable, and democratic relations, as though care, of whatever sort, were sufficient to establish a common identity. And it is likewise mistaken to assume that one kind of care necessarily leads to another. But are Foucauldian self-care and Levinasian care for the Other *only* obstacles to the flourishing of a democratic ethos? If the caring orientation that defines therapeutic and charitable ethics must be largely overcome in order for a new actor (an association of human beings) and a new object (a worldly thing) to emerge, is it nonetheless possible that those dyadic relations of care may also contain a seed that, if cultivated in certain ways, can support democratic care? In other words, does self-care or care for the Other ever offer resources that can be marshaled for this overcoming and ultimately lend support to collective care for worldly conditions?

I argued in chapter 1 against the supposition that simply taking care of oneself fosters or enhances citizens' democratic engagement. If Foucauldian practices of self-care are to have any macropolitical significance, helping to constitute selves who are suited for the demands of associative democratic action, those arts of the self must be activated and continually guided by concern for a worldly thing, an object of public attention, and by the self's desire, however inchoate, to participate more effectively in collective efforts to affect that matter of concern. That is, care for the self may have a part to play in nourishing democratic care for the world, but only if practices of self-care are oriented, from the start, toward associative endeavors that aim to affect worldly conditions. A virtuous circle may be possible, one in which care for the self and care for the world reciprocally interact, but there is little reason to hope that care for the self per se, susceptible as it is to egoist temptations, will generate or enhance associative democratic politics.

If work on the self is initially prompted by collective efforts to publicize a matter of concern and mobilize democratic support on its behalf, then there is reason to believe this reflexive labor may eventually feed back into that democratic movement. Indeed, some associative democratic projects aim explicitly to jar addressees into processes of self-examination and, ideally, self-transformation, processes that can perhaps serve the association's worldly goals. The Welcoming Tennessee Initiative (WTI) is one example. This collaborative project, started in 2005 by the Tennessee Immigrant and Refugee Rights Coalition (TIRRC), focuses on challenging stereotypes and dispelling myths about immigration and immigrants in the state, which has one of the highest rates of immigration in the country. To do so, participants created opportunities for recent immigrants and long-time Tennessee residents to come into direct contact with one other in a variety of settings, including community meetings, film screenings, and church gatherings, designed to facilitate dialogue; they also undertook a media campaign to reach more of the population.[1] The media outreach included fifty billboards throughout the Nashville area, which were meant to grab the attention of viewers, potentially disrupting their current habits of thought and encouraging deeper reflection on the question of immigration. One billboard featured the biblical passage, "I was a stranger and you welcomed me"; another stated, "Welcome the immigrant you once were."[2] The varied strategies of the WTI were intended to help spark individuals to reexamine their beliefs and opinions in order to promote "empathy, hospitality, and neighborly treatment of immigrants in Tennessee."[3] It is difficult to know how many people who attended a WTI event or saw a billboard were prompted to engage in the reflexive relation of questioning and experimentation that William Connolly and others celebrate as democratically significant. There was, however, a measurable shift in public opinion in Tennessee toward supporting routes to legal citizenship in the period WTI undertook its campaign.[4] It is even more difficult to determine whether any of WTI's addressees engaged in micropolitics of the self that in turn inspired them to participate in collective democratic action. Nonetheless, there is reason for hope here, since WTI is but one element of TIRRC's larger, more comprehensive movement and the WTI projects all provided information on TIRCC's multipronged efforts to improve the conditions faced by immigrants in Tennessee. The community education efforts of WTI referenced and publicized the work of TIRRC, a "statewide immigrant and refugee led collaboration" using grass-roots organizing to seek local and national legislative reform, promote two-way immigrant integration processes, combat racial profiling, hold so-called Justice Schools, and mobilize against English-only initiatives, among other programs.[5] Within this configuration, work on the self triggered by WTI's campaigns may help prepare some individuals to join in these associative democratic struggles. The prospect of a mutually supportive dynamic between care for the self and care for the world depends here, as in other cases, on whether an individual's work on herself is spurred by a democratic movement urging care for a worldly thing. This link is crucial. Without such an anchor, work on the self can take many forms—self-indulgent consumerism or the reinforcement of a fundamentalist identity, for example—that do little to foster associative endeavors to make the world a better home and in-between. If, however, the self's reflexive relationship is inspired by democratic action that enacts care for the world, then it can potentially serve as a resource for those worldly endeavors.

What about care for the Other? Might a charitable ethical outlook or activity focused on tending to another's needs harbor elements that can be drawn upon to serve collaborative care for the world? In chapter 2 I insisted that the provision of charity not be mistaken for the practice of democracy. Yet it is hard to agree with Arendt when she declares, "Politics are concerned with the world as such and not with those who live in it."[6] Surely it is unlikely that one would be concerned with the world and willing to expend energy engaging in politics in the absence of any concern for that world's inhabitants. If "the world" and "those who live in it" cannot be as neatly cordoned off from one another as Arendt's remark suggests, then one would do well to consider whether feelings of concern for particular others may bear democratic potential. Can a dyadic relation in which a self is moved to respond to the summons of the Other be transformed into a relation of mutual care for worldly conditions? If so, how? When can a sense of personal responsibility to an Other serve as an opening for the cultivation of a democratic ethics? What kinds of appeals and practices can aid in effecting such a shift?

Two examples are helpful here. First, a video advertisement from 2010 by the Courage Campaign that aired on television in California and was viewed by more than a million people online, is worth consideration. It was designed to elicit viewers' concern for particular individuals, couples, and families yet seeks to direct that concern toward participation in democratic action.[7] The ad was created after the passage of Proposition 8, which made same-sex marriage, previously permitted under state law, illegal in California. The ad, titled "Fidelity" (after the song it features) and also known as the "Don't Divorce . . ." video, consists almost entirely of a series of low-tech snapshots set to a moving, piano-heavy, indie pop song by Regina Spektor. About half of the snapshots are of same-sex couples— at their weddings, on vacation, in familiar portrait poses. The other half of the photographs are of people holding a various handmade signs that read, "Don't Divorce My Moms," "Don't Divorce My Son and Son-in-Law," "Don't Divorce Us," "Don't Divorce My Friends," "Don't Divorce My Uncles," "Don't Divorce My Co-Workers," and so on. Each of these images features one to five people who all, with one exception, look directly into the camera while holding a sign that specifies how they or those close to them would be affected—divorced—by Proposition 8.[8] The cumulative effect of these amateur portraits and homemade signs, in which specific individuals make personal pleas on behalf of specific marriages, is quite arresting. It is difficult not to be struck by the immediacy of the appeal: *this* person, *this* couple will lose something significant if Proposition 8 stands. The ad is clearly structured so as to elicit an emotional, caring response toward particular individuals and families. Indeed, it draws on some familiar techniques used in print and television ads for charitable organizations, which regularly feature images of specific, suffering people, usually children, as part of their call for financial support. What the "Don't Divorce . . ." video seeks to do is not new, then: it tries to evoke viewers' compassion for particular human beings and uses carefully crafted visual representations to do so. Yet the ad is designed to direct that compassionate response into avenues of collective democratic action. When the series of snapshots concludes, the words "Love will prevail" appear on the screen, a statement that can seem apolitical, implying that love is an extra-human force that will ultimately win out, whatever human beings do. But the words that follow reveal the statement to be an incitement to action: "Tell the Supreme Court not to divorce 18,000 California couples." This instruction is followed by the web address for the Courage Campaign, a site which contains information on several actions in which one can participate, ranging from petition-signing and letter-writing campaigns to public protests and attendance at Camp Courage, an activist training program. There is no guarantee that viewers of "Don't Divorce . . ." will be persuaded to join these efforts. Yet the video serves as an important example of how concern for particular others might be activated and directed toward collaborative world-centered projects.

A second, quite different example takes professed concern for the suffering of the world's poor as its starting point but seeks to transform it into democratic demands for the reorganization of global institutions. The powerful work of Thomas Pogge, who has written extensively in academic as well as policy contexts, is driven, first, by a charge of hypocrisy: Americans and others pay lip service to morality, purporting to care about the alleviation of human suffering, but they actually do little to address the profound harms poverty causes throughout the world.[9] Pogge's next move is notably resonant with the questions I discuss here. In *Politics as Usual*, briefs written for the Comparative Research Programme on Poverty, and other writings, Pogge does more than simply allege that existing charitable responses to poverty are inadequate. He also tries to develop a sense of shared, democratic responsibility for the transformation of global institutions. He desires to replace a charitable outlook, according to which the affluent give aid to the needy, with a democratic one, according to which the citizens of the G7 countries (Canada, France, Germany, Italy, Japan, the United Kingdom, and the United States) are accountable for the global order their governments have built. As Pogge convincingly shows, that order's institutional design "systematically produces" deprivation for some and affluence for others.[10] Citizens of the G7 countries, which are all "reasonably democratic," are responsible for this state of affairs and should collectively insist upon "structural reform."[11] While Pogge's argument does not focus primarily on eliciting care for a particular Other, as in the previous example, his work tries to tap into and radically reshape the concern we already, routinely claim to have for others (a concern that seems to drive relatively high rates of charitable giving, including internationally, among Americans).[12] Pogge tries to show that if we really do care about the lives damaged and lost because of poverty, charitable giving will not suffice; a collective democratic response aimed at redesigning global institutions and policies is needed. His work aims to mobilize citizen sentiments toward the transformation of institutions and away from what he terms generous charity.

The efforts of the Courage Campaign's visual media and Pogge's activist scholarship are connected by the fact that each project aims to define and elicit a collectivity of citizens, cast as the responsible agent, and to specify features of worldly conditions as the appropriate objects of their care. In both cases an appeal that draws on but also attempts to rework the viewer's or reader's sense of compassion or concern for others is made. These approaches suggest that the charitable ethical outlook conceptualized and criticized in this book is not entirely opposed to a democratic ethos. It contains a kernel of possibility. Care for others may be invoked and built upon in ways that are politicizing, but only if felt concern can be broadened and directed toward worldly conditions and avenues of collective action to address them.

But if the democratic ethos advocated here can sometimes draw strength from modalities of care that are not yet collaborative or world-centered, it is also important to challenge the sequencing implied by this formulation, a sequencing that is also crucial to arguments made by proponents of therapeutic and charitable ethics. As we saw earlier, work defending Foucauldian- and Levinasian-inspired ethics for democracy tends to suppose that care for the self or for the Other is necessarily prior to and preparatory for what I have called care for the world. But this chronology and the seamlessness it hints at are part of what this book calls into question. Notwithstanding the examples given above, which gesture toward the possibility of politicizing care for the Other(s), a different connection must be contemplated: how collaborative care for the world can enable and support dyadic practices of care. In other words, rather than assume that an individual must start by caring for herself or an Other in order to subsequently move outward into participation in collective action, we should be alert to the ways in which collective action, animated by care for the world, enables other practices of care.

For example, supposing one believes that the creation of what Foucault calls "new forms of subjectivity" is an important project today, perhaps even a strategy for countering contemporary workings of power.[13] It is not necessarily the case that the cultivation of more varied and less normalized individuals is best pursued directly, by engaging in arts of the self. That is, if one accepts what Richard Flathman calls "complementarism"—the view that "robust and widely distributed individualities are productive of group and institutional life, and the latter support and stimulate individualities"—the focus should not be exclusively on the first half of this insight.[14] Also requiring exploration is the possibility that the multiplication of styles of subjectivity may depend to a great extent on collaborative world-centered projects.

That is to say, one ought to ask whether associative democratic politics, guided by the spirit of care for worldly things, can help provide the institutional and cultural supports that foster the emergence of new subjectivities. Michael Warner's astute analysis of queer counterpublics emphasizes the indispensable role such publics play in enabling the development of non-normative selves. "The world-making project of queer life" involves the elaboration of "knowledges, places, practices, languages and learned modes of feeling" that make possible new, queer styles of subjectivity.[15] The power of Warner's analysis lies in his insistence on the public quality of even that dimension of identity that is often taken to be the most personal and private, namely, sexuality. Sexual freedom, Warner argues, involves more than freedom of choice; it requires "access to pleasures and possibilities, since people commonly do not know their desires until they find them."[16] The emergence of diverse individualities, sexual and otherwise, Warner notes, depends on shared cultures that can nurture those individualities into existence. The project of pluralizing forms of subjectivity depends largely on the existence of public supports.[17]

Foucault himself articulated this insight, though without fully pursuing it. In a late interview he clarified that the care of the self, through which an individual attempts to craft a distinctive way of being, is not without its enabling conditions and constraints. The techniques, models, and aspirations that characterize the ethics of self-care are themselves cultural products: "I would say that if I am now interested in how the subject constitutes itself in an active fashion through practices of the self, these practices are nevertheless not something invented by the individual himself. They are models he finds in his culture, and are proposed, suggested, imposed on him by his culture, his society, his social group."[18] What Foucault seems to recognize in this moment—that the conditions of possibility for the ethical practice of self-care are publicly constituted—allows one to appreciate that practices that aspire to care for the world are potentially enabling of "new subjectivities." Self-constitution can be helpfully conceived of as an indirect enterprise, one practiced not only by conscious focus on oneself as an object of care, but also through engagement with others that is directed at changing worldly conditions in ways that make them more amenable to individual experimentation and flourishing.[19]

One's capacity to respond openly and generously to others depends upon broader sociocultural conditions that facilitate and encourage responsiveness and concern—conditions that are shaped less by any particular self than by collective efforts to alter the terms under which humans live. The quality of the dyadic relation between self and other may hinge, importantly, upon the worldly context within which this encounter occurs. Butler offers this insight but backs away from it when she acknowledges that the capacity to respond nonviolently, even hospitably, to the Other depends upon the frames and norms that govern that encounter. As discussed in chapter 2, this attention to schemas of intelligibility would seem to prioritize associative struggles to reshape norms and schemas, recognizing that such efforts are essential to establishing the conditions of possibility for a dyadic encounter characterized by responsiveness and concern. As I argued there, Butler tends to evade the political project this attention to frames, norms, and schemas opens up by instead positing an ethical truth that brings with it an injunction for action. Yet her attention to the way in which every ethical scene is embedded in a set of norms that systematically "derealize" some lives, rendering them ungrievable, should alert one to the importance of challenging and reworking shared cultural frames so that more lives, including foreign, Muslim, impoverished, non-white lives, appear as real and injurable, thereby making a responsive, caring encounter between self and Other more likely.

One example of this kind of world-centered project is Iraq Body Count, a web-based collaborative effort to document the civilian deaths caused by the war in Iraq. The project, as Maja Zehfuss shows, is determined to be more than a "counting tool."[20] The attitude the website conveys toward the information it provides is important: "It is to these all too easily disregarded victims of violence that Iraq Body Count is dedicated and we are resolute that they, too, shall have their memorials."[21] As Zehfuss argues, "The point of Iraq Body Count is not merely to count the dead but to provide memorials, to highlight the grievability of the lives that have been destroyed." Toward this end, the site posts as much detail as possible on "named and identified victims of the war on Iraq," specifying the name, age, sex, place of death, date, and source of information. The site reports, for example, that "Zahraa Husien Khzaieer, a ten-year-old girl, died of gashes in the chest at 'Nassriaa/Baghdad Street' in 2003 and Hashim Kamel Radi, a 22-year-old man, died due to an airstrike on the bus from Baghdad to Nasiriyah in March 2003." Iraq Body Count, despite its name, is resolved to offer more than a tally; its list is offered "in remembrance" and is prefaced by the words, "To those who knew and loved them, we add our sorrow and condolences."[22] It proposes to "interrupt" dominant "frames of war" such as those supplied by the U.S. Department of Defense, which records and publicizes only coalition deaths, primarily by challenging the differentiation between grievable and ungrievable lives that structures mainstream American representations of the Iraqi war.[23] The project, Zehfuss suggests, "intends to subvert the distinction between grievable coalition lives and the Iraqi dead."[24] Iraq Body Count, whose work has received worldwide attention, endeavors to shift, however slightly, reigning schemas that affect "who counts as human" and "whose lives count as lives."[25] This ambition—to create and circulate an alternative cultural frame that disrupts the dominant Western perceptual/normative field—should refocus our attention on the powerful but malleable social context within which every dyadic encounter occurs. The chances for a genuinely ethical response to the Other depend at least as much on that contextual environment as on the attributes of the specific self who faces the Other in need of help. Again, it is important not to assume that the lines of influence run only one way: rather than emphasize, as so many thinkers do, that a more responsive, giving relation to the Other can enhance democratic politics, we should concern ourselves with how world-centered democratic practices can help to create conditions that facilitate more generous relations between particular selves and others.

Finally, another critical connection concerns not the linkages between diverse ethical practices of care, but the relationship between ethos and institutions. The very question of a democratic ethos presupposes that the spirit of a regime, not only its formal features, matters. The argument presented here has defended a specific spirit, one characterized by care for the world as world, as being highly important to and enlivening of associative democracy. Moreover, as I showed in chapter 4, this ethos is already present in some forms of democratic organizing today, though it deserves to be more explicitly elaborated and purposefully pursued.

But one may still wonder how this ethical sensibility can be sustained, much less extended, when so many features of contemporary politics in the United States seem inhospitable, if not hostile, to democratic action that embodies care for the world. Official channels of government offer few opportunities for ordinary citizens to gather for the purpose of discussing and deciding public matters, while associational activities that take place outside of the state apparatus are continually threatened by vigilant policing practices.[26] Corporate power continues to grow, exerting ever more influence on supposedly democratic institutions. And the dominant rhetoric of mass-mediated electoral politics in this country appeals persistently to citizens' self-interest, doing little to bring into view the public world as common object or to cultivate a sense of concern for this entity. How might worldly ethics find expression, here and now?

Such an ethics would seem to depend largely on the existence of institutional spaces and practices that allow democratic actors to assume and enact collective responsibility. Doesn't an ethics oriented toward care of the world require political structures that foster such care and afford opportunities for its exercise? Yet don't the very institutions that might serve to cultivate care of the world depend on such an ethics already being in existence if they are to come into being?

We are in the midst of a powerful paradox famously identified by Jean-Jacques Rousseau in *The Social Contract*. Rousseau's theorization of political founding stresses the extent to which ethics and institutions are mutually dependent upon one another; each one seems to presuppose the other as its condition of possibility. The establishment of a sound democratic system of self-rule, Rousseau explains, seems to require individuals who exhibit a "social spirit" already oriented toward the common good. Yet that orientation would itself seem to be the result of democratic organization: "For a newly formed people to understand the wise principles of politics and to follow the basic rules of statecraft, the effect would have to become the cause; the social spirit which must be the product of social institutions would have to preside over the setting up of those institutions; men would have to have already become before the advent of law that which they become as a result of the law."[27]

Does this bind admit of an escape? Translated into the terms of this project, if an ethics of care for the world might help to inspire and strengthen associative democratic politics, doesn't such an ethics also emerge in and through that very politics? Where does this leave us? Although Rousseau's paradox, I would argue, cannot be resolved, it can be attenuated. The impasse he describes, while genuine, rarely if ever confronts us so starkly. The mutual dependence of ethics and institutions colors every creative political act, every attempt to begin anew, but it is not the fatal trap Rousseau's rendering might imply. We are not in the position of performing a political founding ex nihilo. The situation evoked by Rousseau gains much of its drama from the fact that it is depicted as one in which new laws, practices, and procedures must be invented from scratch, in the absence of any preexisting supports, whether ethical or institutional. We, thankfully or not, do not live in such a vacuum.

Finding ourselves in the midst of things means we can do more than wish for a Rousseauvian Legislator who will set things in motion for us.[28] *In medias res*, Rousseau's riddle loosens its grip a bit. For we do not face an empty political landscape that forces us to make an impossible choice between ethics and institutions. Even if it is a minority feature of contemporary politics in the United States, we nonetheless can find worldly ethics already expressed in institutional life. It is evident in the Beacons Programs, No Más Muertes/No More Deaths, and the Right to the City organizations and projects (see chapter 4). Efforts to care for the world as world—to make the world a more hospitable place for all human beings and to promote democratic practices through which the world can emerge as an in-between—are already happening. One can locate this spirit, for

example, in the work of United for a Fair Economy, a national organization that raises awareness of the harms of concentrated wealth and power,
especially in relation to the racial wealth divide, and advocates progressive
taxation policies. It does so largely through community-based "participatory education" in English and Spanish, which helps to create "popular
educators" who can help foster democratic mobilization on behalf of economic justice.[29] Justice Now, based in California (home to the two largest
women's prisons in the world), works to improve the conditions faced
by women in prison, documenting and challenging human rights abuses
against inmates, especially sexual abuse and the denial of health care.[30]
At the same time they aim to improve prisoners' lives in the present, the
group promotes alternatives to policing and prisons, working toward a
long-term goal of the abolition of prisons. The organization works with
women inmates rather than simply providing services for them: "It's imperative that the prisoners themselves drive the agenda."[31] By cultivating
leadership and activism among inmates, who serve on the group's board
and steer policy and strategy, Justice Now strives not only to address prisoners' basic needs but also to create new avenues for political participation for some of society's most disenfranchised members. Our Water
Commons, based in Minneapolis, is an activist organization working to
bring about "participatory, democratic, community-centered systems" of
water distribution worldwide. In cooperation with other global water justice movements, many of which have successfully challenged governmental privatization efforts, participants advocate the principle that water is a
"commons that belongs to everyone and no one." They seek legal reform
that simultaneously provides greater control of water by local citizens
while strengthening the limits on privatization, pricing, and use, in recognition not only of a human right to water but also of the importance of
fair water distribution for the ecosystems of which all humans are a part.[32]
In these cases and many others, the ethical and the institutional cannot
be detached from one another; care for the world as both a home and an
in-between is enacted in and through democratic counter-institutions.[33]
They are already imperfectly combined.

Whether we join in the activities of these organizations or take inspiration from them to create new ventures, we are far from the abstract,
empty space of Rousseauvian political beginnings. That we are already
located within a messy universe of ethical-institutional entities means we
do not need to imagine the task before us as one of radical invention,

confronting us with an irresolvable riddle: ethics or institutions? We are in the middle of things, and this might turn out to be a good place to be. While collaborative efforts to care for the world may be muted features of contemporary political life, they nonetheless exist. It is surely easier to lament or despair over present conditions, but a commitment to associative democratic politics calls for something else. It requires us to take sustenance from the supports that already exist, so that we might begin where we are.

≟

## INTRODUCTION

1. See *The Turn to Ethics*, ed. Garber, Hanssen, and Walkowitz. Leading examples of this development include Anderson, *The Way We Argue Now*; Bennett, *The Enchantment of Modern Life* and *Vibrant Matter*; Butler, *Giving an Account of Oneself* and *Precarious Life*; Coles, *Rethinking Generosity*; Connolly, *Why I Am Not a Secularist*, *Pluralism*, and *A World of Becoming*; Critchley, *The Ethics of Deconstruction* and *Infinitely Demanding*; Orlie, *Living Ethically, Acting Politically*; White, *The Ethos of a Late Modern Citizen*; and Ziarek, *An Ethics of Dissensus*.

2. William Connolly frequently refers to ethics as being indispensable to democracy. See, for example, *Why I Am Not a Secularist*, 13, 170, 187.

3. For example, many media representations of the Occupy Wall Street (ows) movement in late 2011 emphasized its enactment of an ethos, alternately identified as nonviolent (NPR), leaderless (Huffington Post), do-it-yourself (Jewish Week), and no-demands (Salon.com) in character. Supporters often depicted this ethos as a valuable resource for reinvigorating American democracy. For more theoretical reflections on ows's ethos, see Wendy Brown on its "populist ethos" in "Occupy Wall Street: Return of a Repressed *Res-Publica*" and Richard Grusin on the movement's fostering of a "revolutionary counter-mood" in "Premediation and the Virtual Occupation of Wall Street." But see also George Shulman, "Interpreting Occupy," which argues that academics have mostly interpreted ows in ways that validate "our own preferred frameworks of analysis." Shulman's question, "Must any effort to understand ows make it evidence to confirm what we already (want to) believe?" could easily be raised in relation to the ethos many have attributed to the movement.

4. One might object that what is lacking in the U.S. polity is not the requisite spirit but the institutional arrangements that ensure the exercise of genuinely democratic power. The influence of corporations on U.S. elections, expanded by *Citizens United v. Federal Election Committee* (2010), might, for example, support the claim that citizens act rationally when they decline to participate in democratic politics. Lacking effective sites of democratic decision making, citizens may simply opt out. Yet it is insufficient to insist that structural reform, rather than ethos, is the real issue. This is so not only because of the old but apt Rousseauvian insight regarding the circular relationship between a society's spirit and its institutions. More pointedly still, the institutional problems that might explain citizen dis-

engagement—growing corporate power, an expanded executive branch, an entrenched two-party system, and so on—do not put to rest the question of ethos. Indeed, they may raise it anew: might the absence of effective collective action in response to these conditions lead one back to the problem of a spirit that is missing but that could help mobilize citizens, rendering these mere facts sites of democratic contestation and resistance?

5. As Nikolas Kompridis says, Habermas employs "a very sharp form/content distinction to distinguish a universalistic concept of justice from particular conceptions of the good life" ("From Reason to Self-Realisation?," 333). The moral point of view, according to Habermas, properly guides questions about what is right, while questions about what is good can be answered only within the context of a specific form of life.

6. Some of the most powerful objections to both Habermas's and Rawls's accounts of public reason contend that their approaches to democratic deliberation unwittingly reinforce existing power relations and specifically disadvantage marginalized groups, whose forms of expression may not conform to the normative models of communication they advance. See Young, "Communication and the Other," and Deveaux, *Cultural Pluralism and the Dilemmas of Justice*.

7. Rawls, *Political Liberalism*, 220.

8. Anderson's *The Way We Argue Now* is an exception. She states that ethos has become a "valorized term" in contemporary political theory but says it has been wrongly juxtaposed with reason and aligned with affect (11–12). Anderson challenges this framing (and Foucauldian ethics in particular, which she casts as incoherent) in support of Habermasian discourse ethics, which she claims unites ethics and rationality.

9. The contrast between morality and ethics corresponds roughly to the Hegelian distinction between formal, universal *Moralität* and the more particular, customary *Sittlichkeit*.

10. This is not to say that those involved in the turn to ethics advocate an anything goes approach to political life. Connolly, for example, questions the exclusions generated by Rawlsian public reason, which restrict "new drives of pluralization" (Connolly, *Ethos of Pluralization*, xiv). Yet he also notes that "exclusions, restrictions, and boundaries" are necessary, particularly to restrain fundamentalism. Similarly, Chantal Mouffe argues that "total pluralism" is not possible or desirable and that "some limits need to be put to the kind of confrontation that is going to be seen as legitimate in the public sphere. But the political nature of these limits should be acknowledged instead of being presented as requirements of morality or rationality," as they are for Habermas and Rawls (Mouffe, *The Democratic Paradox*, 93).

11. Connolly maintains that secularist positions that eschew comprehensive conceptions in politics make it difficult for partisans to engage in issues of the day because most participants actually do draw on their metaphysical and religious perspectives. Thus the desire to rid political life of such perspectives may be strategically ineffective. See Connolly, *Why I Am Not a Secularist*, chapter 1. In this regard, the discovery—an apparent surprise to many Democrats—that a majority

of citizens who voted for George W. Bush in 2004 cited moral values as the single most important issue of the election, is instructive. See Katharine Q. Seelye, "Moral Values Cited as a Defining Issue of the Election," *New York Times*, November 4, 2004. Several years later Barack Obama's often moving, morally infused rhetoric leading up to the election of 2008 seemed to express his criticism of the tendency to cede values talk to the right: "In reaction to religious overreach, we equate tolerance with secularism, and forfeit the moral language that would help infuse our policies with a larger meaning" (Obama, *The Audacity of Hope*, 48).

12. *Oxford English Dictionary* (2d ed., 1989). Chamberlain, "From 'Haunts' to 'Character,'" 102. Both the OED and Chamberlain identify Aristotle's *Rhetoric* as a primary text in establishing this meaning of *ethos*. Chamberlain explains that "in most writers of the fifth century BC and later, *ethos* can usually be understood and translated as 'character,'" with the caveat that such character is understood in collective and not strictly individualist terms (101–2).

13. Chamberlain, "From 'Haunts' to 'Character,'" 102.

14. Thomas Corts notes that there has been "confusion of two Greek terms" which are similar in English: ἔθος, meaning simply "custom" or "habit," and ἦθος, meaning "custom, disposition, character." The latter term is the one used by Aristotle, and it is presented as a complement to *nomos* in the ancient Greek tradition. The latter term, Corts notes, also carries a positive connotation, indicating a "good disposition," while the former is "morally neutral and refers to behavioral traits." Corts recommends that scholars transliterate ἔθος as *ethos* and ἦθος as *ēthos* in order to reflect this distinction. In addition, "They might also emphasize the positive moral quality of ἦθος, rather than the behavioral neutrality of its sister term" ("The Derivation of Ethos," 201–2). This book, however, follows the contemporary convention among democratic theorists (and the OED) of using *ethos* to refer to "the characteristic spirit, prevalent tone of sentiment, of a people or a community." See also Chamberlain, "From 'Haunts' to 'Character,'" where he notes that the *Nicomachean Ethics* "explains the connection between *ethos* and *ēthos*" insofar as human virtue is "habituable," that is, susceptible to training and habit (102–3).

15. Chamberlain, "From 'Haunts' to 'Character,'" 102. He notes that "orators can speak to their audience of 'your' or 'our' *ēthē*," indicating a shared moral sensibility.

16. Tocqueville, *Democracy in America*, volume 1, part 2, chapter 9.

17. Work that highlights the significance of virtue in contemporary liberalism includes Macedo, *Liberal Virtues*, and Galston, *Liberal Purposes*.

18. Berkowitz, *Virtue and the Making of Modern Liberalism*.

19. Button, *Contract, Culture, and Citizenship*.

20. Berkowitz, *Virtue and the Making of Modern Liberalism*, x–xii. Button describes this as "the paradox of civic virtue for liberalism": "Liberal societies presuppose and rely on a range of important moral qualities and virtues for their very identity and stability," yet it is hard for liberals to conceive "how those qualities could legitimately be the objects of cultivation," given their commitment to individual freedom and an "overriding concern to limit coercive government" (*Contract, Culture, and Citizenship*, 16).

21. Chamberlain, "From 'Haunts' to 'Character,'" 103. Or at least they are "closely connected" when a society is stable. Both Plato and Aristotle are alert to the difficulties that arise when *ethe* and *nomoi* are no longer mutually reinforcing.

22. A partial exception to this characterization is Machiavelli's portrait of republicanism, which, as Maurizio Viroli argues, follows prior republican thought by emphasizing the rule of law, the principle of civic equality, and the importance of civic virtue but parts company with the humanist and Ciceronian traditions by challenging the value of concord. Viroli, "Machiavelli and the Republican Idea of Politics."

23. This question suggests a project different from Robert Bellah's well-known co-authored book, which borrows Tocqueville's phrase in support of a communitarian, arguably nostalgic vision of American life. Bellah et al., *The Habits of the Heart*.

24. Raymond Geuss has argued strongly against "ethics-first" forms of political theory. But he characterizes ethics quite narrowly as a form of Kantian moral absolutism that regards politics as derivative of an ideal (a view he identifies with Rawls's work). Geuss's criticisms are worth consideration, but he defines *ethics* in a very limited and sometimes even caricatured way that does not begin to capture the diverse conceptualizations of the term by political theorists, many of whom cannot reasonably be charged with the simple-minded idealism Geuss portrays in order to dramatize the merits of his own realism. See Geuss, *Philosophy and Real Politics*.

25. Laclau, "Deconstruction, Pragmatism, Hegemony," 58, 60, 54.

26. Mouffe, "Which Ethics for Democracy?," 91. Elsewhere, however, Mouffe is far from dismissive of ethics: "To secure allegiance and adhesion to [democratic] principles what is needed is the creation of a democratic ethos . . . the mobilization of passions and sentiments, the multiplication of practices, institutions and language games that provide conditions of possibility for democratic subjects and democratic forms of willing" ("Deconstruction, Pragmatism, and the Politics of Democracy," 6).

27. Apostolidis, "Politics and Connolly's Ethics." Although his main argument here is that the "complementarities of ethical and political action" are revealed when Connolly's ethical work is read in connection with the experiences and narratives of immigrant workers, the article nonetheless ends on a cautionary note, warning that theorists should renew their "enthusiasm for interrogating the structural dynamics of power that help order the terrain where ethical practices are deployed."

28. Brown, "Moralism as Anti-Politics." See also Dean, "The Politics of Avoidance," which depicts the turn to ethics as a form of naïve idealism that detracts attention from the critical and oppositional politics in which democratic citizens ought to be engaged. In a related move, Jacques Rancière's "The Ethical Turn of Aesthetics and Politics" casts the ethical turn as an evasion of judgment and distinction making, though this claim is suggested more than fully argued.

29. Shulman, "Acknowledgment and Disavowal as an Idiom for Theorizing Politics."

30. "Action in concert" is Arendt's phrase, which appears throughout her writings and is especially prominent in *The Human Condition*.

31. Ibid. Honig, "The Politics of Ethos," also advances this hypothesis. In a more his-

torical reading of the turn to ethics in the French context, Julian Bourg's *From Revolution to Ethics* documents a paradigm shift following May 1968, in which a new emphasis on ethics (one which persists to this day) appeared in response to the apparent impossibility of political revolution. Although he does not label this development a signal of despair, he does present the shift to the ethical register as a consequence of the failure of institutional overthrow in 1968.

32. On the question of absolutism, Myers, "From Pluralism to Liberalism," demonstrates that the indeterminate ethical outlook articulated by Berlin — that of value pluralism — is misinterpreted and appropriated by contemporary liberals who seek to turn it into a moral foundation sanctioning liberalism. Myers, "Resisting Foucauldian Ethics," shows that the turn to ethics also has the potential to distract from more pressing questions of how to generate collective power. Some of Foucault's influential readers have wrongly emphasized his later work on the ethics of "care for the self" as a strategy for resisting disciplinary power and biopower. This approach, I argue, minimizes Foucault's astute analyses of how discipline and biopower function by "individualizing" and "massifying," respectively, and his related but underappreciated account of the "counter-power" born out of associative activity that can potentially contend with these forces. This neglected but central Foucauldian insight should alert us to the limits of care of the self as a means of reworking existing power relations and redirect our attention to associative strategies instead.

33. Honig observes, "Still, it seems to me, although ethos may be an important part of preparation and receptivity for would-be political actors (themselves already politicized as constituted subjects), it is no match for the worldliness of political engagement" ("The Politics of Ethos," 428). This claim echoes my earlier argument in "The Turn to Ethics and Its Democratic Costs," which conceptualizes the quest for ethos primarily as an evasion of — and threat to — democratic politics.

34. This understanding of politics serves as a counterpoint to what has been termed the "democratic deficit" in contemporary theory, that is, the tendency in recent political thought to emphasize the liberal side of liberal democracy by focusing primarily on questions of individual rights and safeguards against the state at the expense of pursuing questions that concern the distribution of political power and the existence of meaningful opportunities for citizen participation in self-government. I borrow the term "democratic deficit" from Mouffe, *Democratic Paradox* (3–4), though it was in wide circulation during the debates over the design of the European Union.

35. Alexis de Tocqueville famously credits associational activity with saving the "independent and weak" citizens of democracy from helplessness. The "art of association" in which men "combine for great ends" enables individual citizens to produce effects they could not otherwise. Tocqueville, *Democracy in America*, volume 2, part 2, chapters 5–7.

36. Hannah Arendt refers to "co-acting" when she states that action is "never possible in isolation" (*The Human Condition*, 189).

37. Although the existence of certain legal protections such as the right to assemble can help to support the emergence of collective movements, examples of associa-

tive democratic politics among dissidents, as in the Solidarity movement of the 1980s in Poland, indicate that it would be a mistake to rule out the appearance of associative action even in regimes with very limited rights protections. Equally mistaken is the idea that the existence of constitutional rights to speech and assembly, for example, is proof that American political culture is hospitable to the creation and preservation of associational relations. As Michael Rogin has demonstrated, aggressive governmental efforts throughout American history have effectively suppressed associative activities and collective forms of life thought to threaten state power. What Rogin calls the "countersubversive tradition" in the United States involves the state's valorization of "private freedom" and a routine denial of "public freedom," or "the freedom of community members to speak and act together" ("Political Repression in the United States," 65).

38. Arendt, *The Human Condition*, 182.
39. "Art of association" is Tocqueville's well-known phrase, which appears in *Democracy in America*, volume 2, part 2, chapter 5.
40. Held, *Models of Democracy*. Of the eight variants of democracy Held analyzes, seven grant a prominent place to citizens' associative activity. Although the institutional locations and meanings assigned to associations vary, ranging from the citizen councils of classic republicanism to the pressure groups of midcentury pluralism, only the model of democratic elitism grants little to no importance to associational activity.
41. The purpose and meaning ascribed to associational activity vary according to the particular framework within which it is interpreted. Archon Fung's "Associations and Democracy" contains a very useful mapping of the different arguments advanced in support of associational activity. Fung shows that democratic association is credited with making six kinds of contributions, not all of them compatible. (For example, according to some, association is an intrinsic good, but liberals tend to see it as an expression of personal freedom while participatory democrats regard it as a mode of collective self-determination. Still other theories see the practice of association in more instrumental terms, whether as a means of developing certain skills and capacities or as a mechanism for improving the representation of interests.) This diversity should not be surprising, given that the contributions ascribed to associational activity are generated by competing "background ideals," which Fung labels classical liberalism, representative democracy, and participatory democracy.
42. See, for example, Robert F. Worth, "Yemen on the Brink of Hell," *New York Times*, July 20, 2011, and Simon Sebag Montefiore, "Every Revolution Is Revolutionary in Its Own Way," *New York Times*, March 23, 2011.
43. In "A Brief Introduction to Phenomenology and Existentialism" Wrathall and Dreyfus include Arendt, Levinas, and Foucault in their short list of thinkers strongly influenced by phenomenology and existentialism.
44. Although phenomenology and existentialism originally appeared as two distinct strands of twentieth-century European thought, they have "largely merged into a common canon of works and ways of doing philosophy" (ibid., 5). See this same

text for an account of the primary features of "merged" existential phenomenology.

45. Foucault's and Levinas's works feature much more prominently than Arendt's in the recent turn to ethics, perhaps because Arendt does not embrace an explicitly ethical vocabulary. She is also sometimes misread as a thoroughly amoral thinker, though, as I will show, the beginnings of a powerful ethical sensibility—care for the world—run throughout her writings.

46. Kruks, *Retrieving Experience*, 6.

47. This is Wrathall's and Dreyfus's description of Heidegger's shift away from Husserl ("A Brief Introduction to Phenomenology and Existentialism," 3).

48. Ibid., 5.

49. Foucault, "The Ethics of the Concern for Self as a Practice of Freedom," 298.

50. My project explores how the understanding of ethics might productively shift by adopting what Linda Zerilli has called a "world-centered frame." She too identifies this frame with Arendt, though her intervention focuses on the importance of reconceiving freedom as a "world question" rather than a "subject question" for feminist theory and politics. See Zerilli, *Feminism and the Abyss of Freedom*, introduction.

51. I borrow the distinction between a "matter of fact" and a "matter of concern" from Latour, "From Realpolitik to Dingpolitik," 16.

52. Scholem and Arendt, "Eichmann in Jerusalem."

53. Ibid., 51.

54. Ibid., 54.

## 1. CRAFTING A DEMOCRATIC SUBJECT?

1. For example, the antiwar group Code Pink was criticized by some for their activities, which included interrupting and heckling during speeches by officials, including President George W. Bush. Ewen MacAskill, "Debate over US Healthcare Takes an Ugly Turn," *The Guardian*, August 12, 2009; Ian Urbina, "Beyond Beltway, Health Debate Turns Hostile," *New York Times*, August 7, 2009. Popular attention to questions of civility in politics peaked in January 2011 after the assassination attempt on Rep. Gabrielle Giffords and the murder of six others at a public Congress on Your Corner event at a shopping center in Tucson. Helene Cooper and Jeff Zeleny, "Obama Calls for Civility in New Era of American Politics," *New York Times*, January 12, 2011.

2. Myers, "Resisting Foucauldian Ethics." I argue that contemporary theory that champions Foucauldian self-care as a privileged mode of resistance often neglects Foucault's analysis of disciplinary power and biopower, which, if read carefully, should alert one to the limits of the care of the self as a strategy for reshaping power relations.

3. William Connolly is the most influential proponent of this view. See Connolly, *The Ethos of Pluralization*, *Why I Am Not a Secularist*, and *Pluralism*. See also Dumm, *Michel Foucault and the Politics of Freedom*; Orlie, *Living Ethically, Acting Politically*; Simons, *Foucault and the Political*.

4. Foucault, "The Ethics of the Concern for Self as a Practice of Freedom," 263.

5. See especially Detel, *Foucault and Classical Antiquity*; Hadot, "Reflections on the Notion of 'the Cultivation of the Self,'"; O'Leary, *Foucault and the Art of Ethics*. But Hadot also grants that Foucault knowingly "glosses over" some elements of Stoicism, for example, even though he was "well aware of them," because his account of practices of the self is "not only a historical study; it was meant to offer contemporary man a model of life" (226).

6. Dreyfus and Rabinow, *Michel Foucault: Beyond Structuralism and Hermeneutics*, 119.

7. Foucault, "An Aesthetics of Existence," 49.

8. Peter Dews contends that there is a problem with the "reflexive account of self-construction" that appears in Foucault's work on the ancients and in "What Is Enlightenment?" He argues that it seems to require an already-existing self to perform the construction, a requirement that conflicts with Foucault's understanding of the subject "as a construction of power and discourse" (Dews, "The Return of the Subject in Late Foucault," 155). But this claim of contradiction ignores Foucault's analysis of subjectivation (discussed later in this chapter). A slightly different way of countering Dews's claim is offered by Robert Strozier, who says that Foucault consistently theorizes a subject who is "historically constituted" as "self-reflexive" and thereby capable of "using this very constitution as a means to dismantle the strategies of that constitution." A foundational, a priori subject is not the only way to understand the possibility of reflexivity. See Strozier, *Foucault, Subjectivity, and Identity*, chapter 2.

9. "An Aesthetics of Existence" is the title of an interview with Foucault in which he speaks about the importance of an ethics that aims to "give one's life a certain form" (49). In *The History of Sexuality*, vol. 1, Foucault sought to show that sexuality, understood as the epitome of interiority, is itself produced by and in turn furthers discursive practices that seek to uncover a true self hidden beneath appearances. The idea of an ethics that does not focus on a realm of interiority but is manifest in a visible mode of existence may appeal to Foucault as an alternative to that hermeneutic understanding of the self.

10. O'Leary, *Foucault and the Art of Ethics*, 38.

11. Foucault, *The Use of Pleasure*, 11.

12. Foucault, "On the Genealogy of Ethics," 261.

13. Bernstein, "Foucault's Aesthetic Decisionism"; Hadot, "Reflections on the Notion of 'the Cultivation of the Self.'"

14. Flynn, "Truth and Subjectivation in the Later Foucault," 535; O'Leary, *Foucault and the Art of Ethics*, 53–57.

15. O'Leary argues in *Foucault and the Art of Ethics* that Foucault's account of the Greeks tends to overemphasize the aesthetic motivation and neglect the crucial link between self-mastery and political rule over others.

16. Foucault, "The Hermeneutic of the Subject," 94–95.

17. Foucault, *The Use of Pleasure*, 91; Foucault, *The Care of the Self*, 249.

18. Foucault, "The Ethics of the Concern for Self as a Practice of Freedom," 287.

19. Foucault, *The Use of Pleasure*, 91.

20. Ibid., 65–67.

21. Ibid., 68–69.

22. Ibid., 70.

23. The Greek distinction between outer and inner freedom is examined in part 2 of Orlando Patterson's *Freedom*, Volume 1: *Freedom in the Making of Modern Culture*, and in Arendt, "What Is Freedom?" Patterson quotes Philo's *Every Good Man Is Free*, which captures this dualism: "Slavery then is applied in one sense to bodies, in another to souls; bodies have men for masters; souls their vices and passions. The same is true of freedom; one freedom produces security of the body from men of superior strength, the other one sets the mind at liberty from the domination of the passions" (197).

24. Foucault, "The Ethics of the Concern for Self as a Practice of Freedom," 284.

25. Foucault distinguishes between liberation and freedom, noting that most under-standings of liberation wrongly imply an escape from power relations. Foucault recognizes that there are events that can be considered acts of liberation in some sense—as "when a colonized people attempts to liberate itself from its colonizers"—but he claims that what such liberation enables is the creation of "new power relationships," not an escape from power altogether ("The Ethics of the Concern for Self as a Practice of Freedom," 282–83). Moreover, Foucault insists that freedom, understood as an activity rather than a state of affairs, is practiced within that field of power relations. See esp. Foucault, "The Subject and Power."

26. Foucault, "The Ethics of the Concern for Self as a Practice of Freedom," 284.

27. Ibid., 286.

28. One extreme is represented by Eric Paras, who claims that in his late work Foucault abandons his "fire-eating antihumanism" and embraces a "prediscursive," "independent and freestanding subject" (Paras, *Foucault 2.0.*, 4, 14, 101). Dews makes a similar argument in "The Return of the Subject in Late Foucault." My reading is closer to those of Nealon, *Foucault beyond Foucault*, and Ransom, *Foucault's Discipline*. They both interpret Foucault's work on the care of the self as being an extension of his earlier scholarship rather than a clear departure from it.

29. Foucault, "Technologies of the Self," 225.

30. Foucault, "The Ethics of the Concern for Self as a Practice of Freedom," 281–82; Foucault, "An Aesthetics of Existence," 50–51.

31. Foucault, "The Return of Morality," 243.

32. Jane Bennett, for example, says of Foucault's late work on ethics, "A moment of 'freedom' survives within subjectivity after all, it seems" ("'How Is It Then That We Still Remain Barbarians?,'" 656). Thomas Osborne notes that the aesthetics of existence attracts interest because it is regarded as "one of the few things that Foucault is avowedly in favor of" (Osborne, "Critical Spirituality," 60).

33. Foucault, *The History of Sexuality*, vol. 1, 60. See also Foucault, "The Subject and Power," 331.

34. Butler, *The Psychic Life of Power*, 17. For a thoughtful examination of this dynamic in both Foucault and Butler, see Allen, *The Politics of Our Selves*, chapters 3, 4.

35. Butler, *The Psychic Life of Power*, 12, 10. Jon Simons makes this point when he explains that "all subjectifying power endows subjects with some capacities to be agents." Thus, power "enables subjects" (*Foucault and the Political*, 82).

36. Foucault, "An Aesthetics of Existence," 50–51.

37. Foucault, "The Ethics of the Concern for Self as a Practice of Freedom," 291.

38. Bernauer and Mahon, "The Ethics of Michel Foucault," 154.

39. Foucault, *The Use of Pleasure*, 25–32. See also Foucault, "On the Genealogy of Ethics," 263.

40. Foucault, *The Use of Pleasure*, 29–30. Foucault explains that all morality entails a relationship to the self and that this relationship can be examined via four major categories: ethical substance, mode of subjectivation, ethical work, and telos.

41. Ibid., 30. He argues, for example, that Greek ethics approached sexual activity not primarily as a domain of prescriptive and proscriptive rules that applied to all but focused instead on the question of how an individual might stylize his sexual practice in a way that controlled and limited the possible excesses of *aphrodisia*: "The laws against sexual misbehavior were very few and not very compelling. . . . Their theme . . . was an aesthetics of existence" (255).

42. Foucault, "On the Genealogy of Ethics," 254.

43. Ibid., 260.

44. Foucault, *The Use of Pleasure*, 21.

45. Foucault, "On the Genealogy of Ethics," 255, 271.

46. Foucault, *The Use of Pleasure*, 21.

47. Foucault, "On the Genealogy of Ethics," 253. Although the ethics of self-care was practiced almost exclusively in "privileged circles," Foucault notes the exception of early Epicurean groups in Greece whose members were "artisans, small shopkeepers, and poor farmers." Although self-care in this case was still limited to a minority of the population, it had a democratic rather than aristocratic character (*The Hermeneutics of the Subject*, 115).

48. Foucault, *The Use of Pleasure*, 21, 23. In "The Return of Morality," when asked what he thought of the Greeks, Foucault remarked, "Not very much" and commented, with laughter, "All of antiquity seems to me to have been a 'profound error'" (244).

49. Foucault, "On the Genealogy of Ethics," 255.

50. Foucault, "The Ethics of the Concern for Self as a Practice of Freedom," 294–95. He also insists that his inquiry into ancient care of the self not be interpreted as the rediscovery of a lost foundation. Foucault explains, "Nothing is more foreign to me than the idea that, at a certain moment, philosophy went astray and forgot something, that somewhere in its history there is a principle, a foundation that must be recovered." He also remarks in "On the Genealogy of Ethics," "You can't find the solution of a problem in the solution of another problem raised at another moment by other people" (256).

51. In "What Is Enlightenment?" Foucault describes the "attitude" of modernity in terms that echo his depiction of ancient arts of the self. Citing Baudelaire, Foucault says this attitude involves "a mode of relationship that must be established with oneself." Modernity entails an "indispensable asceticism." Indeed, "to be modern is to take oneself as object of a complex and difficult elaboration." This project is one of enlightenment, or a "way out," Foucault says, because it releases us from a status of "immaturity," in which we accept "someone else's authority to lead us" (309, 311, 305).

52. Foucault, *The Use of Pleasure*, 30.

53. Foucault, "An Aesthetics of Existence," 49.

54. Foucault also claims that it is a mistake to suppose that the dissolution of traditional moral codes and prohibitions "solved the problem of ethics." The "problem of an ethics as a form to be given to one's behavior and life" remains ("The Concern for Truth," 263).

55. In contrast to his assertion elsewhere that we are beyond rule-governed morality, Foucault says, "We . . . inherit a secular tradition that sees in external laws the basis for morality. . . . We seek the rules for acceptable behavior in relations with others." Foucault's suggestion nonetheless is that we should question this attachment, not maintain it ("Technologies of the Self," 228).

56. Veyne, "The Final Foucault and His Ethics," 7.

57. Foucault, "On the Genealogy of Ethics," 255–56.

58. Bernauer and Mahon, "The Ethics of Michel Foucault," 147.

59. Foucault, "The Subject and Power," 336.

60. Foucault invites this reading in part because he depicts ancient ethics precisely as non-normalizing in character.

61. Schwartz, "Repetition and Ethics in Late Foucault," 113; Oksala, *Foucault on Freedom*, 168.

62. Flathman, *Freedom and Its Conditions*, 13.

63. Ibid., 33.

64. Smart, "Foucault, Levinas and the Subject of Responsibility," 82.

65. Grimshaw, "Practices of Freedom."

66. Myers, "Resisting Foucauldian Ethics."

67. Foucault mentions both a "politics of ourselves" as a counter to the traditional hermeneutics of the self and the notion of "politics as an ethics," phrases which hint — without doing much more — at the political significance of care for the self ("About the Beginnings of the Hermeneutics of the Self," 222–23; "Politics and Ethics: An Interview," 375).

68. In *The Care of the Self* Foucault argues that the exercise of such care was not a practice of solitude but "a true social practice" involving more or less institutionalized structures, including organized communities, schools, and the guidance of teachers, advisors, and counselors (51–52). See also Foucault, *Hermeneutics of the Self*, especially the lectures of January 20 and 27, in which Foucault addresses the role of "sectarian groups" in ancient ethics as well as the specific others who facilitated care of the self.

69. Foucault, "The Ethics of the Concern for Self as a Practice of Freedom," 284.

70. Ibid., 287.

71. Ibid., 288.

72. Foucault, *The Hermeneutics of the Subject*, 252.

73. Ibid., 298.

74. Ibid., 292. See "The Subject and Power," 346, where Foucault also relies on a contrast between mobility and fixity to differentiate power and domination.

75. Foucault, "The Ethics of the Concern for Self as a Practice of Freedom," 292.

76. Foucault, "Sex, Power and the Politics of Identity," 167.

77. Foucault, *The Use of Pleasure*, 73. Although Foucault spends considerable time on this theme in his writings and lectures, he also speaks of Greek self-care in a more purely aesthetic sense, as though it were primarily about creating a self that exhibits *kalos* (goodness/beauty). This has led O'Leary, for example, to argue that Foucault "downplays" the Greek emphasis on self- and political mastery. See O'Leary, *Foucault and the Art of Ethics*, esp. chapter 2.

78. Foucault, *The Use of Pleasure*, 80–81.

79. Foucault, "The Ethics of the Concern for Self as a Practice of Freedom," 287.

80. In addition to the loosening of the tie between self-care and political rule, Foucault says that in the first two centuries AD care of the self was "freed from its privileged connection to pedagogy" and was no longer seen as a requirement valid at a particular moment in one's life. Instead "'caring about the self' is a rule co-extensive with life" (*The Hermeneutics of the Subject*, 83, 112, 247).

81. Foucault, "Technologies of the Self," 235.

82. Foucault, "On the Genealogy of Ethics," 260.

83. Ibid., 267.

84. Ibid.; Foucault, *The Care of the Self*, 95.

85. Flathman, *Freedom and Its Conditions*, 22–24.

86. Foucault, *The Hermeneutics of the Subject*, 177; see also 83, 126, 192.

87. Foucault, "The Ethics of the Concern for Self as a Practice of Freedom," 287.

88. Simons, *Foucault and the Political*, 123.

89. Dumm, *Michel Foucault and the Politics of Freedom*, 3.

90. On the admission of competing comprehensive views into the public realm, see especially Connolly, *Why I Am Not a Secularist*, chapter 1. The task of "pluralization" is closely tied to what Connolly calls the "politics of becoming," in which "new and unforeseen things surge into being," such as a new cultural identity, an unprecedented rights claim, or an alternative religious faith. Commitment to pluralization requires an attitude of "agonistic respect" and "critical responsiveness" toward instances of the politics of becoming, rather than the simple affirmation of diversity as it currently appears (*Pluralism*, 121–27).

91. In "Agonized Liberalism," Antonio Y. Vázquez-Arroyo provides a powerful critique of this dimension of Connolly's work, arguing that his focus on "democracy as an ethos" overemphasizes the question of civility and fails to consider "structural and institutional aspects of power in contemporary capitalist liberal democracies" (10). Connolly's "strong emphasis on therapeutic strategies" of self-artistry reveals another serious problem, according to Vásquez-Arroyo: "It seems that these practices of the self are hardly intended for those who do not share in power, for the dispossessed. . . . Rather, the strong emphasis placed on forbearance seems directed at those already sharing power, privilege and status: they are asked to practice forbearance to the forces unleashed by the disadvantaged members, to react more generously to new constituencies seeking parity of status and social capital" (15). Although I do not believe that the idea of democratic ethos or democratic culture is necessarily a dead end that forecloses inquiry into things like "constitutional principles, democratic institutions, political economy," as Vásquez-Arroyo

does, I am concerned that the identification of ethics with self-care occludes the worldly contexts that are the sites and objects of democratic action.

92. Connolly, *Pluralism*, 4.

93. Ibid., 122–27.

94. Ibid., 126–27.

95. Ibid., 311; Connolly, *Why I Am Not a Secularist*, 146.

96. Connolly, *Why I Am Not a Secularist*, 145.

97. Ibid., 141.

98. Connolly, *The Ethos of Pluralization*, 69. Graham Longford describes Foucault's ethics as "an art of the contingent self that heightens awareness of the contingencies and differences cross-cutting all identities, thereby helping militate against the indifference, resentment and cruelty toward others which sometimes flow from aggressive attempts to universalize, glorify and defend them." Yet Longford does not address the fact that Foucault never speaks of self-care in this way nor does he explain how this portrait squares with the ideal of mastery that lies at the center of Foucault's ancient ethics (Longford, "Sensitive Killers, Cruel Asthetes, and Pitiless Poets," 574).

99. Connolly, *Why I Am Not a Secularist*, 145–46. In *Pluralism* in particular Connolly casts work upon the self as critical for warding off the tendency to evil in all faiths (14, 19, 27). This tendency consists in the desire to "punish, correct, exclude, or terrorize" those whose beliefs challenge one's own.

100. Connolly, *Why I Am Not a Secularist*, 144.

101. Schoolman and Campbell, "An Interview with William Connolly," 311.

102. Connolly, *Why I Am Not a Secularist*, 146–47.

103. Connolly acknowledges that the "occasion" for arts of the self "often" arises in political contexts, when a "new and surprising movement . . . disturbs dimensions of your identity" (*Why I Am Not a Secularist*, 151). Although this statement is more attenuated than I think it ought to be, it recognizes that self-care is at least often dependent upon political mobilizations for its initiation. I would add, however, that the disturbance of one's identity is unlikely to foster participation in democratic action unless it is accompanied by felt concern for a specific public matter. This is vital if the arts of the self have any hope of being politically, and not just personally, meaningful.

104. Connolly, *The Ethos of Pluralization*, xxvii, 66, 73.

105. "Self-artistry," he notes, may be "spurred into action by specific movements in the politics of becoming" (Connolly, *Why I Am Not a Secularist*, 146).

106. Connolly, *The Ethos of Pluralization*, 73.

107. In this same discussion Connolly states that the macropolitical question "How might the social conditions from which crime emanates be transformed?" should be set aside to ask what might be done through micropolitics to "honor desire and resist the flow of revenge" in individuals. He declares this latter question to be "preliminary" to the other (*The Ethos of Pluralization*, 66).

108. See chapter 3 for a discussion of Bruno Latour's portrait of politicization, which involves the transformation of a "matter of fact" into a "matter of concern."

109. Both quotes taken from interviews with Foucault, cited in Paras, *Foucault 2.0*, 107, 109.

110. Foucault, for example, distinguishes his thinking on the arts of the self from Sartre's notion of authenticity. He says he rejects the idea of a "true self" by emphasizing creativity rather than authenticity. The ancient belief that the "self had to be created as a work of art" is "diametrically opposed" to the idea of discovering one's true self ("On the Genealogy of Ethics," 263, 271).

111. Foucault, *The Hermeneutics of the Subject*, 98.

112. Bernauer and Mahon repeat this assumption in their reading of Foucault's ethics, declaring that commitment to the task of self-creation "will inaugurate new experiences of the self and human solidarity," without any accounting of how solidarity is generated out of individual practices of the arts of the self (Bernauer and Mahon, "The Ethics of Michel Foucault," 155–56).

113. Zerilli, *Feminism and the Abyss of Freedom*, 15.

114. Otherwise sympathetic readers of Foucault have challenged the priority granted to the self's reflexive relation in the name of ethical responsibility to the Other. See Oksala, *Foucault on Freedom*, chapter 9, and Smart, "Foucault, Levinas and the Subject of Responsibility."

115. See, most famously, Lasch, *The Culture of Narcissism*.

116. *The Secret*, a wildly popular DVD and book (the book sold nineteen million copies in the United States and has been translated into forty languages), centers on the claim that an individual's beliefs produce material reality. This profoundly depoliticizing philosophy, touted repeatedly by Oprah Winfrey and other influential celebrities, contends that one's thoughts are the sole determinant of one's experience. See Allen Salkin, "Shaking Riches Out of the Cosmos," *New York Times*, February 25, 2007; Christopher Chabris and Daniel Simons, "Fight 'The Power,'" *New York Times*, September 24, 2010. A more disturbing example of the tendency to overlook social and political practices in favor of a myopic focus on individual disposition can be found in the U.S. Department of Defense's recent foray into positive psychology (Gary Greenberg, "The War on Unhappiness," *Harper's*, September 2010). The goal of this endeavor is to help veterans "learn optimism" (34) and therefore be better equipped to cope with combat and its aftermath. Rather than examine how recent wars have been conducted (e.g., the use of torture, repeated deployments, ill-defined missions) or the social service system available to returning veterans, the army's embrace of positive psychology implies that the problems facing soldiers and veterans are not worldly in character and therefore are best remedied through work on one's inner self.

117. *Micropolitics* sometimes names small-scale intersubjective relations (Connolly, *Why I Am Not a Secularist*, 148) while at other points it denotes more specifically "action on the self" (Connolly, *The Ethos of Pluralization*, 68).

118. Schoolman and Campbell, "An Interview with William Connolly," 329.

119. Connolly, *A World of Becoming*, 91.

120. Heyes, *Self-Transformations*, 112.

121. Ibid., 116.

## 2. LEVINASIAN ETHICS AND DEMOCRACY

1. Oksala, *Foucault on Freedom*, 195. Oksala argues that Foucault is wrong to assume that desirable intersubjective relations will follow from the proper care of the self and insists that Levinas's work is a necessary supplement to Foucault. It is not clear to me, however, that Foucault's and Levinas's views can be integrated to the degree Oksala thinks.

2. Smart, "Foucault, Levinas, and the Subject of Responsibility," 84, 87. There is some structural similarity between Smart's argument and my own, since I claimed in chapter 1 that in order for care of the self to be democratically significant, it must be guided from the start by concern for a public problem. But I disagree with Smart's conclusion that concern for the Other is an adequate supplement to Foucault's ethical approach.

3. Simon Critchley refers to a "motivational deficit" when posing the question of democratic ethics in *Infinitely Demanding*, discussed later in this chapter.

4. Levinas's portrait of ethics also seems to offer an alternative to the formalism and proceduralism of Rawls's and Habermas's Kantian-inspired approaches by stressing a primordial structure of responsibility that escapes formulation in precepts or rules.

5. Critchley, *Infinitely Demanding*, 8.

6. Ziarek, *An Ethics of Dissensus*, 5. Although Ziarek states that the ethics she develops out of Levinas should not be understood as a "recovery of ethics as a new 'ground' of politics," she does not provide the theoretical resources that might enable an understanding of the unconditional as something other than a ground.

7. Levinas, *Totality and Infinity*, 21.

8. Levinas, "The Trace of the Other," 346.

9. Levinas, "Transcendence and Height," 16, 18. Levinas uses "I" and "the Same" interchangeably when speaking of the encounter between self and Other (15). Although some of Levinas's terminology is inconsistent (making translation all the more difficult), he repeatedly identifies *Autrui* as the "human Other." In general, he distinguishes between two forms of otherness, *autre* and *autrui*, although he sometimes capitalizes them and sometimes does not, in keeping with his "rather unsystematic prose style." *Autre*, however, designates anything that is other, including objects, and *autrui* is reserved for human beings (Critchley, "Introduction," 16).

10. Levinas, *Totality and Infinity*, 50.

11. Although Levinas tends to refer to physical being when talking about the face, he does not restrict the reference to the literal face of a person. See, for example, his many references to a scene from Grossman's *Life and Fate*, which Levinas uses as an example of the way the face can signify through the "neck and the back," "the shoulder blades," and the "nape" of the neck (Levinas, "Peace and Proximity," 140). Elsewhere Levinas cautions against understanding "the word *face* . . . in a narrow way" and refers to "the bare arm sculpted by Rodin" as an instance of the human "signifying in its uniqueness" (Levinas, "The Other, Utopia, and Justice," 232).

12. Levinas, "The Other, Utopia, and Justice," 231.

13. Levinas, "Transcendence and Height," 21.

14. Levinas, "Philosophy and Transcendence," 29.

15. Morgan, *Discovering Levinas*, 70.

16. Levinas, "The Proximity of the Other," 101.

17. Levinas describes the self/Other encounter as a "relation without relation" (*Totality and Infinity*, 80). As Colin Davis explains, "It is a relation because an encounter does take place; but it is 'without relation' because that encounter does not establish parity or understanding, the Other remains resolutely Other" (*Levinas*, 45).

18. Levinas, "Difficult Freedom," 251. These biblical figures are often cited by Levinas when he characterizes the Other. See also Levinas, "Transcendence and Height," 17.

19. Levinas, *Totality and Infinity*, 213–14.

20. Levinas refers to the self/Other relation as one of charity throughout his work, but see esp. Levinas, *Entre Nous*, and Robbins, *Is It Righteous to Be?* He also characterizes this relation as one of "total altruism" ("Transcendence and Height, 18).

21. Levinas, *Difficult Freedom*, xiv. Annabel Herzog agrees: "Hunger or destituteness are not formal structures to signify the radical and elusive alterity of the Other; they are not metaphors" ("Is Liberalism 'All We Need'?," 210).

22. Robbins, *Is It Righteous to Be?*, 52. Levinas returns to the topic of fulfilling material needs in a discussion of Heidegger's work, contrasting his own conception of responsibility to the Other with Heidegger's concept of *Fürsorge*: "I don't believe he thinks that giving, feeding the hungry and clothing the naked is the meaning of being or that it is above the task of being," a statement that implies this *is* Levinas's view (Levinas, "Philosophy, Justice and Love," 116).

23. Levinas, *Otherwise Than Being*, 55–56, 64, 72, 74, 77, 79.

24. For a thoughtful reading of Levinas's treatment of Grossman's book, see Morgan, *Discovering Levinas*, chapter 1.

25. In an interview Levinas affirms that to "be for the other" entails being responsible even for someone who is considered an enemy. More pointedly, he declares that the "ss man" has what he "means by a face." This, he acknowledges, is a "very painful" truth (Robbins, *Is It Righteous to Be?*, 55, 208). Yet in an infamous discussion in 1982 after Israel's occupation of Beruit and the massacres in Sabra and Chatila, Levinas denied that "for the Israeli" the Other is "the Palestinian." Here, Levinas, in seeming contradiction to much of his work, specifies that the Other is "the neighbor, one who is not necessarily kin, but who can be." Moreover, he claims that "in alterity we can find an enemy" ("Ethics and Politics," 294).

26. Robbins, *Is It Righteous to Be?*, 55.

27. Levinas, "Substitution," 94.

28. Levinas, "Transcendence and Height," 17.

29. Levinas repeats throughout his work this quote from Dostoevsky: "Each of us is guilty before everyone for everyone, and I more than the others." See, for example, Levinas, *Otherwise Than Being*, 146.

30. Levinas, "Substitution," 90.

31. The most provocative element of Levinas's notion of infinite responsibility, which

does not appear until *Otherwise Than Being*, expands the sense of responsibility one has for the Other to include responsibility for what the Other himself has done. (In this formulation, the responsibility that belongs to the Other but is assumed by the I is a more traditional responsibility for particular deeds that have been committed.) Here, "if the other does something I am the one who is responsible." This means that "I am responsible for the other even when he bothers me, even when he persecutes me" ("The Proximity of the Other," 105). This idea — that the "persecuted one is liable to answer for the persecutor" — is controversial, to say the least. For the purposes of this chapter I do not examine this idea in any depth, focusing instead on the "responsibility for the other" that is a constant throughout Levinas's writings: an unending responsibility for the Other's needs, the responsibility I bear to alleviate suffering. This is also the conception of responsibility that animates efforts to craft a Levinasian democratic ethos.

32. Robbins, *Is It Righteous to Be?*, 55.
33. Levinas, *Totality and Infinity*, 215.
34. Levinas, *Otherwise Than Being*, 118.
35. Morgan, *Discovering Levinas*, 173.
36. Levinas, *God, Death, and Time*, 175; Levinas, "Transcendence and Height," 17.
37. Robbins, *Is It Righetous to Be?*, 117.
38. Ibid., 182.
39. Levinas, "Violence of the Face," 175.
40. See Bernasconi "Rereading *Totality and Infinity*," and Morgan, *Discovering Levinas*, chapter 2, for illuminating discussions of this question.
41. Levinas, "Philosophy and Transcendence," 32.
42. Critchley, "Introduction," 27.
43. Levinas, "Transcendence and Height," 23.
44. The dedication to *Otherwise Than Being* reads as follows: "To the memory of those who were closest among the six million assassinated by the National Socialists, and of the millions on millions of all confessions and all nations, victims of the same hatred of the other man, the same anti-semitism." For Levinas, who described his life and work as "dominated by the presentiment and the memory of the Nazi horror," the devastating disasters of the twentieth century and Western philosophy bear a secret affinity: "The visage of being that shows itself in war is fixed in the concept of totality, which dominates Western philosophy" (*Totality and Infinity*, 21).
45. Levinas's most extreme formulation claims that even "the extermination of living beings" does not affect the face, because the face is "not of the world" (*Totality and Infinity*, 198). As Davis comments, "His reference to extermination is uncomfortably reminiscent of the Holocaust and other modern atrocities. So the belief that the face, in Levinas's very specific philosophical sense, is unharmed seems disturbingly reticent about the countless people who were harmed. Bluntly, the fact that the Other survived Auschwitz unscathed seems incalculably less important than the murder of those who did not" (Davis, *Levinas*, 51).
46. Perpich, *The Ethics of Emmanuel Levinas*, 3.
47. Critchley, "Introduction," 27.

48. Ibid., 12.

49. Davis, *Levinas*, 49.

50. Responsibility cannot be evaded entirely because while murder is always a possibility, even the killing of another, according to Levinas, does not destroy the Other, who in some sense remains inviolable. See note 45 for this chapter concerning the immortality of the face.

51. Critchley, "Introduction," 28.

52. Morgan, *Discovering Levinas*, 278, 282.

53. Robbins, *Is It Righteous to Be?*, 47. Conversely, evil is defined as indifference to the Other (55).

54. Levinas, "Philosophy, Justice and Love," 109. As Diane Perpich points out, although there is disagreement concerning the degree to which Levinas's ethics can be described as normative, the vast majority of secondary work aims to use Levinas's work precisely to support particular normative ends or projects (Perpich, *The Ethics of Emmanuel Levinas*, 9).

55. Robbins, *Is It Righteous to Be?*, 225, 235.

56. Ibid., 231.

57. Enrique Dussel writes that Levinas advances "an anti-politics of the Totality, yet he says nothing about a politics of liberation" (Dussel, "'The Politics' by Levinas," 81).

58. Levinas, *Totality and Infinity*, 21. The specter of Hobbes looms large in Levinas's thought and largely defines the understanding of politics that he juxtaposes to ethics. But Levinas also questions whether it might be possible to refuse Hobbesian egoism in the name of another political possibility. In the closing to *Otherwise Than Being*, Levinas writes, "It is then not without importance to know if the egalitarian and just State in which man is fulfilled (and which is to be set up, and especially to be maintained) proceeds from a war of all against all, or from the irreducible responsibility of the one for all, and if it can do without friendship and faces" (159–60).

59. Levinas, "Transcendence and Height," 23.

60. Levinas, "Uniqueness," 195.

61. Levinas, "Dialogue on Thinking-of-the-Other," 202.

62. Robbins, *Is It Righteous to Be?*, 133.

63. Levinas, *Otherwise Than Being*, 157. Here Levinas seems to describe the appearance of the third party in chronological terms, as though it comes after the face-to-face encounter, disrupting it. But Levinas also denies that such a division exists, indicating that the third party is actually there from the start (*Totality and Infinity*, 213). Robert Bernasconi argues, "If Levinas, perhaps somewhat clumsily, attempted at times to express the relation of the ethical to the political by according a chronological priority of the face of the Other over the third party, his more careful formulations avoided casting it within a narrative idiom" (Bernasconi, "The Third Party," 80).

64. Levinas, "Peace and Proximity," 168.

65. Levinas, "The Other, Utopia, and Justice," 229; Levinas, "Uniqueness," 195. See also Levinas, *Otherwise Than Being*, 157–58; Levinas, "Philosophy, Justice and Love," 104–5; and Levinas, "The Proximity of the Other," 101.

66. Peperzak, *To the Other*, 168.

67. Levinas, *Totality and Infinity*, 213.

68. Levinas, *Otherwise Than Being*, 158. At one point in *Totality and Infinity*, Levinas also positions the third party, another Other, in a slightly more specific sense, as he "whom in the midst of his destitution the Other already serves" (157). This indicates that the Other who obliges me is also under an infinite obligation because he too is faced by another Other. The third party is Other to "my" Other.

69. Levinas, "The Proximity of the Other," 107.

70. Levinas, *Otherwise Than Being*, 159.

71. Levinas, "The Other, Utopia, and Justice," 229.

72. Levinas, "Philosophy, Justice, and Love," 104.

73. Robbins, *Is It Righteous to Be?*, 67.

74. Levinas, "The Proximity of the Other," 101–2. See also Levinas, "Peace and Proximity," 142.

75. Levinas, "Uniqueness," 195. See also Levinas, "Dialogue on Thinking-of-the-Other," 202–3, concerning the task of comparison ushered in by the third.

76. See Levinas, "Philosophy, Justice and Love," 105, and Levinas, "Uniqueness," 195, among others.

77. Robbins, *Is It Righteous to Be?*, 67.

78. Caygill, *Levinas and the Political*, 3.

79. Herzog, "Is Liberalism 'All We Need'?," 211–13.

80. Bernasconi, "The Third Party," 83; Morgan, *Discovering Levinas*, 24.

81. Herzog, "Is Liberalism 'All We Need'?"

82. Levinas, "Useless Suffering," 94.

83. Levinas, "Philosophy, Justice, and Love," 105.

84. Robbins, *Is It Righteous to Be?*, 100.

85. Ibid., 132.

86. Levinas, "Peace and Proximity," 144.

87. Levinas, "The Proximity of the Other," 108.

88. Alford, "Levinas and Political Theory," 157.

89. Ibid., 164.

90. Simmons, "The Third," 98.

91. Wingenbach, "Refusing the Temptation of Innocence," 230; Davis, *Levinas*, 53.

92. As Tocqueville famously worried, the existence of an "immense protective power" that "foresees and supplies [citizens'] necessities" may constitute a novel form of despotism, within which citizens are a flock of "timid and hardworking animals" and the government is "the shepherd" (Tocqueville, *Democracy in America*, vol. 2, part 4, chapter 6).

93. Critchley, *Infinitely Demanding*, 8.

94. Critchley, however, seems to mis-ascribe this element of approval to Levinas himself (ibid., 57, 61).

95. Ibid., 49, 51.

96. Ibid., 62.

97. Ibid., 11.

98. Ibid., 113. Critchley also cites mobilizations against intervention in Iraq by the

United Kingdom and the United States, protests at the Republican National Convention in 2004, and groups like Pink Bloc and Billionaires for Bush as examples of "direct democratic action."

99. Ibid., 93.

100. Ibid., 125–26.

101. Rancière, "Does Democracy Mean Something?," esp. 59–61.

102. Critchley, *Infinitely Demanding*, 94, 119, 120. To Critchley, *democratization* refers to a mobile, ongoing struggle for "true democracy." It involves "working in common at a certain distance from the state, working toward control of the place from which one acts and speaks, working together in a situation as a political subject committed to a plan, a place, a space, a process" (115, 118).

103. In earlier writing Critchley tended to characterize Levinasian ethics in these terms. See Critchley, "Five Problems in Levinas's View of Politics." In *Infinitely Demanding*, ethics has not lost its disruptive power, but it is bound up with a kind of politics and is not only the hiatus of politics.

104. Critchley borrows the phrase "true democracy" from Marx to signify "a truth that no state incarnates" but toward which "democratization" forever aspires (Critchley, *Infinitely Demanding*, 115). He characterizes "the ethical experience of infinite responsibility at the heart of subjectivity" as "metapolitical" (119).

105. Critchley claims that *metapolitical* should not be construed as prepolitical or nonpolitical, but he provides no defense of this supposed distinction (*Infinitely Demanding*, 120).

106. Poppendieck, *Sweet Charity?*, 253. Poppendieck envisions the possibility of "turning kitchens and pantries into free spaces, places where people can meet and interact across the gulf of social class and the divisions of race and ethnicity, not as givers and receivers . . . but as . . . fellow citizens." She cites rare efforts to transform charitable food giving into cooperative endeavors of self-determination (316–17).

107. Ibid., 5.

108. Ibid., 270.

109. Ibid., 290.

110. Ibid., 5.

111. Ibid., 12, 296.

112. This term, from Tocqueville, looms large in the political science literature on civic education and civic skills in relation to political participation.

113. Putnam's *Bowling Alone* forwards a rather amorphous notion of social capital, inconsistently used both descriptively and normatively and identified with participation in community organizations such as the Rotary and Elks clubs, bowling leagues, and choirs as well as with conventional forms of political participation such as voting and petition signing. Putnam's book purports to track the decline in American social capital since 1965, which he claims is evident on these social and political fronts. Among many problems with Putnam's argument, his basic contention that Americans became less engaged in collective life after 1965 is deeply suspect since that date marks the advent of some of the most important social movements in U.S. history. By focusing on bridge clubs and dinner parties, on the one hand, and voting and petition signing, on the other, Putnam arguably

misses the most interesting forms of American civic engagement of the last century. Moreover, if we take those excluded social movements and forms of direct democratic action seriously, Putnam's suggestion that a decline in certain kinds of localized group memberships is mirrored by and even contributes to political disaffection is thrown into question.

114. Brady, Verba, and Schlozman, "Beyond SES." See also Verba, Schlozman, and Brady, *Voice and Equality.* "Civic skills," according to the authors, are a resource (along with time and money) that can explain differing levels of political activity among citizens, especially activities requiring time, such as working on a campaign, contacting government officials, protesting, engaging in informal community activity, and serving on local governing boards or attending board meetings. Civic skills, they say, are partly "acquired and honed" in the nonpolitical institutions of adult life, including the workplace, voluntary associations, and churches ("Beyond SES," 273). For such skills to be developed in nonpolitical organizations, however, specific opportunities to learn, improve, and maintain skills must be available: "Simply being involved with nonpolitical institutions does not foster political activity" (280–81). Thus, the type of involvement is key. Only certain "skill-acts" such as writing a letter, going to a meeting where decisions are made, planning or chairing a meeting, or giving a presentation or speech develop "competencies" that can help explain political participation. Many forms of participation in charitable organizations, in which volunteers execute predefined tasks, are unlikely to involve such skill-acts.

115. Eliasoph, *Avoiding Politics.* Eliasoph's three case studies—of volunteer groups, recreational groups, and activist groups—reveal what she calls a "shrinking circle of concern" among citizens. Although the volunteers, members of an antidrug organization and a parents' group supporting a local high school, sometimes revealed "deeper political awareness" when "backstage," in their work together they continued to focus attention on tasks that they defined as unpolitical and as "close to home," unconnected to the broader world. Eliasoph shows that their participation was often limited to "lending a hand to pre-set projects" (50) (such as fundraising) rather than engaging in discussion about what ends should be pursued. Activity focused on helping individuals "one person at a time" rather than on transforming institutions of group life (55). In fact, "in group meetings, volunteers never drew connections between their everyday acts of charity and public issues" (24). Her persuasive account of "political evaporation" raises a significant challenge to volunteering as the "hegemonic image of good citizenship" (25). See also Eliasoph, *Making Volunteers,* which is also rooted in participant research and confirms the earlier analysis of the depoliticizing character of volunteer activity. Here the focus is on so-called Empowerment Projects, hybrid entities funded by government, nonprofit, and private funds which aim to "transform people" and cure social ills by "empowering" those who are currently marginalized (by including them, however unequally, in volunteer organizations). The provision of narrow, hierarchical aid to the needy is combined with an emphasis on self-transformation as the route to collective social change, a mixture that seems to blend what I have called therapeutic ethics with charitable ethics.

116. See esp. Eliasoph, *Making Volunteers*, chapter 5.

117. Ibid., 92–94.

118. Theda Skocpol notes that volunteer efforts are often "professionally coordinated or one-shot sporadic undertakings" that, though worthy, involve people "'doing for' others—feeding the needy at church soup kitchens, tutoring children at an after-school clinic, or guiding visitors at a museum exhibit—rather than 'doing with' fellow citizens as ongoing members of a shared group" (*Diminished Democracy*, 227). In addition, even in charitable volunteer organizations that explicitly aim to include disadvantaged as well as more privileged people among their participants, social inequality continues to materialize and structure the relations between them, as Eliasoph shows. For example, among youth volunteers who were supposed to be working together as equals in civic engagement projects, disadvantaged youth, constantly exposed to public speeches about them, often "spoke of themselves as outcomes and variables; they understood that they were the main problem to solve," while nondisadvantaged youth assumed "they were supposed to solve the problems" of others (Eliasoph, *Making Volunteers*, 20).

119. Poppendieck, *Sweet Charity*, 19.

120. Butler and Connolly, "Politics, Power and Ethics." Butler has also written, "I have worried that the return to ethics has constituted an escape from politics, and I've also worried that it's meant a certain heightening of moralism and this has made me cry out, as Nietzsche cried out about Hegel, 'Bad air! Bad air!'" ("Ethical Ambivalence," 15). Among those who identify an ethical turn in Butler's own *oeuvre*, though with quite varied assessments of its meaning, are Mills, "Normative Violence, Vulnerability, and Responsibility"; Dean, "Change of Address: Butler's Politics at Sovereignty's Deadlock"; Boucher, "The Politics of Performativity."

121. Lloyd, *Judith Butler*, esp. chapter 6, and Chambers and Carver, *Judith Butler and Political Theory*, esp. chapter 4.

122. Butler, "1999 Preface," vii–xxviii.

123. Lloyd, *Judith Butler*, 134.

124. See Mills, "Normative Violence, Vulnerability and Responsibility," for an interesting reading of Butler that posits a contradiction between her earlier analysis of subjectification as a process involving "normative violence" and her later call for a "nonviolent ethics." Mills argues that Butler's explicitly ethical work, by celebrating nonviolence as such, departs from her previous conceptualization of normative violence without addressing this shift. According to Butler's earlier work, all norms, which "we cannot do without," are constraining and exclusionary (as well as enabling). Mills claims that Butler's nonviolent ethics is at odds with this account of norms as being necessarily violent. I think Mills is right about the further question this insight begs: Are there perhaps two different modes or types of violence at issue here? What exactly is normative violence and "can it be thought in a way that allows for a nonviolence in its midst"? (152). Though Mills articulates this important question, she does not pursue it.

125. Butler, *Precarious Life*, 134. See also Butler, *Giving an Account of Oneself*, 100, on "common vulnerability."

126. Butler's focus on common vulnerability is echoed by Stephen K. White's empha-

sis on mortality—or "our subjection to death"—as a source of connection and equality among human beings that can support a modern ethos. He argues that an appreciation of our universal mortality can enhance the "presumptive generosity" we show toward others. Like Butler, White tends to present mortality as an absolute universal, without exploring how mortality is figured, signified, or variously politicized in ways that encourage or discourage the egalitarian democratic politics he supports. See White, *The Ethos of a Late Modern Citizen*. See also Honig, "Antigone's Two Laws," for an insightful conceptualization of "mortalist humanism" as a key dimension of the "ethical turn." She identifies this resurgent form of humanism with the work of Butler, White, and Nicole Loraux.

127. Butler, *Frames of War*, 54.
128. Butler, *Precarious Life*, xii. *Interdependency* means "the subject that I am is bound up with the subject that I am not" (Butler, *Frames of War*, 40).
129. Butler, *Precarious Life*, 31.
130. Ibid., 22–27.
131. Ibid., 22.
132. Vázquez-Arroyo, "Responsibility, Violence, and Catastrophe," 102, 101.
133. Shulman, "Acknowledgement and Disavowal as an Idiom for Theorizing Politics."
134. Butler, *Frames of War*, 25. The distinction between precariousness and precarity is also conceptualized by Butler as a distinction between universal and differential vulnerability (*Precarious Life*, 39, 32, 44). Vázquez-Arroyo charges Butler with disavowing "any socio-political analysis of vulnerability" which would involve addressing "the various degrees of vulnerability that political subjects experience in scenes of power that are mediated by structural inequalities of class, gender, and status" ("Responsibility, Violence, and Catastrophe," 102). He does not address Butler's notion of precarity or explain whether the distinction she draws between precariousness and precarity is at all useful in this regard.
135. Butler, *Frames of War*, 22.
136. Ibid., 14.
137. Ibid., 2; see also 22, where precariousness "imposes . . . ethical obligations." In a different formulation, precariousness "grounds" positive social obligations (22).
138. Ibid., 180.
139. Ibid., 179.
140. On the notion of derealization, see esp. Butler, *Precarious Life*, 33–34.
141. Other readers of Butler affirm a chronology according to which Butler's ethics are preparatory for politics. For example, although Sara Rushing asserts that Butler does not prioritize ethics over politics, she claims in "Preparing for Politics" that Butler conceptualizes an ethics of generosity, humility, patience, and restraint that "precedes and informs" political interactions.
142. Shulman, "Acknowledgment and Disavowal as an Idiom for Theorizing Politics."
143. Butler, *Frames of War*, 23.
144. Lloyd, *Judith Butler*, 154–55. The phrase "struggles against the norm" is from Butler, *Undoing Gender*, 13.
145. Lloyd, "Toward a Cultural Politics of Vulnerability," 103–4.
146. Honig makes a similar point when she wagers that "only in a world as seemingly

bereft as our own of meaningful political engagement, a world in which way too much time is spent in the (proverbial) gym, could ethos seems such a promising alternative way" to the lessons of self-decentering supplied by political participation ("The Politics of Ethos," 428). Despair figures somewhat differently but also prominently in the "reversal of the flow of time" that Rancière attributes to the ethical turn. He alleges that recent work focused on the category of ethics is not "turned towards an end to be accomplished" but is "turned towards the catastrophe behind us," the Holocaust ("The Ethical Turn of Aesthetics and Politics," 192).

147. Shulman, "Acknowledgment and Disavowal as an Idiom for Theorizing Politics." Shulman is here contrasting James Baldwin's conceptualization of disavowal and acknowledgment, which he interprets as thoroughly political, with Butler's. Noting that Baldwin understood that only collective action "could force whites to count blacks as real," Shulman argues, "Community originates, if at all, when public performance of 'no justice, no peace' compels a response; ethical 'acknowledgement' might *follow* such a political moment but rarely (ever?) precedes it."

148. Critchley, *Infinitely Demanding*, 40, 56.

149. Shulman, "Acknowledgment and Disavowal as an Idiom for Theorizing Politics." Shulman argues that Butler does not avow the politics of her own definition of vulnerability, which conceives of it almost exclusively in terms of state violence and not, say, of climate change or economic dispossession. He further points out that Butler fails to recognize "that acknowledgment of mortal precariousness does not yield only one outcome." The meaning of *precariousness* is politically contingent, as any reading of Hobbes will show.

150. The adoption of a world-centered vocabulary is not, on its own, enough to shift one from the intimacy of the charitable dyad to the complexity of associational activity among coactors who aim to affect the conditions of their lives. Luce Irigaray, for example, uses the language of world in *Sharing the World* to describe a (potentially hospitable) self/Other relation that involves a confrontation between two utterly unique worlds. Thus, despite the title of her book, Irigaray's approach privileges a dyadic encounter between two beings understood to occupy entirely distinct, singular worlds (1, 3, 63, 68, 86, 70). Save for one fleeting reference to "a new world" that might exist between otherwise wholly separate subjects (23), there is no account in this work of the world as something which exceeds any particular subject or subjects and which can both link and separate persons (see chapters 3 and 4).

## 3. DEMOCRATIC ETHICS OF CARE

1. The democratic ethos defended here involves turning from "the question of the subject" to "the question of the world." This is Linda Zerilli's description of the reorientation she pursues in relation to the meaning of feminist freedom (*Feminism and the Abyss of Freedom*, introduction). The question of the subject in ethical thought, as I've tried to show, actually takes two forms, depending on whether the self or the Other is cast as the focal point. But in both cases, the significance of the extrasubjective world, which I argue is the recipient of a distinctively democratic practice of care, is obscured.

2. Regarding the title of the book, see the letter written to Karl Jaspers by Arendt on August 6, 1955, in Arendt and Jaspers, *Correspondence 1926–1969*, 263–64. The idea of *amor mundi*, though not always referred to by this name, is especially important to Arendt's arguments concerning "world-alienation" in chapter 6 of *The Human Condition* and to her distinction between conscience as a form of concern for the self and political action as a form of concern for the world in "Civil Disobedience" and in the essays collected in *Responsibility and Judgment*.

3. For other efforts to expand on Arendt's conception of *amor mundi*, though quite different from this project, see Biskowski, "Practical Foundations for Political Judgment"; Breen, "Agonism, Antagonism, and the Necessity of Care"; Chiba, "Hannah Arendt on Love and the Political." Although all three articles claim to interpret and develop Arendt's notion of "love for the world," only Biskowski carefully theorizes the second half of the term, *mundi*, so as to specify what is distinctive about care, love, or concern directed at the world rather than at other persons.

4. Arendt praises Gotthold Ephraim Lessing for "always taking sides for the world's sake" ("On Humanity in Dark Times," 7–8). Her account of civil disobedience stresses that such associative activity expressed concern for the fate of the world. Arendt uses the examples of individual conscientious objection and collective civil disobedience (in response to the Vietnam War) to illustrate her distinction between moral and political action, identified with care for the self and care for the world, respectively. Thoreau serves as the representative of a moral outlook directed at keeping one's hands clean and maintaining personal integrity by abstaining from conduct that would offend one's conscience. Arendt contrasts this type of moral action with political action undertaken by a group that aims to transform a worldly practice, policy, or law ("Civil Disobedience," 58–68).

5. Arendt does not present an ethics as such, yet the argument I make here, which engages with Arendt's thought to conceptualize a worldly ethics, challenges readings which allege that Arendt's conception of politics is simply amoral. Benhabib, *The Reluctant Modernism of Hannah Arendt*, and Kateb, *Hannah Arendt*, for example, criticize Arendt for failing to provide any moral foundations to guide and constrain politics. While it is true that Arendt rejects the notion of an absolute normative ground that sanctions political life, her work as a whole, I believe, is animated by a distinctive ethical outlook—*amor mundi*—which is too often overlooked. Though this idea cannot provide the universal "metanorms" Benhabib seeks or the transcendent moral principles Kateb desires, it is important to appreciate that a powerful ethical sensibility informs Arendt's account of politics.

6. For example, in Noddings's *Caring*, a mother's care for her child is treated as paradigmatic of caring as such and serves as a model for the ethics of Eros, or feminine spirit, she advances.

7. Nel Noddings, who helped inaugurate the inquiry into care ethics, explicitly rejected the extension of such ethics to political life, claiming that "nonrational" care cannot survive institutionalization. Although many other care theorists have criticized this view, the model of an individual caregiver (implicitly or explicitly gendered as feminine) and a particularly dependent person (a baby, an elderly

parent) continues to dominate. For example, Virginia Held argues for the political relevance of care but does so largely by analogizing the state to a caregiver/ mother. Her theory does not address the possibility of care for conditions enacted by citizens in association with one another and, indeed, barely addresses whether the welfare state she defends involves or requires democratic participation of any kind (Held, *The Ethics of Care*).

8. Tronto, *Moral Boundaries*, 103.

9. Ibid., 107.

10. Ibid., 175.

11. Ibid., x.

12. Arendt, *The Human Condition*, 52. The language of world is prominent in Martin Heidegger's work as well. Arendt gives Heidegger credit for his central conception of human existence as being-in-the-world, noting that this understanding seems to challenge the philosophical tradition's concern with "man in the singular" and disregard for human plurality. Heidegger's idea of being-in-the-world has the merit, Arendt thinks, of pointing toward the reality of our life "together with others" and thereby decentering the singular subject (Arendt, "Concern with Politics in Recent European Philosophical Thought," 443). The promise of this innovation goes unfulfilled, however, according to Arendt, because Heidegger's hostile portrait of *Das Man* supports "an ideal of the self that measured authenticity in terms of a *withdrawal* from social relations" (Villa, *Arendt and Heidegger*, 232). Arendt charges that "the most essential character of the [Heideggerean] Self is its absolute Self-ness, its radical separation from all its fellows" (Arendt, "What Is Existential Philosophy?," 181). According to this view, Heidegger's thought, despite its ostensibly this-worldly character, paradoxically expresses modern worldlessness.

13. Arendt, *The Human Condition*, 2.

14. Pitkin, *The Attack of the Blob*, 303n93.

15. Arendt, *The Origins of Totalitarianism*, 301. The concept of world building challenges Mary Dietz's claim that political instrumentality is "always formulated negatively" by Arendt (Dietz, "The Slow Boring of Hard Boards," 885n25).

16. Arendt, *The Human Condition*, 9. See also Arendt, "Introduction into Politics," 107.

17. Arendt, *The Human Condition*, 257–73.

18. Matt Richtel, "Hooked on Gadgets and Paying a Mental Price," *New York Times*, June 6, 2010.

19. Timothy Morton, for example, rejects the language of world, along with that of Nature and the environment, on the grounds that these terms connote an "alien and alienated" out there, separate from human beings, and thereby betray the "ecological thought" — the total interconnection of everything (Morton, *The Ecological Thought*, 5; see also 30).

20. In this respect world is not entirely unlike Sartre's understanding of the milieu, described by Iris Young as "the already-there set of material things and collectivized habits against the background of which any particular action occurs" (Young, "Gender as Seriality," 726).

21. Tocqueville, *Democracy in America*, vol. 2, 510.

22. Arendt, "Introduction into Politics," 128.

23. Arendt, "What Is Freedom?," 156. The uncertainty of outcomes is emphasized by Arendt's conception of action as being irreversible and unpredictable. On changing the world, see esp. *The Human Condition*, chapter 5, and Arendt, "Civil Disobedience," 77.

24. Heidegger, "The Thing," 174. See also *Oxford English Dictionary*, 2d ed., first sense: "a meeting, assembly, esp. a deliberative or juridical assembly, a court, a council."

25. Heidegger, "The Thing," 165–86.

26. Coles, "Moving Democracy," 234.

27. Ibid., 229–35.

28. Latour, "From Realpolitik to Dingpolitik," 16.

29. Pitkin, "Justice: On Relating Private and Public," 329.

30. Rancière, *Disagreement*, 55. He sometimes presents this "assertion of a common world" as an act that occurs in connection with the collision of two incommensurable orders or worlds (42–43).

31. Ibid., 51.

32. Ibid., 52.

33. Ibid., 12, xii.

34. Ibid., 58, 53.

35. Ibid., 50.

36. Ibid., 58.

37. Rancière, Lecture, Northwestern University, April 1, 2003.

38. Barr, *Political Machines*, chapter 8.

39. Rancière, *Disagreement*, 56–58, and Rancière, "Does Democracy Mean Something?," 60.

40. Gomart and Hajer, "Is *That* Politics?," 46–47.

41. Marres, "No Issue, No Public," chapter 4.

42. Latour writes, "We don't assemble because we agree, look alike, feel good, are socially compatible, or wish to fuse together," but "because we are drawn together by divisive matters of concern" ("From Realpolitik to Dingpolitik," 23).

43. Bennett, *Vibrant Matter*, viii.

44. Ibid., 122.

45. Ibid., xvii.

46. On the term *actant*, see Latour, *Pandora's Hope*, 180. *Collective* is his term for a confederation of actants that generate effects (*Politics of Nature*, 61). Latour argues that the idea of the collective should replace the "civil war" expressed in the subject/object opposition with a more accurate portrait of "civil collaboration" between humans and nonhumans (ibid., 73).

47. Latour, *Pandora's Hope*, 182. See also Latour, *Politics of Nature*, 237, on association.

48. Latour, *Pandora's Hope*, 180.

49. Bennett, *Vibrant Matter*, 23.

50. Ibid., 24.

51. Bennett argues against the tendency to depict the array of nonhuman entities as a structure, a representation that suggests a "stolid whole" that acts either as a constraint on human agency or as an enabling background for it (*Vibrant Matter*, 29,

35). She asks what would happen if we saw nonhuman materialities as "bona fide participants rather than as recalcitrant objects, social constructs, or instrumentalities" (62).

52. Bennett, *Vibrant Matter*, 108. She pushes this point further, arguing that the "scope of democratization can be broadened to acknowledge more nonhumans in more ways, in something like the ways in which we have come to hear the political voices of other humans formerly on the outs" (109).

53. Bennett makes this point when she amends her account of "thing-power," noting that it lends itself to "an atomistic rather than congregational understanding of agency" (*Vibrant Matter*, 20).

54. I am using the category human in a relatively uncritical way throughout, though I believe one should be cautious about treating present-day divisions between humans and nonhumans as fixed and immovable. For a consideration of the historically variable construction of the category human, see Fernandez-Armesto, *Humankind: A Brief History*.

55. I take the term *coexistentialism* from Timothy Morton. It captures the insight that "existence is always co-existence": we live in a condition of "radical intimacy" (*The Ecological Thought*, 47). This outlook is shared by Morton, Bennett, and Latour, even though the term is not.

56. Bennett, *Vibrant Matter*, 95–96. Although Bennett, following Darwin, acknowledges that worms' contributions to human history and culture are unplanned, she cites Darwin's claim that worms do not simply follow impulse but make what seem to be free, unpredictable decisions (96).

57. Bennett at times suggests that anthropomorphism, though problematic, is an important way of challenging anthropocentrism, so that a "chord is struck between person and thing (*Vibrant Matter*, 120). Steven Shaviro echoes this point: "A certain cautious anthropomorphism is necessary in order to avoid anthropocentrism" ("The Universe of Things" online, unpaginated).

58. Bennett, *Vibrant Matter*, 104, 108.

59. Ibid., 103.

60. Marres, "No Issue, No Public," 54. See also Marres, "Frontstaging Nonhumans," esp. 191–99. See Dewey, *The Public and Its Problems*, 47, 13.

61. Dewey, *The Public and Its Problems*, 39. Dewey does not acknowledge any difference between those who are affected by an action and those who form as a public seeking redress for that problem. He seems to conflate "the affected" with those who insist that a matter be "cared for," eliding the fact that many may be affected by a problem (and thus amount to a certain kind of collectivity) without there being any organized response to it.

62. Ibid., 16.

63. Ibid., 21.

64. The most influential text in this regard is Olson, *The Logic of Collective Action*.

65. See, for example, Seyd and Whitely, *Labour's Grass Roots*; Schlozman, Verba, and Brady, "Participation's Not a Paradox"; Wilson, *Political Organizations*. These texts all expand the category of incentives that are held to influence citizen participation in collective action and thereby challenge rational choice approaches.

66. Wilson, *Political Organizations*, chapter 3. His understanding of purposive incentives is echoed by Seyd's and Whitely's conceptualization of "collective incentives," according to which individuals not only assess their immediate personal costs and benefits but also think about group welfare and collective goods. Although Seyd and Whitely acknowledge that these sorts of motivations are susceptible to the "free rider" problem formulated by Olson, they argue that, contra Olson, people regularly "think collectively rather than individually" and therefore may "rationally" choose to work with others if associative action appears more capable of achieving the outcomes they identify as collective goods (Seyd and Whitely, *Labour's Grass Roots*, chapter 4).

67. Markell, "The Rule of the People," 12, 7. Markell's analysis emphasizes events in particular as occasions for democratic response, building on his interpretation of Arendt's notion of beginning as a way of marking the irrevocability of actual events. Without disputing this very compelling account of Arendtian beginning, I think it makes sense to extend Markell's insight regarding action as a "second rather than a first step" to a range of worldly phenomena, not all of which are specific, episodic events but which can and do serve as "occasions for response."

68. Scholz, *Political Solidarity*, 21–27, 33–38. Scholz cites a particular goal as the source of the bond among participants in political solidarity, but she also specifies that the goal must involve challenging injustice (21). Scholz's "political solidarity" is restricted to projects with social justice as their end (54). Identifying the practice of solidarity with certain substantive ends may be worthwhile (I do something similar in chapter 4 when I elaborate upon care for the world as a normative project). Yet Scholz tends to write as though social justice is a self-evident end that allows one to distinguish good from bad forms of collective organizing.

69. Ibid., 125.

70. The term *project-related* is from Rippe, "Diminishing Solidarity," 355.

71. Allen, "Solidarity after Identity Politics," 112. Other modes of resistance practiced by the Danish people included the government's refusal to hand over German Jews who had sought refuge in Denmark (on the grounds that they were no longer German citizens), widespread hiding of Jews by non-Jewish Danes, and the payment by wealthy Danish citizens for Jews to enter Sweden, where they could receive work permits. Allen argues that this case exemplifies a form of solidarity that is especially relevant to feminism, according to which "one need not 'be' a woman to join in the collective effort to resist women's subordination" (ibid.).

72. Dean, *Solidarity of Strangers*, 17–22.

73. Dean's "affectional" solidarity misses the possibility of shared rather than reciprocal emotions among participants. James Jasper distinguishes between reciprocal emotions, or "participants' ongoing feelings toward each other," to which Dean refers, and shared emotions, which are held by a group at the same time. These shared emotions do not have other group members as their object, but, as I would put it, a worldly thing (Jasper, "The Emotions of Protest," 417).

74. Dean does briefly dismiss what she regards as "tactical solidarity" in which a coalition forms in pursuit of certain goals, claiming that solidarity is thereby "reduced to a means" (*Solidarity of Strangers*, 27).

75. Marres, "No Issue, No Public," 47, 29. See also Marres, "Issues Spark a Public into Being."

76. Marres, "No Issue, No Public," 98, 129, for the World Bank's EIR as an example of such a disputed object. Although Marres cites Dewey for his insights into how publics are generated in response to issues, her account stresses the contentious character of publics in ways that defy Dewey's theory. She puts it mildly: "Dewey did not sufficiently appreciate that actors are likely to be *antagonistically* implicated in an issue" (89). See also Marres, "Issues Spark a Public into Being," 215–16.

77. Marres, "No Issue, No Public," 58, 130.

78. Ibid., 133, 128. According to Marres, a public must entail open disagreement—the expression of "exclusive attachments"—or it is not a genuine public. For an issue such as climate change to be publicized, for example, means that "the oil company can't be ignored or downplayed; the constraints it puts on addressing climate change must be taken seriously, and vice versa" (130). There is an unacknowledged tension, however, between the stress Marres places on controversy and antagonism as defining features of a public and her emphasis on the "settlement" of issues as the very purpose of democratic struggle. If settlement is the telos of democratic action, how is this end to be combined with the desire to keep issues open to the widest possible range of perspectives?

79. Marres, "No Issue, No Public," 129. She says that the issue networks that formed on the Internet around the EIR were "publics-in-the-making" (133). The EIR was "framed as an object of concern in accessible media such as the web" and the "divergences between actors' various attachments, and indeed their mutual exclusivity, were made manifest" (129). Yet Marres does not think a genuine public came into existence because of the relatively limited involvement of "lay citizens" in a controversy in which corporations and NGOs played the key roles (133).

80. The suggestion that failure to endorse a particular model of ethics on offer is tantamount to endorsing a Kantian command morality can be found in Bennett, *The Enchantment of Modern Life*, 152, and Connolly, *Why I Am Not a Secularist*, 150.

81. According to the United Nations, more than one billion people are hungry—or, in bureaucratic parlance, suffer from food insecurity—throughout the world. In the United States, thirty-six million people suffer from hunger, according to the USDA.

82. Namely, grains are disproportionately grown to make feed for animals (to be consumed by the world's wealthy) rather than to be used as food for humans.

83. As I pointed out in chapter 2, hunger appears regularly in Levinas's writings as a characteristic of the Other to whom I am called to respond.

## 4. PARTISANSHIP FOR THE WORLD

1. Lawrence Biskowski believes that Arendt's notion of world is endowed with "substantive moral content" and that *amor mundi* is meant to serve as an "ethical foundation" for action and judgment. Although I think Biskowski relies on an overly foundational vocabulary that is at odds with Arendt's account of judging, his core claim, namely, that Arendt believes amor mundi can and should orient politics, is apt (Biskowski, "Practical Foundations for Political Judgment," 870).

2. As I will argue, when Arendt refers to the world as being common, she too is

making a normative claim, to the effect that the world *should* serve to connect and separate us.

3. Arendt, "On Humanity in Dark Times," 16; Arendt, *The Human Condition*, 52.

4. The very idea of home has been persuasively challenged by feminist critics, including Bonnie Honig in "Difference, Dilemmas, and the Politics of Home." Honig draws on De Lauretis, "Eccentric Subjects," and Reagon, "Coalition Politics," to challenge the "phantasmatic imaginary of home" ("Difference, Dilemmas, and the Politics of Home," 270). Honig says that the "dream of home" conceals the extent to which home is in many cases not a site of safety where "life is preserved" and "people are fed." Indeed, the idealized vision of home not only neglects the realities of conflict and suffering that often characterize experiences of home life but may support the drive to violently bring "the dream of unitariness or home into being," at the level of both individual and nation (268, 270). Despite the problems that attend the concept of home, I use it here in relation to world in ways that are intended to challenge its privatized and exclusionary connotations. In addition, theorizing the world as simultaneously a shared home and in-between, as a potential site of nurturance as well as a space of contestation, resonates with Honig's persuasive call for home to be "recast in coalitional terms as the site of necessary nurturing but also strategic, conflicted, and temporary alliances" (269).

5. As David Beetham notes, three criteria are often used to evaluate any human rights claim: Is the invoked right "fundamental, universal, and clearly specifiable?" (*Democracy and Human Rights*, 210).

6. Amartya Sen referred to "freezing a list of capabilities for all societies" as a "denial of the reach of democracy," quoted in Srivivasan, "No Democracy without Justice," 457.

7. This is the list provided by Beetham, *Democracy and Human Rights*, 116. As Beetham notes, this list offers "a minimum agenda of economic and social rights" which is narrower than the array laid out in the UN's International Covenant on Economic, Social and Cultural Rights (1976). Beetham's list is very similar to what Sen calls "elementary capabilities": "being able to avoid such deprivations as starvation, under-nourishment, escapable morbidity and premature mortality." These elementary capabilities are part of a more comprehensive set of "substantive freedoms" that include, for example, literacy, which is part of Beetham's minimum (Sen, *Development as Freedom*, 36).

8. These two claims do not provide an exhaustive account of the implications or consequences of needs deprivation. For example, these arguments center the effects deprivation has on those who directly experience it. But a growing body of research documents the significant, though indirect, effects of severe poverty in the context of concentrated wealth, as in the United States. Here, the effects are on the democratic regime itself, as economic inequality threatens to undermine political equality. The widening economic gap in the United States, for example, has been shown repeatedly to generate oligarchic forms of government and to distort political decision making in favor of the richest citizens. See Bartels, *Unequal Democracy*; Gilens, "Inequality and Democratic Responsiveness"; Winters and Page, "Oligarchy in the U.S.?"

9. For discussion of the notion of a fully human life, see esp. Nussbaum, *Women and Human Development*, 70–74.

10. Proponents of the capabilities approach echo advocates of social and economic rights who insist that these rights must be included in a comprehensive set of human rights if more conventional, widely acknowledged political rights are to be truly exercisable. From this viewpoint, it is somewhat ironic that welfare rights are referred to as second-generation rights (in reference to having been added relatively recently to an expanding domain of human rights) when they appear to name the very precondition for the realizability of first-generation rights.

11. Capabilities, which concern what someone is able to do or be, are distinct from functions. As Nussbaum explains, "We shoot for capabilities, and those alone. Citizens must be free to determine their own course after that" (*Women and Human Development*, 87). This insistence on capabilities as the proper goal rests uneasily with Nussbaum's skepticism toward people's actual, often "mistaken" desires, expressed in the same book, 135–61 *passim*.

12. Ibid., 53–54.

13. Berlin, "Introduction," xlvi.

14. Arendt, *On Revolution*, 63, 68.

15. Arendt, *The Human Condition*, 28, 30.

16. Ibid., 30, 25, 30–31.

17. Ibid., 119–20. See also 83, where Arendt argues that the Greeks "felt it necessary to possess slaves because of the slavish nature of all occupations that served the needs for the maintenance of life."

18. Ibid., 45, 47.

19. Arendt, *On Revolution*, 60.

20. Ibid., 60–61.

21. Reinhardt, *The Art of Being Free*, 153.

22. Arendt, *On Revolution*, 94.

23. Reinhardt, *The Art of Being Free*, 151; Arendt, *The Human Condition*, 8.

24. Arendt, *On Revolution*, 60.

25. Reinhardt, *The Art of Being Free*, 153. The language of dictate and rule also contrasts with Arendt's depiction of political equality as a matter of *isonomy*, or no-rule. See Arendt, *On Revolution*, 30, and Arendt, *The Human Condition*, 220–30.

26. Arendt, *On Revolution*, 69. Arendt is quoting John Adams, *Discourses on Davila*.

27. Beltrán, "Going Public," 605.

28. Arendt, "Public Rights and Private Interests," 106–7.

29. Arendt, "Freedom and Politics," 202. See also Arendt, "What Is Freedom?" and *The Life of the Mind*, esp. 195–217.

30. Arendt, "On Hannah Arendt," 317–18.

31. Fraser, *Unruly Practices*, 161.

32. Ibid., 160. Fraser challenges the view that Arendt often seems to hold, of needs as "self-evident and beyond dispute" (ibid., 145). Honig argues, however, in "Toward an Agonistic Feminism," that because resistability is the sine qua non of Arendt's politics, her work supplies resources for challenging the boundaries she herself tries to establish, such as those between the private and the public.

33. Fraser, *Unruly Practices*, 166.

34. For information on AEC, see www.chicagoantieviction.org and Don Terry, "Foreclosed Home Is a Risky Move for Homeless Family," *New York Times*, June 25, 2011.

35. AEC's definition of housing as a human right is linked to its advocacy of the idea of adverse possession, which holds that land should belong to the people who live and work there. This concept is used by AEC to challenge foreclosures and evictions and to argue that those occupying and tending to a residence (even if not legal owners or renters) are entitled to live there. See Yana Kuchinoff, "The Chicago Anti-Conviction Campaign: Building a Movement from the Ground Up," *truthout*, November 17, 2010, available at www.truthout.org. AEC is also affiliated with Take Back the Land, a national network of organizations working to "elevate housing to the level of a human right"; it endorses breaking "immoral laws which allow banks to gain billions in profit while human beings are made homeless." See www.takebacktheland.org.

36. www.chicagoantieviction.org.

37. Ibid.

38. I would suggest, for example, that making the world a home also requires treating and protecting certain goods as collective, not privately owned, assets. Although the commons is used to refer to quite different sorts of potentially communally shared goods, including parks, the Internet, libraries, minerals, airwaves, and patents (some of which are rather more finite than others), the general idea of the commons is valuable for specifying resources that are best regarded as a form of shared wealth or common property, which ought to be protected from market enclosure. For a general—and polemical—defense of the commons, see Bollier, *Silent Theft*. For a discussion of the importance of protecting public space in particular from privatization, see Kohn, *Brave New Neighborhoods*.

39. John Alexander writes that Sen's readers tend to neglect the "institutional emphasis" of his thought, focusing on capabilities as "individual benefits" without paying adequate attention to the problem of "creating and sustaining the right type of institutions for the development of human capabilities" (Alexander, "Ending the Liberal Hegemony," 19–20).

40. Arendt, "On Humanity in Dark Times," 13.

41. Arendt, *The Human Condition*, 53.

42. Ibid., 52.

43. Reinhardt, *The Art of Being Free*, 144. In *The Human Condition* Arendt contrasts the commonality she traces to a mediating world with accounts that locate commonality in the nature of men (57–58).

44. See esp. Arendt, *The Human Condition*, chapter 6, where "world-alienation" defines the modern age.

45. Arendt, *The Human Condition*, 53.

46. Arendt, "Introduction into Politics," 128, 167.

47. Ibid., 175, 106.

48. Although some readers question Arendt's commitment to democratic politics (see, for example, Wolin, "Hannah Arendt"), interpreters such as Jeffrey Isaac and Alan Keenan have persuasively defended Arendt's democratic commitments. Against

the charge of elitism leveled at Arendt by Wolin, for example, Isaac's "Oases in the Desert" demonstrates that the categories of mass and elite in Arendt's work correspond to two different kinds of democratic politics rather than to two discrete classes of people—one large-scale and representative, the other localized and direct—and that the elite Arendt endorses in her celebration of the council system is best read as an example of grass-roots democratic politics. See also Keenan, *Democracy in Question*.

49. Arendt, "The Crisis in Culture," 223.

50. Arendt, "Introduction into Politics," 128–29. Arendt also declares here that "living in a real world and speaking with one another about it are basically one and the same."

51. Ibid., 175.

52. Arendt, "On Humanity in Dark Times," 24.

53. Ibid., 26, 30.

54. Arendt, "Philosophy and Politics," 80–82.

55. Arendt, "Freedom and Politics," 197.

56. Arendt, *The Human Condition*, 57, and "On Humanity in Dark Times," 31.

57. Arendt, "Introduction into Politics," 128.

58. Curtis, *Our Sense of the Real*, 91.

59. Arendt, "Thoughts on Politics and Revolution," 232.

60. As Tim Hayward points out in "Anthropocentrism," the term is sometimes used to describe a feature of human being-in-the-world that seems unavoidable. Insofar as humans are engaged in thinking and judgment, they necessarily think and judge as humans; they cannot escape this perspective. This means that even if, say, humans extend moral concern to nonhumans (as many do), they inevitably rely on human reference points to do so. Thus, anthropocentrism in this sense refers more precisely to the anthropogenic character of our concepts and values.

61. Human chauvinism refers to the tendency to specify relevant differences between beings in ways that invariably favor humans. See Routley and Routley, "Against the Inevitability of Human Chauvinism." Speciesism, akin to racism and sexism, refers to arbitrary discrimination on the basis of species (Hayward, "Anthropocentrism," 52). Hayward makes the important point that it is a mistake to define anthropocentrism as "excessive concern with humans" (the real problem, he says, is lack of concern with nonhumans), because the practices that are usually thereby criticized (hunting a species to extinction, destroying a forest to build a road, etc.) actually are in the interests of "one quite narrowly-defined group" and do not benefit humans as such (57–58).

62. There is extensive debate among environmental ethicists over whether nonhumans can be said to have interests. Peter Singer, for example, argues that the capacity to experience pleasure or pain is the criterion for ascribing interests to a being and thus that all mammals, birds, and probably vertebrates have interests, while other animals are dubious and plants are excluded ("Not for Humans Only").

63. *Mesh* is Timothy Morton's term, used in *The Ecological Thought* to capture the

totality in which humans and nonhumans, organic and inorganic matter are entangled. Although Morton rejects the terminology of world and life world for problematically distancing humans from a habitat or environment, I nonetheless use *mesh* here as a rough synonym for world in my sense.

64. This approach is at odds with Morton's *The Ecological Thought*, in which he contends that "we need reasons for acting that aren't bound up with self-interest" (119). On the other hand, Morton writes, "Since everything depends upon everything else, we have a very powerful argument for caring about things. The destruction of some things will affect other things" (35). Despite the vagueness of this statement, it seems to leave room for the possibility that concern for human survival might lead people to care about nonhuman entities.

65. Bennett, *Vibrant Matter*, ix–x.

66. For example, critics of the strongly nonanthropocentric view question the fruitfulness of ongoing metaphysical debates about the possibility of proving the existence of intrinsic value (a major preoccupation among environmental ethicists) and also wager that purely nonanthropocentric arguments are unlikely to be persuasive in policy contexts. See Light, "Contemporary Environmental Ethics."

67. Ibid., 436.

68. Ibid., 441.

69. Ibid., 444–45.

70. Ibid., 446, 434. In "Convergence and Contextualism," Bryan Norton argues in a similar vein that there is "convergence" among environmentalists who hold anthropocentric and nonanthropocentric views. In most policy contexts, consensus among environmentalists, despite disagreement in basic values, is possible, according to Norton. For a critique that charges Norton with neglecting the most difficult cases in which an anthropocentric argument in favor of environmental protection is not possible (for example, concerning the fate of the Delhi Sands fly in California), see Rolston, "Converging versus Reconstituting Environmental Ethics."

71. There is a growing consensus that problems of global hunger are best understood not as a function of inadequate supply but as the result of political and social arrangements. See Lappé, Collins, and Rosset, *World Hunger*; Patel, *Stuffed and Starved*; Thurow and Kilman, *Enough*. Concerning declining bee populations and possible causes, see Elizabeth Kolbert, "Stung: Where Have All the Bees Gone?," *The New Yorker*, August 6, 2007; Alison Benjamin, "Why Bees Matter," *The Guardian*, August 14, 2008; "Pesticides Linked to Bee Decline, Say Green Groups," *The Guardian*, August 6, 2010. In 2010 a major study found that two infections seemed to be working together in cases of colony collapse, but it still appears that there are "complex interactions between a number of factors, pathogens, environmental, beekeeping practices and other stressors, which are causing honey bee losses" (Ian Douglas, "Study Finds Causes of Colony Collapse Disorder in Bees," *Telegraph*, October 8, 2010).

72. This view has been most famously articulated in the context of U.S. politics by Peter Bachrach, whose work argues that the surest route to the alleviation of

poverty is through changes in the structure of power and the ability of poor people to participate in decision-making institutions. See Bachrach and Baratz, *Power and Poverty*.

73. White, *Democracy, Justice and the Welfare State*, 5. White borrows the term "needs interpretation" from Fraser, *Unruly Practices*.

74. From UN Doc. E/C.12/1992/2, quoted in Beetham, *Democracy and Human Rights*, 107.

75. Nussbaum, *Women and Human Development*, 149, 152 (emphasis added). To my mind, the tactic of conceptual separation does not avoid paternalism; it merely attempts to console people with a false, idealized vision of ex nihilo constitution making according to which philosophers set things right, so that ordinary people can then be permitted to "pursue their own desires" (which will now be "more adequately informed") (161).

76. Ibid., 144. Nussbaum states that "an independently justified list of substantive goods" is required to establish a "foundation" for society (155, 160).

77. Ibid., 160, 159.

78. Some interpreters criticize Sen on this point, arguing on behalf of Nussbaum's "philosophical position" rather than in support of Sen's "democratic position." Those terms are from Claassen, "Making Capability Lists," which endorses the "philosophical position." See also Srivivasan, "No Democracy without Justice."

79. Crocker, *Ethics of Global Development*, 305.

80. Claassen says this is the "predominant objection" raised by Sen's democratic position to the philosophical position articulated by Nussbaum (Claassen, "Making Capability Lists," 3).

81. This is Srivivasan's gloss on Sen's commitments (Srivivasan, "No Democracy without Justice, 457), which lead Sen to "stand up against any proposal of a grand mausoleum to one fixed and final list of capabilities" (Sen, "Human Rights and Capabilities," 160).

82. Sen, *Development as Freedom*, xiii.

83. Brettschneider argues most forcefully against conceptions of democracy that are either strictly outcome-oriented or procedural, represented by Ronald Dworkin and Jeremy Waldron, respectively. Brettschneider wavers, however, on whether Waldron's procedural account of democracy is pure or impure (Brettschneider, *Democratic Rights*, 146n12).

84. Although Brettschneider claims to advance an account of democracy that "embraces the tension" between procedure and substance, he also minimizes the sense of friction and loss his own theory seems to point toward by advocating a balancing technique for addressing conflicts between procedural and substantive goods. Such balancing is made possible, in Brettschneider's theory, by the fact that the same three values—equality of interests, political autonomy, and reciprocity—are held to be the source of democracy's procedural and substantive commitments. Brettschneider conceives of the balancing operation as an objective calculation which determines whether more or less of the same value-set is lost in competing scenarios. Balancing thereby involves assessing fully commensurable options, according to a common measure. This, in turn, allows Brettschneider

to imply that there is a single correct answer in cases of conflict: one need only choose the route that "minimizes loss." Though there is a "loss to democracy" here, it is not a tragic loss, on Brettschneider's view, since one can be assured one has simply retained more of a good thing than if an alternative decision had been made. Although neither author puts the problem in quite these terms, Thomas Christiano and Alex Zakaras offer criticisms of Brettschneider's view that speak to this tendency to assume that there is a right answer in all cases in which democracy's procedural and substantive requirements collide. See Thomas Christiano's review of Brettschneider's book in *The Journal of Politics*, which charges Brettschneider with ignoring the real disagreements that can attend specific cases, even if one accepts his three core values as definitive. See also Zakaras, "Against Democratic Contractualism," which posits that Brettschneider is able to offer this neat and tidy account of conflict resolution only by relying on a troubling notion of what is a "reasonable" interpretation of democratic values, a maneuver Zakaras alleges fails to respect "real people" (56–57).

85. Brettschneider's approach has the merit of confirming some basic intuitions most people have about what democracy involves — for example, it seems to affirm the conviction that harm is done to democracy and not to some other value or good if, say, a majority acts so as to disenfranchise some percentage of the citizen population (*Democratic Rights*, 12–13).

86. Ibid., 158.

87. Brettschneider conceptualizes this loss most clearly in his reflections on judicial review in chapter 7 of *Democratic Rights*. Here a loss to democracy may be owing to a democratically made decision that violates a substantive right or to a nondemocratic decision, such as one issued by a high court, which overturns a majoritarian decision in order to protect a substantive right.

88. White, *Democracy, Justice, and the Welfare State*, 37–46. White's work draws on Nancy Fraser's idea of the "politics of needs interpretation" as well as on Joan Tronto's efforts to develop a democratic ideal of care that does not succumb to paternalism. For a critical account of the fate of similar efforts during the War on Poverty, see Nancy Naples, "From Maximum Feasible Participation to Disenfranchisement."

89. White, *Democracy, Justice, and the Welfare State*, 164.

90. Ibid., 138.

91. See Corbett, "The Civil Initiative." Jim Corbett was a leader in the Sanctuary movement, along with John Fife, a cofounder of No Más Muertes. Although the idea of civil initiative, like many arguments on behalf of civil disobedience, invokes the notion of a higher law that trumps positive law, practitioners of civil initiative stress that it is primarily concerned with upholding "the Law," not with disobedience to positive law. Nonetheless, many members of No Más Muertes have been ticketed and some arrested for littering because they left drinking water along known migrant trails in the Arizona desert. Two other activists were charged with human trafficking for leading two ailing migrants to the organization's medical base camp. (The charges were dismissed.) See Stephen Lemmons, "Blood's Thicker Than Water: As Thousands Die in the Arizona Desert as a Result

of U.S. Border Policy, an Army of Activists Intervenes," *Phoenix New Times*, February 25, 2010, and www.nomoredeaths.org.

92. In *Arizona et al. v. United States* (2012), the Supreme Court upheld the centerpiece of Arizona's immigration law—the "show me your papers" provision—while declaring three of its provisions unconstitutional.

93. Lefebvre, "The Right to the City." See Soja, *Seeking Social Justice*, for discussion of Lefebvre's idea as well as its recent reappropriation. For a diagnosis of the anti-democratic effects of contemporary city-building practices, see Bickford, "Constructing Inequality."

94. Harvey, "The Right to the City," *International Journal of Urban and Regional Research*. See also Harvey, "The Right to the City," *New Left Review*.

95. See www.righttothecity.org.

## EPILOGUE

1. www.welcomingtn.org and Michael Jones Correa, "All Immigration Is Local: Receiving Communities and Their Role in Successful Immigrant Integration," September 2011. Available at www.americanprogress.org.

2. Travis Loller, "Group Hopes to Temper Debate with Billboards," *The Tennessean*, July 28, 2006.

3. www.welcomingtn.org. The site describes a range of techniques used by WTI to make Tennessee a more "welcoming state."

4. Janell Ross, "Group Seeks Straight Talk on Immigrants," *The Tennessean*, June 16, 2009.

5. See www.tnimmigrant.org. More detailed information on these projects and others can be found there.

6. Arendt, "Freedom and Politics," 200.

7. The video is available through YouTube and the Courage Campaign's website: www.couragecampaign.org/page/s/divorce.

8. This exceptional image is very striking: two male firefighters in uniform, with their backs to the camera, stand in front of a fire engine, and a small child between them holds each of their hands. Text on the windshield of the fire engine reads, "Please don't divorce us! We have a beautiful thing here. In fact, everyone should be so lucky."

9. Pogge's argument echoes in part Norman Geras's claim that the contemporary sociopolitical world, marked by the hegemony of liberal capitalism, is defined by a "contract of mutual indifference," according to which there is a shared expectation among human beings neither to give nor receive aid. Suffering is acceptable, Geras argues, within this (distorted) "moral logic" (Geras, *The Contract of Mutual Indifference*, 41, 74). Though Geras is less focused than Pogge on the heightened and unique responsibility of citizens of developed countries and on the specific global institutional changes that they ought to seek in order to alleviate needless suffering, his central idea of generalized indifference supports Pogge's opening salvo in *Politics as Usual*: that widespread, preventable suffering and death are routinely tolerated even by those who profess to be moral.

10. Pogge, *Politics as Usual*, esp. chapters 1 and 2. In chapter 2 Pogge demonstrates that

the World Trade Organization, the International Monetary Fund, and the World Bank are "designed so that they systematically contribute to the persistence of severe poverty" (26).

11. Pogge, *Politics as Usual*, 27, 54.

12. Charitable giving levels as a percentage of GDP are significantly higher in the United States than in other developed nations. See "CAF Briefing Paper: International Comparisons of Charitable Giving," available at www.cafonline.org. See also "Giving USA 2010," researched and published by the Center on Philanthropy at Indiana University, available at www.aafrc.org. According to Pogge, it is more rational for an affluent person who wants to address poverty to support structural reform than to give donations (*Politics as Usual*, 54).

13. Foucault, "The Subject and Power," 336.

14. Flathman, *Willful Liberalism*, 8. Flathman contends that complementarism is correct; individuality and plurality are interwoven and "advantage one another." Yet Flathman's subsequent claim runs counter to my own, for Flathman asserts that "the complementarisms that dominate in liberal theory and practice" (which he does not name specifically) tend to "too readily assume that [individualities] will be taken care of by, will themselves come along with, group and associational life" (ibid.). My point, spurred on by a commitment to associative democratic politics that Flathman would likely view with skepticism, is instead that it is too frequently assumed that the focused cultivation of individualities will additively result in an invigorated and transformed public life.

15. Warner, *The Trouble with Normal*, 177, 139.

16. Ibid., 7.

17. George Kateb, in a decidedly different vein, argues that the self-conscious crafting of individuality is a project that requires the support of democratic culture. Starting from the position that "democracy's most elevated justification lies in its encouragement of individuality," Kateb alleges that the exemplary forms of individuality explored by Emerson, Thoreau, and Whitman are possible only within a democratic setting: a "political artifice" sustains these thinkers' admirable individualities (Kateb, "Democratic Individuality and the Claims of Politics," 78, 105). Yet the individualities elaborated by these thinkers would seem to be self-defeating since they often involve skepticism toward, if not withdrawal from, the very political system that serves as their condition of possibility. Kateb does not seem particularly worried about this vulnerability, noting that "as long as there are countless people willing to take part [in democratic activities], there can be no duty to do so, no matter how sharply indebted one felt" (ibid., 105). Assuming democratic participation by "countless others" (who do not come to disdain or outgrow the democratic system, as do those most honorific individualists) allows Kateb to remain undisturbed by the prospect that the individuality he cites as democracy's greatest achievement might also contribute to its ruin.

18. Foucault, "The Ethics of the Concern for Self as a Practice of Freedom," 291.

19. John Dewey articulated a dialogic understanding of self and society, affirming the importance of self-creation while stressing its indirect character. As Richard Schusterman argues, "Although Dewey gives teleological priority to the indi-

vidual, society precedes and shapes its constitution. . . . This social construction of the self is central to Dewey's argument that personal self-realization requires an active public life: If 'the mental and moral structure of individuals, the pattern of their desires and purposes' depend largely on the habits, thoughts, and values that society encourages, then improving our society seems essential to improving the quality of the selves we realize" ("Pragmatism and Liberalism between Dewey and Rorty," 400, quoting Dewey, *Individualism Old and New*, 81). In this article and elsewhere, Schusterman draws attention to Dewey's account of self-creation as largely an indirect undertaking. See also Schusterman, "Putnam and Cavell on the Ethics of Democracy."

20. Zehfuss, "Subjectivity and Vulnerability," 67.

21. www.iraqbodycount.net. Quoted in Zehfuss, "Subjectivity and Vulnerability," 67.

22. Ibid. Quotes from Iraq Body Count can be found at www.iraqbodycount.net/names.htm.

23. In an interview, Butler talks about the importance of interrupting the cultural frames by which we presently live, though she presents the task in an oddly passive way: "We have to come against the limit of the cultural frames in which we live. . . . We have to *let those frames get interrupted* by other frames" (Power, "The Books Interview: Judith Butler" [emphasis added]).

24. Zehfuss, "Subjectivity and Vulnerability," 68.

25. Those quotes are posed as questions by Butler in *Precarious Life*, 20.

26. "'Proactive arrests,' covert surveillance, and psychological tactics," for example, were used by police at nonviolent demonstrations that took place at the World Economic Forum in New York in 2002. FBI investigations that began in the early 2000s targeted critics of the Bush administration and antiwar activists (the latter pursued in the name of antiterrorism). The violent and militarized response of police forces to peaceful Occupy protesters throughout the United States in 2011 and 2012 has also been well documented. These are just a few contemporary examples of what Michael Rogin calls the tradition of "political repression" in the United States, that is, repeated and coordinated efforts by the state to disrupt and render ineffectual citizen association. See "Police Memos Say Arrest Tactics Calmed Protest," *New York Times*, March 17, 2006; Eric Lichtblau, "Large Volume of F.B.I. Files Alarms U.S. Activist Groups," *New York Times*, July 18, 2005; Colin Moynihan, "F.B.I. Searches Antiwar Activists' Homes," *New York Times*, September 24, 2010; Norm Stamper, "Paramilitary Policing from Seattle to Occupy Wall Street," *The Nation*, November 9, 2011; Michael Rogin, "Political Repression in the United States."

27. Jean Jacques Rousseau, *The Social Contract*, trans. Maurice Cranston (New York: Penguin Books, 1968), book 2, chapter 7.

28. For two provocative readings of the democratic significance of the Rousseauvian Legislator, see Johnston, *Encountering Tragedy*, and Honig, *Democracy and the Foreigner*. Both Johnston and Honig portray the Legislator as the *deus ex machina* in a founding fiction that would seem to threaten the "democratic credentials" of the order he founds (Johnston, *Encountering Tragedy*, 52). Johnston reads this fiction as disabling of democratic politics because it tends to ascribe the task of mainte-

nance rather than innovation to its citizens (Johnston, *Encountering Tragedy*, 71). Yet Honig locates unexpected potential in Rousseau's myth, arguing that the foreignness of the foreign-founder might be read as a "marker of the law's alienness to the people who live by it." This sense of alienation, Honig contends, might be worth preserving insofar as "the positive side of 'alienation' . . . marks a gap in legitimation, a space that is held open for future refoundings, augmentations, and amendment" (Honig, *Democracy and the Foreigner*, 30–31).

29. See www.faireconomy.org.

30. See www.jnow.org and "A World without Prisons: Improving Prisoners' Lives and Transforming the Justice System," available at www.leadershipforchange.org.

31. "A World without Prisons," 2. One of Justice Now's cofounders, Cynthia Chandler, describes a fundamental principle of the organization's work: "We can't advocate for anyone until they tell us what they need" (2).

32. See www.ourwatercommons.org. Several global populist movements (involving some combination of NGOs, unions, and political parties) have successfully challenged governmental privatization policies by insisting on the recognition of water and energy as specifically public goods. See Hall, Lobina, and de la Motte, "Public Resistance to Privatization in Water and Energy," for a thorough discussion of the struggles that have taken place in a number of countries, both developed and developing, over attempts at privatization.

33. As I use it here, *counter-institution* refers to an organization located outside the state's institutional matrix that serves as a venue for the experiences of discussion, decision making, and action among citizens. Counter-institutions in this sense are roughly synonymous with the semiautonomous associations and organizations of what is sometimes called democratic civil society. These counter-institutions have also been conceived of as a "parallel polis," an idea borrowed from the Czech Charter 77 movement. The notion of a parallel polis is meant to signify "the cultivation of democratized practices and institutions that would shadow those of the state: information networks, forms of education, trade unions, foreign contacts, and economy" (Euben, "The Polis, Globalization, and the Politics of Place," 282).

# BIBLIOGRAPHY

Alexander, John. "Ending the Liberal Hegemony: Republican Freedom and Amartya Sen's Theory of Capabilities." *Contemporary Political Theory* 9, no. 1 (2010).

Alford, C. Fred. "Levinas and Political Theory." *Political Theory* 32, no. 2 (2004).

Allen, Amy. *The Politics of Our Selves: Power, Autonomy, and Gender in Contemporary Critical Theory.* New York: Columbia University Press, 1998.

———. "Solidarity after Identity Politics: Hannah Arendt and the Power of Feminist Theory." *Philosophy and Social Criticism* 25, no. 1 (1999).

Anderson, Amanda. *The Way We Argue Now.* Princeton: Princeton University Press, 2005.

Apostolidis, Paul. "Politics and Connolly's Ethics: Immigrant Narratives, Racism, and Identity's Contingency." *Theory and Event* 11, no. 3 (2008). muse.jhu.edu/journals/theory_and_event/.

Arendt, Hannah. "Civil Disobedience." *Crises of the Republic.* New York: Harcourt Brace, 1972.

———. "Concern with Politics in Recent European Philosophical Thought." *Essays in Understanding 1930–1954.* New York: Harcourt Brace, 1994.

———. "The Crisis in Culture." *Between Past and Future: Eight Exercises in Political Thought.* New York: Viking Press, 1968.

———. "Freedom and Politics." *Freedom and Serfdom: An Anthology of Western Thought,* ed. Albert Hunold. Dordrecht: Reidel, 1961.

———. *The Human Condition.* Chicago: University of Chicago Press, 1958.

———. "Introduction into Politics." *The Promise of Politics,* ed. Jerome Kohn. New York: Schocken Books, 2005.

———. *The Life of the Mind.* New York: Harcourt Brace Jovanovich, 1978.

———. "On Hannah Arendt." *Hannah Arendt: The Recovery of the Public World,* ed. Melvyn A. Hill. New York: St. Martin's Press, 1979.

———. "On Humanity in Dark Times: Thoughts on Lessing." *Men in Dark Times.* New York: Harcourt, Brace and World, 1968.

———. *On Revolution.* New York: Viking Press, 1963.

———. *The Origins of Totalitarianism.* New York: World Publishing, 1951.

———. "Philosophy and Politics." *Social Research* 57, no. 1 (1990).

———. "Public Rights and Private Interests." *Small Comforts for Hard Times: Humanists on Public Policy,* ed. Michael J. Mooney and Florian Stuber. New York: Columbia University Press, 1977.

————. *Responsibility and Judgment*. Edited by Jerome Kohn. New York: Schocken Books, 2003.

————. "Thoughts on Politics and Revolution." *Crises of the Republic*. New York: Harcourt Brace Jovanovich, 1972.

————. "What Is Existential Philosophy?" *Essays in Understanding 1930–1954*, ed. Jerome Kohn. New York: Harcourt Brace, 1994.

————. "What Is Freedom?" *Between Past and Future: Eight Exercises in Political Thought*. New York: Penguin Books, 1968.

Arendt, Hannah, and Karl Jaspers. *Correspondence 1926–1969*. New York: Harcourt Brace Jovanovich, 1992.

Bachrach, Peter, and Morton Baratz. *Power and Poverty: Theory and Practice*. New York: Oxford University Press, 1970.

Barr, Andrew. *Political Machines: Governing a Technological Society*. London: Athlone Press, 2001.

Bartels, Larry M. *Unequal Democracy: The Political Economy of the New Gilded Age*. Princeton: Princeton University Press, 2008.

Beetham, David. *Democracy and Human Rights*. Cambridge: Polity Press, 1999.

Bellah, Robert, Richard Madsen, William M. Sullivan, Ann Swidler, and Steven M. Tipton. *The Habits of the Heart: Individualism and Commitment in American Life*. New York: Perennial Library, 1985.

Beltrán, Cristina. "Going Public: Hannah Arendt, Immigrant Action, and the Space of Appearance." *Political Theory* 37, no. 5 (2009).

Benhabib, Seyla. *The Reluctant Modernism of Hannah Arendt*. Thousand Oaks, Calif.: Sage Publications, 1996.

Bennett, Jane. *The Enchantment of Modern Life: Attachments, Crossings, and Ethics*. Princeton: Princeton University Press, 2001.

————. "'How Is It Then That We Still Remain Barbarians?' Foucault, Schiller, and the Aestheticization of Ethics." *Political Theory* 24, no. 4 (1996).

————. *Vibrant Matter: A Political Ecology of Things*. Durham: Duke University Press, 2010.

Berkowitz, Peter. *Virtue and the Making of Modern Liberalism*. Princeton: Princeton University Press, 1999.

Berlin, Isaiah. "Introduction." *Four Essays on Liberty*. New York: Oxford University Press, 1969.

Bernasconi, Robert. "Rereading *Totality and Infinity*." *The Question of the Other*, ed. Arleen B. Dallery and Charles E. Scott. Albany: SUNY Press, 1989.

————. "The Third Party: Levinas on the Intersection of the Ethical and the Political." *Journal of the British Society for Phenomenology* 30, no. 1 (1999).

Bernauer, James W., and Michael Mahon. "The Ethics of Michel Foucault." *The Cambridge Companion to Foucault*, ed. Gary Gutting. Cambridge: Cambridge University Press, 1994.

Bernstein, Richard. "Foucault's Aesthetic Decisionism." *Telos* 67 (1986).

Bickford, Susan. "Constructing Inequality: City Spaces and the Architecture of Citizenship." *Political Theory* 28, no. 3 (2000).

Biskowski, Lawrence. "Practical Foundations for Political Judgment: Arendt on Action and World." *Journal of Politics* 55, no. 4 (1993).

Bollier, David. *Silent Theft: The Private Plunder of Our Common Wealth.* New York: Routledge, 2002.

Boucher, Geoff. "The Politics of Performativity: A Critique of Judith Butler." *Parrhesia* 1 (2006).

Bourg, Julian. *From Revolution to Ethics: May 1968 and Contemporary French Thought.* Montreal: McGill-Queen's University Press, 2007.

Brady, Henry, Sidney Verba, and Kay Lehman Schlozman. "Beyond SES: A Resource Model of Participation." *American Political Science Review* 89, no. 2 (1995).

Breen, Keith. "Agonism, Antagonism, and the Necessity of Care." *Law and Agonistic Politics,* ed. Andrew Schapp. Aldershot: Ashgate, 2009.

Brettschneider, Corey. *Democratic Rights: The Substance of Self-Government.* Princeton: Princeton University Press, 2007.

Brown, Wendy. "Moralism as Anti-Politics." *Politics Out of History.* Princeton: Princeton University Press, 2001.

———. "Occupy Wall Street: Return of a Repressed *Res-Publica.*" *Theory and Event* 14, no. 4 (2011 Supplement). muse.jhu.edu/journals/theory_and_event/.

Butler, Judith. "1999 Preface." *Gender Trouble.* New York: Routledge, 2006.

———. "Ethical Ambivalence." *The Turn to Ethics,* ed. Marjorie Garber, Beatrice Hanssen, and Rebecca Walkowitz. New York: Routledge, 2000.

———. *Frames of War: When Is Life Grievable?* London: Verso, 2009.

———. *Giving an Account of Oneself.* New York: Fordham University Press, 2003.

———. *Precarious Life: The Powers of Mourning and Violence.* New York: Verso, 2006.

———. *The Psychic Life of Power: Theories in Subjection.* Palo Alto: Stanford University Press, 1997.

———. *Undoing Gender.* New York: Routledge, 2004.

Butler, Judith, and William Connolly. "Politics, Power, and Ethics: A Discussion between Judith Butler and William Connolly." *Theory and Event* 4, no. 2 (2000). muse.jhu .edu/journals/theory_and_event/.

Button, Mark. *Contract, Culture, and Citizenship: Transformative Liberalism from Hobbes to Rawls.* University Park: Pennsylvania State University Press, 2008.

Caygill, Howard. *Levinas and the Political.* New York: Routledge, 2002.

Chamberlain, Charles. "From 'Haunts' to 'Character': The Meaning of *Ēthos* and Its Relation to Ethics." *Helios* 11, no. 2 (1984).

Chambers, Samuel, and Terrell Carver. *Judith Butler and Political Theory: Troubling Politics.* New York: Routledge, 2008.

Chiba, Shin. "Hannah Arendt on Love and the Political: Love, Friendship, and Citizenship." *Review of Politics* 57, no. 3 (1995).

Christiano, Thomas. "Review of *Democratic Rights: The Substance of Self-Government* by Corey Brettschneider." *Journal of Politics* 71, no. 4 (2009).

Claassen, Rutger. "Making Capability Lists: Philosophy versus Democracy." *Political Studies* 59, no. 3 (2011).

Coles, Romand. "Moving Democracy: The Political Arts of Listening, Traveling, and

Tabling." *Beyond Gated Politics: Reflections for the Possibility of Democracy*. Minneapolis: University of Minnesota Press, 2005.

———. *Rethinking Generosity: Critical Theory and the Politics of Caritas*. Ithaca: Cornell University Press, 1997.

Connolly, William. *The Ethos of Pluralization*. Minneapolis: University of Minnesota Press, 1995.

———. *Pluralism*. Durham: Duke University Press, 2005.

———. *Why I Am Not a Secularist*. Minneapolis: University of Minnesota Press, 1999.

———. *A World of Becoming*. Durham: Duke University Press, 2010.

Corbett, Jim. "The Civil Initiative." *Goatwalking*. New York: Viking, 1991.

Corts, Thomas. "The Derivation of Ethos." *Speech Monographs* 35, no. 2 (1968).

Critchley, Simon. *The Ethics of Deconstruction*. Edinburgh: Edinburgh University Press, 1999.

———. "Five Problems in Levinas's View of Politics and the Sketch of a Solution to Them." *Political Theory* 32, no. 2 (2004).

———. *Infinitely Demanding: Ethics of Commitment, Politics of Resistance*. London: Verso, 2007.

———. "Introduction." *The Cambridge Companion to Levinas*, ed. Robert Bernasconi and Simon Critchley. Cambridge: University of Cambridge Press, 2002.

Crocker, David A. *Ethics of Global Development: Agency, Capability, and Deliberative Democracy*. Cambridge: Cambridge University Press, 2008.

Curtis, Kimberley. *Our Sense of the Real: Aesthetic Experience and Arendtian Politics*. Ithaca: Cornell University Press, 1999.

Davis, Colin. *Levinas: An Introduction*. Notre Dame: University of Notre Dame, 1996.

Dean, Jodi. "Change of Address: Butler's Politics at Sovereignty's Deadlock." *Judith Butler's Precarious Politics*, ed. Terrell Carver and Samuel Chambers. New York: Routledge, 2008.

———. "The Politics of Avoidance." *Hedgehog Review* (summer 2005).

———. *Solidarity of Strangers: Feminism after Identity Politics*. Berkeley: University of California Press, 1996.

De Lauretis, Teresa. "Eccentric Subjects: Feminist Theory and Historical Consciousness." *Feminist Studies* 16, no. 1 (1990).

Detel, Wolfgang. *Foucault and Classical Antiquity: Power, Ethics, and Knowledge*. Cambridge: Cambridge University Press, 2005.

Deveaux, Monique. *Cultural Pluralism and the Dilemmas of Justice*. Ithaca: Cornell University Press, 2000.

Dewey, John. *The Public and Its Problems*. Denver: Alan Swallow, 1927.

Dews, Peter. "The Return of the Subject in Late Foucault." *Michel Foucault: Critical Assessments*, ed. Barry Smart. Vol. 5. London: Routledge, 1995.

Dietz, Mary. "'The Slow Boring of Hard Boards': Methodical Thinking and the Work of Politics." *American Political Science Review* 88, no. 4 (1994).

Dreyfus, Hubert, and Paul Rabinow. *Michel Foucault: Beyond Structuralism and Hermeneutics*. Chicago: University of Chicago Press, 1983.

Dumm, Thomas L. *Michel Foucault and the Politics of Freedom*. Newbury Park, Calif.: Sage Publications, 1996.

Dussel, Enrique. "'The Politics' by Levinas: Towards a 'Critical' Political Philosophy." *Difficult Justice: Commentaries on Levinas and Politics*, ed. Asher Horowitz and Gad Horowitz. Toronto: University of Toronto Press, 2006.

Eliasoph, Nina. *Avoiding Politics: How Americans Produce Apathy in Everyday Life*. Cambridge: Cambridge University Press, 1998.

———. *Making Volunteers: Civic Life after Welfare's End*. Princeton: Princeton University Press, 2011.

Euben, Peter. "The Polis, Globalization, and the Politics of Place." *Democracy and Vision: Sheldon Wolin and the Vicissitudes of the Political*, ed. Aryeh Botwinick and William Connolly. Princeton: Princeton University Press, 2001.

Fernandez-Armesto, Felipe. *Humankind: A Brief History*. Oxford: Oxford University Press, 2004.

Flathman, Richard E. *Freedom and Its Conditions: Discipline, Autonomy, and Resistance*. New York: Routledge, 2003.

———. *Willful Liberalism*. Ithaca: Cornell University Press, 1992.

Flynn, Thomas. "Truth and Subjectivation in the Later Foucault." *Journal of Philosophy* 82, no. 10 (1985).

Foucault, Michel. "About the Beginnings of the Hermeneutics of the Self." *Political Theory* 21, no. 2 (1993).

———. "An Aesthetics of Existence." *Politics, Philosophy, Culture: Interviews and Other Writings, 1977–1984*, ed. Lawrence D. Kritzman, New York: Routledge, 1988.

———. *The Care of the Self*. New York: Vintage Books, 1988.

———. "The Concern for Truth." In *Politics, Philosophy, Culture: Interviews and Other Writings, 1977–1984*, ed. Lawrence D. Kritzman. New York: Routledge, 1988.

———. "The Ethics of the Concern for Self as a Practice of Freedom." *Ethics: Subjectivity and Truth*, ed. Paul Rabinow. *The Essential Works of Foucault, 1954–1984*. New York: New Press, 1997.

———. "The Hermeneutic of the Subject." *Ethics: Subjectivity and Truth*, ed. Paul Rabinow. *The Essential Works of Foucault, 1954–1984*. New York: New Press, 1997.

———. *The Hermeneutics of the Subject: Lectures at the Collège de France, 1981–1982*. New York: Picador, 2005.

———. *The History of Sexuality*. Vol. 1. New York: Vintage, 1990.

———. "On the Genealogy of Ethics." *Ethics: Subjectivity and Truth*, ed. Paul Rabinow. *The Essential Works of Foucault, 1954–1984*. New York: New Press, 1997.

———. "Politics and Ethics: An Interview." *The Foucault Reader*. New York: Vintage Books, 1984.

———. "The Return of Morality." *Foucault Live: Interviews 1961–1984*, ed. Sylvére Lotringer. New York: Semiotext(e), 1996.

———. "Sex, Power and the Politics of Identity." *Ethics: Subjectivity and Truth*, ed. Paul Rabinow. *The Essential Works of Foucault, 1954–1984*. New York: New Press, 1997.

———. "The Subject and Power." *Power*, ed. James D. Faubion. *The Essential Works of Foucault, 1954–1984*. New York: New Press, 2000.

———. "Technologies of the Self." *Ethics: Subjectivity and Truth*, ed. Paul Rabinow. *The Essential Works of Foucault, 1954–1984*. New York: New Press, 1997.

———. *The Use of Pleasure*. New York: Vintage Books, 1985.

————. "What Is Enlightenment?" *Ethics: Subjectivity and Truth*, ed. Paul Rabinow. *The Essential Works of Foucault, 1954–1984*. New York: New Press, 1997.

Fraser, Nancy. *Unruly Practices: Power, Discourse, and Gender in Contemporary Social Theory*. Minneapolis: University of Minnesota Press, 1989.

Fung, Archon. "Associations and Democracy: Between Theories, Hopes, and Realities." *Annual Review of Sociology* 29 (2003).

Galston, William. *Liberal Purposes: Goods, Virtues, and Diversity in the Liberal State*. Cambridge: Cambridge University Press, 1991.

Garber, Marjorie, Beatrice Hanssen, and Rebecca Walkowitz, eds. *The Turn to Ethics*. New York: Routledge, 2000.

Geras, Norman. *The Contract of Mutual Indifference: Political Philosophy after the Holocaust*. London: Verso, 1999.

Geuss, Raymond. *Philosophy and Real Politics*. Princeton: Princeton University Press, 2008.

Gilens, Martin. "Inequality and Democratic Responsiveness." *Public Opinion Quarterly* 69, no. 5 (2005).

Gomart, Emilie, and Maarten Hajer. "Is *That* Politics? For an Inquiry into Forms in Contemporary Politics." *Social Studies of Science and Technology: Looking Back, Ahead*, ed. Bernward Joerges and Helga Nowotny. Dordrecht: Kluwer Academic Publishers, 2003.

Grimshaw, Jean. "Practices of Freedom." *Up against Foucault: Explorations of Some Tensions between Foucault and Feminism*, ed. Caroline Ramazanoglu. New York: Routledge, 1993.

Grusin, Richard. "Premediation and the Virtual Occupation of Wall Street." *Theory and Event* 14, no. 4 (2011 Supplement). muse.jhu.edu/journals/theory_and_event/.

Hadot, Pierre. "Reflections on the Notion of 'the Cultivation of the Self.'" *Michel Foucault: Philosopher*, ed. T. J. Armstrong. New York: Routledge, 1992.

Hall, David, Emanuele Lobina, and Robin de la Motte. "Public Resistance to Privatization in Water and Energy." *Development in Practice* 15, nos. 3, 4 (2005).

Harvey, David. "The Right to the City." *International Journal of Urban and Regional Research* 27, no. 4 (2003).

————. "The Right to the City." *New Left Review* 53 (October 2008).

Hayward, Tim. "Anthropocentrism: A Misunderstood Problem." *Environmental Values* 6 (1997).

Heidegger, Martin. "The Thing." *Poetry, Language, Thought*. New York: Harper and Row, 1971.

Held, David. *Models of Democracy*. 2d ed. Palo Alto: Stanford University Press, 1996.

Held, Virginia. *The Ethics of Care: Personal, Global, and Political*. New York: Oxford University Press, 2006.

Herzog, Annabel. "Is Liberalism 'All We Need'? Levinas's Politics of Surplus." *Political Theory* 30, no. 2 (2002).

Heyes, Cressida. *Self-Transformations: Foucault, Ethics, and Normalized Bodies*. Oxford: Oxford University Press, 2007.

Honig, Bonnie. "Antigone's Two Laws: Greek Tragedy and the Politics of Humanism." *New Literary History* 41, no. 1 (2010).

———. *Democracy and the Foreigner*. Princeton: Princeton University Press, 2001.

———. "Difference, Dilemmas, and the Politics of Home." *Democracy and Difference: Contesting the Boundaries of the Political*, ed. Seyla Benhabib. Princeton: Princeton University Press, 1996.

———. "The Politics of Ethos." *European Journal of Political Theory* 10, no. 3 (2011).

———. "Toward an Agonistic Feminism: Hannah Arendt and the Politics of Identity." *Feminist Interpretations of Hannah Arendt*, ed. Bonnie Honig. University Park: Pennsylvania State University Press, 1995.

Irigaray, Luce. *Sharing the World*. London: Continuum, 2008.

Isaac, Jeffrey. "Oases in the Desert: Hannah Arendt on Democratic Politics." *American Political Science Review* 88, no. 1 (1994).

Jasper, James. "The Emotions of Protest: Affective and Reactive Emotions in and around Social Movements." *Sociological Forum* 13, no. 3 (1998).

Johnston, Steven. *Encountering Tragedy: Rousseau and the Project of Democratic Order*. Ithaca: Cornell University Press, 1999.

Kateb, George. "Democratic Individuality and the Claims of Politics." *The Inner Ocean: Individualism and Democratic Culture*. Ithaca: Cornell University Press, 1992.

———. *Hannah Arendt: Politics, Conscience, Evil*. Totowa, N.J.: Rowman and Allanheld, 1983.

Keenan, Alan. *Democracy in Question: Democratic Openness in a Time of Political Closure*. Palo Alto: Stanford University Press, 2003.

Kohn, Margaret. *Brave New Neighborhoods: The Privatization of Public Space*. New York: Routledge, 2004.

Kompridis, Nikolas. "From Reason to Self-Realization? Axel Honneth and the 'Ethical Turn' in Critical Theory." *Contemporary Perspectives in Critical and Social Philosophy*, ed. John Rundell, Danielle Petherbridge, and Jan Bryant. Leiden: Brill, 2004.

Kruks, Sonia. *Retrieving Experience: Subjectivity and Recognition in Feminist Politics*. Ithaca: Cornell University Press, 2001.

Laclau, Ernesto. "Deconstruction, Pragmatism, Hegemony." *Deconstruction and Pragmatism*, ed. Chantal Mouffe. London: Routledge, 1997.

Lappé, Frances Moore, Joseph Collins, and Peter Rosset. *World Hunger: 12 Myths*. New York: Grove Press, 1998.

Lasch, Christopher. *The Culture of Narcissism: American Life in an Age of Diminishing Expectations*. New York: W. W. Norton, 1979.

Latour, Bruno. "From Realpolitik to Dingpolitik." *Making Things Public*, ed. Bruno Latour and Peter Weibel. Cambridge: MIT Press, 2005.

———. *Pandora's Hope: Essays on the Reality of Science Studies*. Cambridge: Harvard University Press, 1999.

———. *Politics of Nature: How to Bring the Sciences into Democracy*. Cambridge: Harvard University Press, 2004.

Lefebvre, Henri. "The Right to the City." *Writings on Cities*, ed. Eleanor Kofman and Elizabeth Lebas. Cambridge, Mass.: Blackwell, 1996.

Levinas, Emmanuel. "Dialogue on Thinking-of-the-Other." *Entre Nous: On Thinking-of-the-Other*. New York: Columbia University Press, 1998.

————. "Difficult Freedom." *The Levinas Reader*, ed. Seán Hand. Oxford: Wiley-Blackwell, 2001.

————. *Difficult Freedom: Essays on Judaism*. Translated by Seán Hand. Baltimore: Johns Hopkins University Press, 1990.

————. *Entre Nous: On Thinking-of-the-Other*. New York: Columbia University Press, 1999.

————. "Ethics and Politics." *The Levinas Reader*, ed. Seán Hand. Oxford: Wiley-Blackwell, 2001.

————. *God, Death and Time*. Palo Alto: Stanford University Press, 2001.

————. "The Other, Utopia, and Justice." *Entre Nous: On Thinking-of-the-Other*. New York: Columbia University Press, 1999.

————. *Otherwise Than Being*. Translated by Alphonso Lingis. Pittsburgh: Duquesne University Press, 1981.

————. "Peace and Proximity." *Alterity and Transcendence*. New York: Columbia University Press, 1999.

————. "Philosophy and Transcendence." *Alterity and Transcendence*. New York: Columbia University Press, 1999.

————. "Philosophy, Justice, and Love." *Entre Nous: On Thinking-of-the-Other*. New York: Columbia University Press, 1999.

————. "The Proximity of the Other." *Alterity and Transcendence*. New York: Columbia University Press, 1999.

————. "Substitution." *Basic Philosophical Writings*, ed. Adriaan Peperzak, Simon Critchley, and Robert Bernasconi. Bloomington: Indiana University Press, 1996.

————. *Totality and Infinity: An Essay on Exteriority*. Translated by Alphonso Lingis. Pittsburgh: Duquesne University Press, 1969.

————. "The Trace of the Other." *Deconstruction in Context: Literature and Philosophy*, ed. Mark C. Taylor. Chicago: University of Chicago Press, 1986.

————. "Transcendence and Height." *Basic Philosophical Writings*, ed. Adriaan Peperzak, Simon Critchley, and Robert Bernasconi. Bloomington: Indiana University Press, 1996.

————. "Uniqueness." *Entre Nous: On Thinking-of-the-Other*. New York: Columbia University Press, 1998.

————. "Useless Suffering." *Entre Nous: On Thinking-of-the-Other*. New York: Columbia University Press, 1998.

————. "Violence of the Face." *Alterity and Transcendence*. New York: Columbia University Press, 1999.

Light, Andrew. "Contemporary Environmental Ethics: From Metaethics to Public Philosophy." *Metaphilosophy* 33, no. 4 (2002).

Lloyd, Moya. *Judith Butler: From Norms to Politics*. Cambridge: Polity Press, 2007.

————. "Toward a Cultural Politics of Vulnerability." *Judith Butler's Precarious Politics*, ed. Samuel Chambers and Terrell Carver. New York: Routledge, 2008.

Longford, Graham. "Sensitive Killers, Cruel Aesthetes, and Pitiless Poets: Foucault, Rorty, and the Ethics of Self-Fashioning." *Polity* 33, no. 4 (2001).

Macedo, Stephen. *Liberal Virtues: Citizenship, Virtue, and Community in Liberal Constitutionalism*. New York: Oxford University Press, 1990.

Markell, Patchen. "The Rule of the People: Arendt, *Archê*, and Democracy." *American Political Science Review* 100, no. 1 (2006).

Marres, Noortje. "Frontstaging Nonhumans: Publicity as a Constraint on the Political Activities of Things." *Political Matter: Technoscience, Democracy, and Public Life*, ed. Bruce Braun and Sarah J. Whatmore. Minneapolis: University of Minnesota Press, 2010.

———. "Issues Spark a Public into Being: A Key but Often Forgotten Point of the Lippmann-Dewey Debate." *Making Things Public*, ed. Bruno Latour and Peter Weibel. Cambridge: MIT Press, 2005.

———. "No Issue, No Public." Ph.D. diss., University of Amsterdam, 2005.

Mills, Catherine. "Normative Violence, Vulnerability, and Responsibility." *differences* 18, no. 2 (2000).

Morgan, Michael L. *Discovering Levinas*. Cambridge: Cambridge University Press, 2007.

Morton, Timothy. *The Ecological Thought*. Cambridge: Harvard University Press, 2010.

Mouffe, Chantal. "Deconstruction, Pragmatism, and the Politics of Democracy." *Deconstruction and Pragmatism*, ed. Chantal Mouffe. New York: Routledge, 1996.

———. *The Democratic Paradox*. London: Verso, 2000.

———. "Which Ethics for Democracy?" *The Turn to Ethics*, ed. Marjorie Garber, Beatrice Hanssen, and Rebecca Walkowitz. New York: Routledge, 2000.

Myers, Ella. "From Pluralism to Liberalism: Rereading Isaiah Berlin." *Review of Politics*, no. 72 (2010).

———. "Resisting Foucauldian Ethics: Associative Politics and the Limits of the Care of the Self." *Contemporary Political Theory* 7, no. 2 (2008).

———. "The Turn to Ethics and its Democratic Costs." Ph.D. diss., Northwestern University, 2006.

Naples, Nancy. "From Maximum Feasible Participation to Maximum Disenfranchisement." *Social Justice* 25, no. 1 (1998).

Nealon, Jeffrey T. *Foucault beyond Foucault: Power and Its Intensifications since 1984*. Palo Alto: Stanford University Press, 2007.

Noddings, Nel. *Caring: A Feminine Approach to Ethics and Moral Education*. Berkeley: University of California Press, 1984.

Norton, Bryan. "Convergence and Contextualism: Some Clarifications and a Reply to Steverson." *Environmental Ethics* 19 (1997).

Nussbaum, Martha Craven. *Women and Human Development: The Capabilities Approach*. Cambridge: Cambridge University Press, 2000.

Obama, Barack. *The Audacity of Hope*. New York: Vintage Books, 2008.

Oksala, Johanna. *Foucault on Freedom*. Cambridge: University of Cambridge Press, 2005.

O'Leary, Timothy. *Foucault and the Art of Ethics*. London: Continuum, 2002.

Olson, Mancur. *The Logic of Collective Action: Public Goods and the Theory of Groups*. Cambridge: Harvard University Press, 1965.

Orlie, Melissa. *Living Ethically, Acting Politically*. Ithaca: Cornell University Press, 1997.

Osborne, Thomas. "Critical Spirituality: On Ethics and Politics in the Later Foucault." *Foucault contra Habermas: Recasting the Dialogue between Genealogy and Critical Theory*, ed. Samantha Ashenden and David Owen. London: Sage Publications, 1999.

Paras, Eric. *Foucault 2.0: Beyond Power and Knowledge*. New York: Other Press, 2006.

Patel, Raj. *Stuffed and Starved: The Hidden Battle for the World Food System*. Brooklyn: Melville House, 2008.

Patterson, Orlando. *Freedom*. Volume 1 of *Freedom in the Making of Western Culture*. New York: Basic Books, 1991.

Peperzak, Adriaan. *To the Other: An Introduction to the Philosophy of Emmanuel Levinas*. West Lafayette: Purdue University Press, 1993.

Perpich, Diane. *The Ethics of Emmanuel Levinas*. Palo Alto: Stanford University Press, 2008.

Pitkin, Hanna. *The Attack of the Blob: Hannah Arendt's Concept of the Social*. Chicago: University of Chicago Press, 1998.

———. "Justice: On Relating Private and Public." *Political Theory* 9, no. 3 (1981).

Pogge, Thomas. *Politics as Usual: What Lies Behind the Pro-Poor Rhetoric*. Cambridge: Polity Press, 2010.

Poppendieck, Janet. *Sweet Charity? Emergency Food and the End of Entitlement*. New York: Penguin, 1998.

Power, Nina. "The Books Interview: Judith Butler." *New Statesman* (August 2009).

Putnam, Robert. *Bowling Alone: The Collapse and Revival of American Community*. New York: Simon and Schuster, 2000.

Rancière, Jacques. *Disagreement: Politics and Philosophy*. Translated by Julie Rose. Minneapolis: University of Minnesota Press, 1998.

———. "Does Democracy Mean Something?" *Dissensus: On Politics and Aesthetics*. London: Continuum, 2010.

———. "The Ethical Turn of Aesthetics and Politics." *Dissensus: On Politics and Aesthetics*. London: Continuum, 2010.

———. Lecture at Northwestern University, April 1, 2003.

Ransom, John S. *Foucault's Discipline: The Politics of Subjectivity*. Durham: Duke University Press, 1997.

Rawls, John. *Political Liberalism*. New York: Columbia University Press, 1996.

Reagon, Bernice Johnson. "Coalition Politics: Turning the Century." *Home Girls: A Black Feminist Anthology*. New York: Kitchen Table–Women of Color Press, 1983.

Reinhardt, Mark. *The Art of Being Free: Taking Liberties with Tocqueville, Marx, and Arendt*. Ithaca: Cornell University Press, 1997.

Rippe, Klaus Peter. "Diminishing Solidarity." *Ethical Theory and Moral Practice* 1, no. 1 (1998).

Robbins, Jill. *Is It Righteous to Be? Interviews with Emmanuel Levinas*. Palo Alto: Stanford University Press, 2001.

Rogin, Michael. "Political Repression in the United States." *Ronald Reagan, the Movie and Other Episodes in American Political Demonology*. Berkeley: University of California Press, 1987.

Rolston, Holmes, III. "Converging versus Reconstituting Environmental Ethics." *Nature in Common: Environmental Ethics and the Contested Foundations of Environmental Policy*, ed. Ben A. Minteer. Philadelphia: Temple University Press, 2009.

Rousseau, Jean Jacques. *The Social Contract*. Translated by Maurice Cranston. New York: Penguin Books, 1968.

Routley, Richard, and Val Routley. "Against the Inevitability of Human Chauvinism." *Ethics and Problems of the 21st Century*, ed. Kenneth E. Goodpaster and Kenneth M. Sayre. Notre Dame: Notre Dame University Press, 1979.

Rushing, Sara. "Preparing for Politics: Judith Butler's Ethical Dispositions." *Contemporary Political Theory* 9, no. 3 (2010).

Schlozman, Kay, Sidney Verba, and Henry Brady. "Participation's Not a Paradox: The View from American Activists." *British Journal of Political Science* 25 (1995).

Scholem, Gershom, and Hannah Arendt. "'Eichmann in Jerusalem': An Exchange of Letters between Gershom Scholem and Hannah Arendt." *Encounter* 22 (January 1964).

Scholz, Sally. *Political Solidarity*. University Park: Pennsylvania State University Press, 2008.

Schoolman, Morton, and David Campbell. "An Interview with William Connolly." *The New Pluralism: William Connolly and the Contemporary Global Condition*, ed. David Campbell and Morton Schoolman. Durham: Duke University Press, 2008.

Schusterman, Richard. "Pragmatism and Liberalism between Dewey and Rorty." *Political Theory* 22, no. 3 (1994).

———. "Putnam and Cavell on the Ethics of Democracy." *Political Theory* 25, no. 2 (1997).

Schwartz, Michael. "Repetition and Ethics in Late Foucault." *Telos* 117 (1999).

Sen, Amartya. *Development as Freedom*. New York: Anchor Books, 2000.

———. "Human Rights and Capabilities." *Journal of Human Development* 6, no. 2 (2005).

Seyd, Patrick, and Paul Whitely. *Labour's Grass Roots*. Oxford: Oxford University Press, 1992.

Shaviro, Steven. "The Universe of Things." *Theory and Event* 14, no. 3 (2011). muse.jhu.edu/journals/theory_and_event/.

Shulman, George. "Acknowledgment and Disavowal as an Idiom for Theorizing Politics." *Theory and Event* 14, no. 1 (2011). muse.jhu.edu/journals/theory_and_event/.

———. "Interpreting Occupy." *Possible Futures*, December 20, 2011. www.possible-futures.org.

Simmons, William. "The Third: Levinas' Theoretical Move from An-Archical Ethics to the Realm of Justice and Politics." *Philosophy and Social Criticism* 25, no. 6 (1992).

Simons, Jon. *Foucault and the Political*. New York: Routledge, 1995.

Singer, Peter. "Not for Humans Only: The Place of Nonhumans in Environmental Issues." *Environmental Ethics: An Anthology*, ed. Andrew Light and Holmes Rolston III. Malden, Mass.: Blackwell, 2002.

Skocpol, Theda. *Diminished Democracy: From Membership to Management in American Civic Life*. Norman: Oklahoma State University Press, 2004.

Smart, Barry. "Foucault, Levinas, and the Subject of Responsibility." *The Later Foucault: Politics and Philosophy*, ed. Jeremy Moss. London: Sage Publications, 1998.

Soja, Edward W. *Seeking Spatial Justice*. Minneapolis: University of Minnesota Press, 2010.

Srivivasan, Sharath. "No Democracy without Justice: Political Freedom in Amartya Sen's Capability Approach." *Journal of Human Development* 8, no. 3 (2007).

Strozier, Robert M. *Foucault, Subjectivity, and Identity: Historical Constructions of Subject and Self*. Detroit: Wayne State University Press, 2002.

Thurow, Roger, and Scott Kilman. *Enough: Why the World's Poorest Starve in an Age of Plenty*. New York: PublicAffairs, 2009.

Tocqueville, Alexis de. *Democracy in America*. Translated by George Lawrence. New York: Harper and Row, 1966.

Tronto, Joan. *Moral Boundaries: A Political Argument for an Ethic of Care*. New York: Routledge, 1993.

Vázquez-Arroyo, Antonio Y. "Agonized Liberalism: The Liberal Theory of William E. Connolly." *Radical Philosophy* 127 (2004).

———. "Responsibility, Violence, and Catastrophe." *Constellations* 15, no. 1 (2008).

Verba, Sidney, Kay Lehman Schlozman, and Henry Brady. *Voice and Equality: Civic Voluntarism in American Politics*. Cambridge: Harvard University Press, 1995.

Veyne, Paul. "The Final Foucault and His Ethics." *Critical Inquiry* 20 (1993).

Villa, Dana R. *Arendt and Heidegger: The Fate of the Political*. Princeton: Princeton University Press, 1996.

Viroli, Maurizio. "Machiavelli and the Republican Idea of Politics." *Machiavelli and Republicanism*, ed. Gisela Bock, Quentin Skinner, and Maurizio Viroli. Cambridge: Cambridge University Press, 1991.

Warner, Michael. *The Trouble with Normal: Sex, Politics, and the Ethics of Queer Life*. New York: New Press, 1999.

White, Julie Anne. *Democracy, Justice, and the Welfare State: Reconstructing Public Care*. University Park: Pennsylvania State University Press, 2000.

White, Stephen K. *The Ethos of a Late Modern Citizen*. Cambridge: Harvard University Press, 2009.

Wilson, James Q. *Political Organizations*. Princeton: Princeton University Press, 1995.

Wingenbach, Ed. "Refusing the Temptation of Innocence: Levinasian Ethics as Political Theory." *Strategies* 12, no. 2 (1999).

Winters, Jeffrey A., and Benjamin I. Page. "Oligarchy in the United States?" *Perspectives on Politics* 7, no. 4 (2009).

Wolin, Sheldon. "Hannah Arendt: Democracy and the Political." *Salmagundi* 60 (1963).

Wrathhall, Mark A., and Hubert L. Dreyfus. "A Brief Introduction to Phenomenology and Existentialism." *A Companion to Phenomenology and Existentialism*, ed. Hubert L. Dreyfus and Mark A. Wrathall. Malden, Mass.: Blackwell, 2006.

Young, Iris Marion. "Communication and the Other: Beyond Deliberative Democracy." *Intersecting Voices: Dilemmas of Gender, Political Philosophy, and Policy*. Princeton: Princeton University Press, 1997.

———. "Gender as Seriality: Thinking about Women as a Social Collective." *Signs* 19, no. 3 (1994).

Zakaras, Alex. "Against Democratic Contractualism." *Representation* 47, no. 1 (2011).

Zehfuss, Maja. "Subjectivity and Vulnerability: On the War with Iraq." *International Politics* 44 (2007).

Zerilli, Linda M. G. *Feminism and the Abyss of Freedom*. Chicago: University of Chicago Press, 2005.

Ziarek, Ewa. *An Ethics of Dissensus: Postmodernity, Feminism and the Politics of Radical Democracy*. Palo Alto: Stanford University Press, 2001.

INDEX

=

actants, 99–103
Adams, John, 117–18
agency, 98–103, 132
*Ahabath Israel* (love of the Jewish people), 18–19
Alexander, John, 185n39
Alford, C. Fred, 67
Allen, Amy, 106, 181n71
alterity. *See* the Other
*amor mundi* (love of the world), 87–88, 112, 177nn2–3, 182n1
Anderson, Amanda, 154n8
anthropocentrism, 126–28, 180n57, 186nn60–61, 187n66, 187n70
anthropomorphism, 180n57
antiroad protests, 95–96, 101
Apostolidis, Paul, 156n27
Arendt, Hannah, 53, 157n36; on *amor mundi*, 87–88, 177nn2–3, 177n5, 182n1; on democratic politics, 124–26, 185n48; and existential phenomenology, 14–15; on mediation, 123–26; and perspectivalism, 97; on poverty, 112–21; in relation to care for the world, 2, 105–6; on the world, 10, 17–19, 89–93, 112, 142, 177n4, 178n12, 185n43
arts of the self. *See* care for the self
assemblages, 99–103
association. *See* associative democracy
associative democracy, 2, 10, 40, 104–10, 140, 157n37, 158n41; definition of, 11–13; in relation to charitable ethics, 13–14, 16, 55, 61–62, 71–75, 83–83; in relation to therapeutic ethics, 13–15,

24, 42–45, 48–52; in relation to worldly ethics, 14, 16–19, 50–52, 86, 92–98, 108–10, 135–38; suppression of, 148, 157n37, 192n26

Bachrach, Peter, 187n72
Barry, Andrew, 95–96
Beacons project, 135–36, 149
Beetham, David, 183n5, 183n7
Beltrán, Cristina, 118
Benhabib, Seyla, 177n5
Bennett, Jane, 99–103, 127, 161n32, 179n51, 180nn52–53, 180nn56–57
Berkowitz, Peter, 7
Berlin, Isaiah, 115, 157n32
Bernasconi, Robert, 66, 170n63
Bernauer, James, 32, 166n112
Bernstein, Richard, 26
Biskowski, Lawrence, 177n3, 182n1
Brady, Henry, 74, 173n114
Brettschneider, Corey, 133–34, 188nn83–84, 189n85
British Petroleum oil spill, 90, 103
Brown, Wendy, 9, 153n3
Bourg, Julian, 156n31
Butler, Judith: on frames and norms, 76, 174n124, 192n23; on Levinasian precariousness and politics, 5, 16, 55, 68, 76–83, 146–47, 175n134, 176n149; on the subject, 30; and the turn to ethics, 76, 174n120
Button, Mark, 7, 155n20

California initiative and referendum system, 134–35

capabilities, 113–15, 119, 122, 131–32, 183nn6–7, 184nn10–11, 185n39, 188n81; versus functions, 184n11

care ethics: feminist, 88–89, 177nn6–7

care for the Other, 2, 14, 53–62; as asymmetrical, 57, 63, 78–79, 168n20; as charitable ethics, 16, 54–55, 68–75, 83–83, 85, 89, 140; Critchley's account of, 68–71; democratic relevance of, 54–55, 61–62, 70–75, 167n6; and intersubjective relations, 62–68, 167n1; Levinas's account of, 56–60, 62–68, 70, 168n22, 168n31; and "the third," 62–68, 86; versus care for the self, 53–54. *See also* the Other

care for the self, 2, 14, 21; Connolly's account of, 40–52, 164n91, 165n99, 165n103; contemporary significance of Foucauldian style of, 31–39; democratic relevance of, 39–52, 140–42, 145–46, 163n67, 165n103; Foucault's account of, 23–31, 145–46, 160nn8–9, 162nn40–41, 162n50, 165n98, 166n110; in Greco-Roman context, 24–32, 34–39, 162nn47–48, 164n77, 164n80; and intersubjective relations, 34–39, 163n68, 166n112, 167n1; as therapeutic ethics, 15–16, 45–52, 85; versus care for the Other, 53–54

care for the world, 2, 10–11, 16–19, 51–52, 86–89, 149–51, 177n4; as care for conditions, 11, 24, 55, 73, 109–10, 125; as care for the world as in-between, 112–13, 122–26; as care for the world as home, 112–22, 126; as care for worldly things, 89–98; as enabling other forms of care, 145–48, 191n14; examples of, 109–10, 135–38, 149–50; and relationship between its two normative aims, 130–38

Carver, Terrell, 76

Chamberlain, Charles, 155n12, 155n14, 156n21

Chambers, Samuel, 76

charitable ethics, 173n115; as discouraging associative democracy, 16, 54–55, 68–75, 82–83, 89, 140. *See also* care for the Other

Chicago Anti-Eviction Campaign (AEC), 120–21, 185n35

Christian morality, 30–32

Christiano, Thomas, 188n84

*Citizens United v. Federal Election Committee*, 153n4

civic republicanism, 6–8

civil disobedience, 189n91; Arendt on, 88, 177n2, 177n4

Claassen, Rutger, 188n78, 188n80

coaction, 8, 12, 17, 72, 86, 89, 112, 157n36

coexistentialism, 101, 127–30, 178n19, 180n55

Coles, Romand, 94

colony collapse, 129, 187n71

commonality: contentious form of, 2, 14, 19, 96–98, 104, 108, 135, 179n42, 182n76, 182n78; of political objects, 11, 50, 70, 95, 106–8; of the world, 90, 93–95, 112–13, 122–26, 138, 185n43

commons, the, 150, 185n38, 193n32

compassion, 53

Connolly, William: on Foucauldian arts of the self and democratic politics, 15–16, 23–24, 40–52, 141, 164nn91, 165n99, 165n103, 166n117; on pluralization, 5, 40–43, 154n10–11, 164n90

Corbett, Jim, 189n91

Corts, Thomas, 155n14

Courage Campaign, 142–44

Critchley, Simon, 5, 16, 54–55, 60, 68–71, 74–76, 82–83, 172nn104–5

Crocker, David A., 132

Curtis, Kimberley, 125

Danish Resistance, 106, 181n71

Davis, Colin, 60–61, 67, 168n17, 169n45

Dean, Jodi, 106–7, 156n28, 181nn73–74

democracy: as ailing, 1–2, 9–10, 54, 68–69, 157n34, 175n146; in Arendt's thought, 124–26, 185n48; and individuality, 145–46, 191n14, 191n17; pluralist, 40–43; radical, 79, and Rousseau, 148–51, 192n28; spirit of, 3, 10, 16, 22, 138, 149–50, 153n4; as substantive versus procedural, 133–35, 188nn83–84, 189n87. *See also* associative democracy

democratic ethos, 2–17, 22–23, 176n1;

Foucauldian, 23–24, 39–52; Levinasian, 53–55, 68–83. *See also* care for the world

democratization, 82, 125–26, 172n102, 172n104, 180n52, 180n52; in relation to material conditions, 130–38

Derrida, Jacques, 70

Dewey, John, 17, 104–5, 107, 180n61, 182n76, 191n19

Dews, Peter, 160n8, 161n28

Dillard, Annie, 111

*Dingpolitik* (Latour), 97, 108

discipline, 33–34, 48–49, 157n32

Dostoevsky, Fyodor, 168n29

Dumm, Thomas, 39–40

Dussel, Enrique, 170n57

dyadic ethical relations, 2, 14, 16, 18, 63, 77, 80, 83, 86, 139, 146

economic rights, 113–15, 130, 183n7, 184n10

Eliasoph, Nina, 74, 173n115, 174n118

enlightenment: Foucault on, 162n51

*ethos*: meaning of the term in ancient Greek context, 6, 8, 28, 35, 155n12–15

existential phenomenology, 14–15, 158n44

Extractive Industries Review (EIR), 96–97, 101, 108, 182n79

face, the (Levinas): of the enemy, 168n25; as expressing universal precariousness, 76–78, 81; as indestructible, 169n45; as nonliteral, 167n11; in relation to politics, 66; as revealing humanity, 63; as revealing the Other, 56–59, 62

Flathman, Richard, 33, 145, 191n14

Flynn, Thomas, 26

Foucault, Michel: as advocate of therapeutic ethics, 2, 15, 45–47; on ancient care for the self, 23–31, 37–39, 160n9, 162nn40–41, 162nn47–48, 162nn50–51, 163n68, 164n77, 166n110; on care for the self in contemporary contexts, 31–39, 145–46, 163nn54–55, 163nn67, 166n112, 167n1; Connolly's reading of, 40–52; and existential phenomenology, 14–15; on freedom, 27–30, 161n25; on power, 33–34, 48–49,

157n32, 159n2; on subjectivation, 28–30, 160n8

foundationalism, 9–10, 54–55, 66, 81–82, 157n32, 162n50, 167n6

frames, 80, 82, 146–47, 192n23

Fraser, Nancy, 94, 120, 132, 184n32

freedom: care for the self as a practice of, 23, 27–30, 35, 46, 48; inner versus outer, 27–28, 161n23; as opposed to necessity, 116–17; as public, 118–19, 157n37; real versus formal, 114–15, 183n7; sexual, 145; versus liberation, 161n25

French Revolution, 116–17

Fung, Archon, 158n41

Geuss, Raymond, 156n24

God: as mediating object for Jewish community, 18–19

Gomart, Emilie, 96

Greco-Roman ethics. *See* care for the self: in Greco-Roman context

Grimshaw, Jean, 34

Grusin, Richard, 153n3

Habermas, Jürgen, 4–5, 154n5–6

Hajer, Maarten, 96

Harvey, David, 137

Hayward, Tim, 186nn60–61

Heidegger, Martin, 14, 85, 92, 168n22, 178n12

Held, David, 13, 158n40

Held, Virginia, 177n7

hermeneutics of the self, 25, 160n9, 163n67

Herzog, Annabel, 66, 168n21

Heyes, Cressida, 48–49

hierarchy: in charitable relations, 16, 54, 63, 68, 71–72, 78–79, 114, 130, 135, 173n115; democratic challenges to, 135–38

Hoeksche Waard, 96, 101

Holocaust, 18, 56–57, 106, 169nn44–45, 175n146

Honig, Bonnie, 10–11, 157n33, 174n126, 175n146, 183n4, 184n32, 192n28

human rights, 114, 183n5, 183n7, 184n10, 185n35

hunger, 57–58, 72, 109–10, 114, 117–18, 168n21, 168n22, 182nn81–83, 187n71

institutions: and counter-institutions, 150, 193n233; in relation to ethos, 148–51
Iraq Body Count, 147–48
Irigaray, Luce, 176n150
Isaac, Jeffrey, 185n48

Jasper, James, 181n73
Johnston, Steven, 192n28
justice, 53; in Levinas's work, 65–67
Justice Now, 150

Kateb, George, 177n5, 191n17
Kompridis, Nikolas, 154n5

Laclau, Ernesto, 9
Latour, Bruno, 17, 85, 94, 97, 99–101, 108, 127, 179n42, 179n46
Lawrence v. Texas, 131
Lefebvre, Henry, 137
Levinas, Emmanuel, 5, 11, 13–16, 167n11, 169n44; as advocate of charitable ethics, 2, 71–75, 83; Butler's reading of, 75–83; Critchley's reading of, 68–71, 74–75, 83; on ethics in relation to politics, 62, 65–68, 170n58; on responsibility to the Other, 53–62, 167n1, 167n4, 167n9, 168n17, 168n22, 168n25, 170n54; on the third, 62–65, 170n63, 171n68
liberalism: and ethics, 7–8
Light, Andrew, 128
Lloyd, Moya, 76, 81
Longford, Graham, 165n98
Loving v. Virginia, 131

Mahon, Michael, 32, 166n112
Markell, Patchen, 105, 181n67
Marres, Noortje, 96–97, 104, 107–8, 182n76, 182nn78–79
material needs: Arendt on, 116–21, 184n32; and charitable ethics, 68, 72; and economic rights or capabilities, 113–15, 122, 130–32; as enabling political participation, 115, 117–22, 184n10; of the Other, 57–58, 68, 168n22; in

relation to making the world a home, 113–15, 120–22, 135–38; and welfare administration, 130–31
matter of concern, 17, 45, 50, 73, 95, 112, 123, 126, 140; versus matter of fact, 94, 101, 104, 110
mediation: by the world and worldly things, 12, 17, 50, 86, 104, 107–13, 122–26, 185n43
micropolitics, 47–48, 166n117; in relation to macropolitics, 15, 23–24, 42, 46–52, 165n107
Mills, Catherine, 174n124
morality, 4, 9; versus ethics, 5, 30–32, 154n9, 162nn40–41, 163nn54–55, 167n4
Morgan, Michael, 56–58
Morton, Timothy, 178n19, 180n55, 186n63, 187n64
Mouffe, Chantal, 9, 154n10, 156n26

nature, 90, 100, 178n19
Nazism, 18, 55–57, 106, 169n44
Nealon, Jeffrey T., 161n28
needs. See material needs
needs interpretation, 120, 130, 132, 136
nihilism, 54, 68–69
No More Deaths/No Más Muertes, 136–37, 149, 189n91
Noddings, Nel, 177nn6–7
nonhumans, 91, 179n51, 180n54; from an anthropocentric perspective, 126–27, 186nn60–62; from a coexistentialist perspective, 126–30, 187n64; as producing effects, 98–103, 179n46
normalization. See discipline
norms, 76, 80–81, 146–47, 174n124
Norton, Bryan, 128, 187n70
Nussbaum, Martha: on capabilities, 114, 131–33, 184n11, 188n75, 188n78

Obama, Barack, 154–55n11
objects. See worldly things
Occupy Wall Street (ows), 154n3, 192n26
Oksala, Johanna, 33, 54, 167n1
O'Leary, Timothy, 25–26, 160n15
oligarchy, 183n8
Olson, Mancur, 105, 181n66

ontological priority: of care for the self, 21, 39; of care for the Other, 53–54

Osborne, Thomas, 161n32

the Other, 167n9; as empirical versus metaempirical, 59–60; as enemy, 57, 168n25; as indestructible, 60, 169n45, 170n50; the face of, 56, 59, 66, 76, 78, 81, 167n11, 168n25, 169n25; radical alterity of, 55–56, 168n17; as revealing precariousness, 76–78; self's encounter with, 53–56, 167n17; self's failure to respond to, 60–61, as source of subjectivity, 58–59; as a summons to responsibility, 56–58. *See also* care for the Other

Our Water Commons, 150

Paras, Eric, 161n28

paternalism: in context of welfare, 130, 189n88; of democratic despotism, 171n92; as quality of charitable ethics, 68, 114; in relation to human capabilities, 131–32, 188n75; as risk of democratic ethos, 8

People for the Ethical Treatment of Animals, 94

Perpich, Diane, 60, 170n54

Philo, 161n23

Pitkin, Hanna, 90, 94

Plato, 27, 38

pluralism, 3–5

pluralization, 5, 40–43, 164n90

Pogge, Thomas, 143–44, 190nn9–10, 191n12

political participation: and decline in civility, 21–22; lack of, 3, 9–10, 175n146; material conditions of, 115, 117–22, 184n10; motivation for, 105, 180n65, 181n66; and relation to secondary associations, 73–74, 172n113, 173nn114–15, 174n118. *See also* associative democracy

politicization, 93–95; of care for the self and care for the Other, 139–44

Poppendieck, Janet, 72–75, 172n106

poverty, 115–21, 183n8, 187n72, 191n12. *See also* material needs

power: in Butler's work, 30, 80–81; expansion of democratic forms of, 125–26, 130–31; in Foucault's work, 28–29, 36–37, 157n32, 159n2; in relation to compassion, 53

precariousness, 76–82, 146–47, 174n126, 175n134, 176n149

public(s), 12, 104, 107–8, 182n76, 182nn78–79

Putnam, Robert, 73–74, 172n113

queer counterpublics, 145–46

Rancière, Jacques, 70, 94–96, 156n28, 175n146, 179n30

Ransom, John S., 161n28

Rawls, John, 4–5, 154n6

reflexive relationship. *See* care for the self

Reinhardt, Mark, 116–17, 123

responsibility to the Other. *See* care for the Other

Right to the City movement, 137–38, 149

Rogin, Michael, 157n37, 192n26

Rousseau, Jean-Jacques, 148–50, 192n28

rule: absence of, 184n25; of the self, 27; over others, 37–39

Rushing, Sara, 175n141

Schlozman, Kay Lehman, 74, 173n114

Scholem, Gershom, 18–19

Scholz, Sally, 106, 181n68

Schusterman, Richard, 191n19

Schwartz, Michael, 33

self-interest, 16, 35, 54, 62; informed by coexistentialism, 126–30; 187n64

Sen, Amartya: on capabilities, 114, 132–33, 183n7, 185n39, 188n78, 188nn80–81

Seyd, Patrick, 181n66

Shaviro, Steven, 180n57

Shulman, George, 9–10, 77, 83, 153n3, 176n147, 176n149

Simmons, William, 67

Simons, Jon, 39, 161n35

Singer, Peter, 186n62

Skocpol, Theda, 174n118

Smart, Barry, 54

solidarity, 12, 75, 77, 104–8, 181n68, 181n71, 181nn73–74

spirit: of democracy, 3, 10, 16, 22, 138, 149–50, 153n4

subjectivation, 28–30, 160n8

subjectivity: Foucault on new forms of, 32–34, 145; Levinasian view of, 58

techniques of the self. *See* care for the self

Tennessee Immigrant and Refugee Rights Coalition (TIRRC), 140–41

therapeutic ethics, 45–47, 140, 145, 164n91, 166n116, 173n115; as discouraging associative democracy, 15–16, 47–52, 85, 87, 89. *See also* care for the self

*thing*: meaning of, 92–93. *See also* worldly things

third, the (third party): in Levinas's thought, 62–68, 86, 170n63, 171n68

third terms. *See* worldly things

Tocqueville, Alexis de, 6, 92, 157n35, 171n92

totality, 56, 169n44

Tronto, Joan, 88–89

turn to ethics, 1–2, 156n31, 159n45; in Butler's work, 76; criticisms of, 9–10, origins of, 2–8; versus return to ethics, 8–9

United for a Fair Economy, 150

United Nations, 131

Vásquez-Arroyo, Antonio, 77, 164n91, 175n134

Verba, Sidney, 74, 173n114

Veyne, Paul, 32

Viroli, Maurizio, 156n22

volunteerism, 72, 74, 173nn114–15, 174n118

vulnerability. *See* precariousness

Warner, Michael, 145–46

Welcoming Tennessee Initiative, the (WTI), 140–41

White, Julie Anne, 130, 135, 189n88

White, Stephen K., 174n126

Whitely, Paul, 181n66

Wingenbach, Ed, 67

world, the, 2, 17; in Heidegger's thought, 178n12; as in-between, 112–13, 122–26, 185n43; meaning of, 89–92, 100, 122; as recipient of care, 86–87, 89, 109–10, 122, 135–38, 149–51, 176n1; as shared home, 112–22, 183n4, 185n38. *See also* worldly things

world-building, 50, 90, 103, 112, 145, 178n15

worldlessness, 123, 178n12

worldly ethics. *See* care for the world

worldly things, 2, 100–101; defining qualities of, 92–98; as mediating associational relations, 12, 17, 50, 86, 104, 107–9, 111; as recipients of care, 11, 14, 19, 135, 181n73. *See also* world, the

Zakaras, Alex, 188n84

Zehfuss, Maja, 147

Zerilli, Linda, 46, 159n50, 176n1

Ziarek, Ewa, 54, 167n6

Ella Myers is Assistant Professor of Political Science and
Gender Studies at the University of Utah.

Library of Congress Cataloging-in-Publication Data
Myers, Ella, 1976–
Worldly ethics : democratic politics and
care for the world / Ella Myers.
p. cm.
Includes bibliographical references and index.
ISBN 978-0-8223-5385-0 (cloth : alk. paper)
ISBN 978-0-8223-5399-7 (pbk. : alk. paper)
1. Democracy—Moral and ethical aspects. 2. International
relations—Moral and ethical aspects. 3. Citizenship—
Moral and ethical aspects. 4. Political participation—
Moral and ethical aspects. I. Title.
JC423.M96 2013
172—dc23    2012033712